Case Studies in Information Technology, People and Organisations

edited by

Karen Legge, Chris W Clegg and Nigel J Kemp

NCC Blackwell
MANCHESTER • OXFORD

British Library Cataloguing in Publication Data
Legge, K.
  Case Studies in Information Technology, People and Organisations
  1. Information technology
  I. Title II. Clegg, C. III. Kemp, N.
  004

ISBN: 1–85554–078–9

© NCC BLACKWELL LIMITED, 1991

First published in 1991 by NCC Blackwell Limited, 108 Cowley Road, Oxford, OX4 1JF, England.

Editorial Office, The National Computing Centre Limited, Oxford House, Oxford Road, Manchester M1 7ED, England.

Typeset in Palatino/Futura by Bookworm Typesetting and printed by Hobbs the Printers of Southampton.

ISBN 1–85554–078–9

Preface

Between 1983 and 1984, the three of us edited a book of case studies on issues in organisational behaviour, personnel management and industrial relations. Not only did we thoroughly enjoy working together and with our 40 contributors, but the very positive reactions of colleagues and students to the cases (and the problem-solving they involved) stimulated us to have another go. This time, though, we felt a unifying theme would have some merit. Information technology (IT) appears to be an area of vital importance for the foreseeable future, and all three of us have researched its organisational implications. It seemed an obvious focus.

So here they are: 25 original research-based case studies, written and edited by 39 leading IT researchers and practitioners largely (but not exclusively) from the UK. These studies focus on the human and organisational aspects of a wide range of applications. Our contributors generally reject technological determinism in favour of a managerial choice, while recognising that this choice may be constrained by technological parameters and bargaining power. As in our previous book, these cases are chiefly concerned with organisational behaviour and human resource management. They highlight such concepts as competitive advantage, culture, organisational and work system design, power, conflict, interest groups, the labour process, control and change management.

Thanks are due to many people, not least to Tim Goodfellow and Alyn Shipton of Basil Blackwell and Marcia Lamb of NCC Blackwell for their encouragement and patience. Our secretaries and families have perhaps shown even greater patience. Above all we thank our contributors for sharing the fruits of their research and bearing with our editorial suggestions. This book, and the accompanying teachers' manual, are theirs rather than ours. We hope you enjoy using it as much as we have enjoyed compiling it.

KL, CWC, NJK
February 1991

List of contributors

Gordon Allison is Research Associate at the HUSAT Research Institute, Loughborough University of Technology.

Greg J Bamber is Reader at the Graduate School of Management, University of Queensland, Australia.

John R Bessant is Professor at the Centre for Business Research, Brighton Polytechnic.

David Boddy is Reader in Management Studies at the Glasgow Business School, University of Glasgow.

David A Buchanan is Professor in Human Resource Management at the Department of Management Studies, Loughborough University of Technology.

Joanna F Buckingham is Research Fellow at the Centre for Business Research, Brighton Polytechnic.

Bernard Burnes is Research Officer at Manchester School of Management, University of Manchester Institute of Science and Technology.

Jon Clark is Professor in Industrial Relations, Department of Sociology and Social Policy, University of Southampton.

Chris W Clegg is Senior Research Fellow at the MRC/ESRC Social and Applied Psychology Unit, University of Sheffield.

Leela Damodaran is Senior Research Fellow at the HUSAT Research Institute, Loughborough University of Technology.

Patrick Dawson is Lecturer in Organisational Studies at the Graduate School of Management, University of Adelaide, Australia.

Mike Fitter is Senior Research Fellow at the MRC/ESRC Social and Applied Psychology Unit, University of Sheffield.

Arthur Francis is Senior Lecturer at the Management School, Imperial College of Science and Technology, London.

Chris Hendry is Senior Research Fellow at the Centre for Corporate Strategy and Change, Warwick Business School, University of Warwick.

Heather J Hopkins is Senior Lecturer in Organisational Behaviour in the Business School, Bolton Institute of Higher Education

Nigel J Kemp is Organisational Effectiveness Consultant at Shell International Petroleum Company Ltd, Shell Centre, London.

Dian Kjaergaard is Associate Professor at the Institut fur Informatik og Økonomistyring, Copenhagen School of Economics and Business Administration, Denmark.

David Knights is Senior Lecturer at Manchester School of Management, University of Manchester Institute of Science and Technology.

Peter Le Quesne is Research Officer at London Business School.

Frank Land is Professor of Information Management at London Business School.

Russell D Lansbury is Professor in the Department of Industrial Relations, University of Sydney, Australia.

Mark Lansdale is Lecturer in Psychology and Information Technology at the Department of Human Sciences, Loughborough University of Technology.

Karen Legge is Professor of Behaviour in Organisations in the Department of Behaviour in Organisations, the Management School, University of Lancaster.

Geoff Lockett is Professor of Management Science and Information Management at Manchester Business School, University of Manchester.

Ian McLoughlin is Lecturer in Industrial Relations at the Centre for Management and Business Studies, Brunel University.

Robin Martin is Research Fellow at the MRC/ESRC Social and Applied Psychology Unit, University of Sheffield.

Wally S Mueller is Professor at the School of Psychology, Curtin University of Technology, Western Australia.

Fergus Murray is Research Fellow at Manchester School of Management, University of Manchester Institute of Science and Technology.

Ian Newman is Senior Lecturer in Computing Studies at the Department of Computer Studies, Loughborough University of Technology.

Michael Noon is Lecturer in Organisational Behaviour at Cardiff Business School, University of Wales College of Cardiff.

C Wendy Olphert is Principal Scientist at the HUSAT Research Institute, Loughborough University of Technology.

Margaret Patrickson is Senior Lecturer in Organisational Behaviour at Elton Mayo School of Management, South Australian Institute of Technology, South Australia.

Paul R Sparrow is Human Resources Consultant at PA Consulting Group, Birmingham.

Tom Stewart is Managing Director of System Concepts Ltd, London.

Gillian Symon is Research Scientist at the MRC/ESRC Social and Applied Psychology Unit, University of Sheffield.

Carole Truman is Research Fellow at the Department of Social and Economic Studies, University of Bradford.

Toby D Wall is Assistant Director at the MRC/ESRC Social and Applied Psychology Unit, University of Sheffield.

Janette Webb is Lecturer in Organisational Studies at the Department of Business Studies, University of Edinburgh.

Indrajit Wijegunaratne is based at Balwyn North, Victoria, Australia.

Contents

Introduction

Karen Legge, Chris Clegg and Nigel Kemp

This book comprises 25 original case studies focusing on the people and organisational aspects of a wide range of information technology (IT) applications. Cases are drawn from many areas: manufacturing, financial services, retailing and distribution, communications services and the public sector. This companion teachers' manual contains sets of theoretical notes and answers to the questions on each case in the students' book. The case studies and the notes that accompany them have been written and edited by 39 of the leading researchers and practitioners in this field. Most are from the UK, and each study describes a real situation of which the writer has detailed first-hand experience.

There are two justifications for a book of this kind. The first is that IT is simply too important to remain the exclusive preserve of technologists: we leave them to it at our peril! The strategies that guide IT development are of major importance. So are its subsequent design, implementation, use and evaluation in organisations. These issues may be vital to the well-being of the people involved and the effectiveness of the organisations in which they work. Put another way, people and their organisations both affect and are affected by IT. As such these are hugely significant areas of enquiry, education and action.

One justification for the format of this book is that the case method is an exciting and highly effective way of exploring and learning about these issues. This is especially so when the subject matter is complex and interdependent. This is certainly true of the links between IT and the individual and organisational issues that form the core of this text.

Our objectives, then, are to provide multi-faceted learning and teaching materials for a wide range of students and tutors. These will enable them to identify the key technical, people and organisational issues, and the interrelations between them. These topics are approached from a variety of theoretical perspectives in a way that encourages lively discussion and debate.

The rest of this introduction is organised in four parts. First we describe the format of a typical case study and a typical entry in the teacher's manual. Second, we describe the structure and organisation of the book as a whole, and how we believe it can most effectively be used. Third, we try to characterise the different sorts of users who we think could benefit from this book. Finally, we provide a brief outline of the major substantive individual and organisational issues raised by IT and addressed in this book.

A TYPICAL CASE STUDY AND TEACHERS' MANUAL ENTRY

A typical case study is presented in three parts. First, the authors carefully describe a real-life problem involving the application of IT within an organisation. Most cases are quite short (usually around 4000 words), and each should be an easy and enjoyable read. Next you will find a set of tasks or questions, sometimes involving roleplay. These tasks may take an hour or a day, but most will involve group work followed by a plenary discussion of ideas and suggestions from the groups. Finally, there is a short list of essential reading for students, and a list of additional references.

The teacher's manual provides additional material on each case to help the tutor, and is normally organised in four parts. It begins with a short summary of the theoretical background, identifying the key issues, ideas and concepts raised by the case study. The second section gives a brief account of what happened next, wherever this is possible; it may, for instance, describe the outcomes of some prescribed interventions. The third section gives the case writer's suggested answers to the tasks and questions in the students' book. Finally there is a further list of background reading that may be helpful to the tutor, and possibly to the students as well. We must emphasise that the manual is meant as a tool to help the busy tutor; it is not intended to prescribe a 'correct' set of views, or definitive answers. We hope that users of these books will develop their own ideas and their own insights.

THE BOOK'S STRUCTURE AND HOW TO USE IT

The 25 case studies are divided into two broad areas:

   – Section I: Manufacturing sector;

   – Section II: Service and information sectors.

Table 0.1 shows the additional subdivisions within each main area. If, for instance, you are interested in the *Financial services* sector, the table will refer you to cases 11–14.

CASE AND SECTOR	SETTING	TECHNOLOGY	PHASE/TIMING			CONCEPTS AND KEY ISSUES
			DESIGN STRATEGY PLANNING	IMPLEMENTATION AND CHANGE	USE AND EVALUATION	
SECTION I: MANUFACTURING SECTORS						
Production systems						
Case 1: Belma Joints	Mechanical Engineering	CNC, Robots, JIT	▓	▓		Organisational history & context; culture & climate; labour process; competitive advantage; work system design; change management; HRM strategy and implementation; JIT.
Case 2: Engineering & Manufacturing Ltd (EML)	Light Engineering Factory	CADCAM	▓		▓	User participation & appropriation; human-centred systems; interest groups; soft systems methodology; impact on users & organisations.
Case 3: Kandu	Engineering Factory	CAD	▓	▓		Strategic choice; organisational learning; organisation & work system design; change management.
Case 4: Paragon Electronics plc	Computer Manufacturer	CNC		▓	▓	Job & work system design; psychological & organisational impact.
Case 5: Oliver Tools	Engineering Factory	CNC		▓	▓	Organisational culture; labour process; job & work system design; industrial relations; role play.
Case 6: Brandwear Clothing Ltd	Retail Factory	CNC, DNC		▓	▓	Sexual division of labour; equal opportunities; payment systems; job design; skills & training.

Table 0.1   The Structure of This Book

CASE AND SECTOR	SETTING	TECHNOLOGY	PHASE/TIMING			CONCEPTS AND KEY ISSUES
			DESIGN STRATEGY PLANNING	IMPLEMENTATION AND CHANGE	USE AND EVALUATION	
Information Processing & Distribution systems						
Case 7: International Computers Ltd	Computer Manufacturer	Minis, mainframes, total business solutions	▓			Competitive advantage; culture & organisational design; organisational learning; change management; HRM strategy & implementation
Case 8: Silica Tele Test	Manufacturer of computer based test equipment	Processing, tracking, planning & materials handling systems	▓▓	▓		Strategic choice; culture & politics; competitive advantage; labour process; work system design; control systems
Case 9: Clever Control Ltd	Manufacturer of Process Control Systems	CAPM, MIS		▓	▓	Systems implementation; change management; functional integration & co-ordination; champions & stakeholders; culture & history; impact on organisation
Case 10: Booths Ltd	Confectionery Wholesaler	MIS		▓	▓	System usability; job quality; change management; user centred design; impact on people & organisations

Table 0.1   The Structure of This Book

CASE AND SECTOR	SETTING	TECHNOLOGY	PHASE/TIMING			CONCEPTS AND KEY ISSUES
			DESIGN STRATEGY PLANNING	IMPLEMENTATION AND CHANGE	USE AND EVALUATION	
SECTION II: SERVICE & INFORMATION SECTORS Financial Services						
Case 11: General Insurance J9	Distributed Insurance Company	MIS E-mail	▨	▨	▨	Strategy, structure & systems; control & autonomy; co-ordination; information usage; roles & relationships.
Case 12: A Life Insurance Company	Insurance Company Head Office	MIS	▨	▨		Structure, power, politics, culture; competitive advantage; material & symbolic resources; career paths; interest groups.
Case 13: MBank	Merchant Bank	IPSE	▨	▨	▨	Systems standards; systems implementation; organisation requirements; technical & social issues; change management.
Case 14: National Community Bank	Bank Branch & Credit Offices	Decision Support System (PCs)		▨	▨	Change management; decentralisation; sub-cultures; social & technical co-requisites for implementation and adoption; interest groups; system complexity; impact on users.

Table 0.1   The Structure of This Book

CASE AND SECTOR	SETTING	TECHNOLOGY	PHASE/TIMING			CONCEPTS AND KEY ISSUES
			DESIGN STRATEGY PLANNING	IMPLEMENTATION AND CHANGE	USE AND EVALUATION	
Retail and Distribution						
Case 15: Airfuels Ltd	Oil distribution & supply	MIS, Hardware, Software	▓			Organisational structure & politics; globalisation; organisational design; change management.
Case 16: FoodCo	Warehousing food retail	MIS, Materials handling	▓	▓		Strategy; management style; trust; choice; organisational & work system design; industrial relations; human resource management; comparative outcomes.
Case 17: Headco	Retail head office	PCs, WPs		▓	▓	Ergonomics; health & safety; end-user participation; training; trade-offs between commercial and human factors.

Table 0.1　The Structure of This Book

CASE AND SECTOR	SETTING	TECHNOLOGY	PHASE/TIMING			CONCEPTS AND KEY ISSUES
			DESIGN STRATEGY PLANNING	IMPLEMENTATION AND CHANGE	USE AND EVALUATION	
Communications Services						
Case 18: TXE4 Exchange System	British Telecom	Semi-electronic Exchange System	▓			Strategic choice; coordination; culture & control; privatisation; industrial relations & negotiation; work organisation; supervisory roles; selection & training.
Case 19: The *Evening News*	Provincial Newspaper	PCs, Direct input		▓		Strategic choice; power, conflict, interest groups; negotiation; management style & control; implementation phases; theory of action.
Case 20: Digital Exchange Systems	British Telecom	Integrated digital exchange systems		▓		Contingency theory; design space; action theory; culture; competitive advantage; negotiation; skill polarisation; roles; conflict.

Table 0.1   The Structure of This Book

CASE AND SECTOR	SETTING	TECHNOLOGY	PHASE/TIMING			CONCEPTS AND KEY ISSUES
			DESIGN STRATEGY PLANNING	IMPLEMENTATION AND CHANGE	USE AND EVALUATION	
Public Sector						
Case 21: New Times Medical Centre	Medical Practice	Micro-based information systems		▨		Organisational change, work system design; stakeholders & negotiation; roleplay; planning; technology as change catalyst.
Case 22: Payfund	National Payments Administration	Integrated information systems	▨			Sociotechnical systems; quality of working life; job design; structured design & implementation methods.
Case 23: Oasis Palm Project	Collaborative University & Business Design Team	IKBS Software Engineering	▨			Collaborative research & design; project management; inter-organisational politics, stakeholders; technical, social & commercial issues.
Case 24: Training Access Points	Training Agency	Databases, Prototypes	▨			System design; user requirements; acceptability; prototypes; evaluating design and systems.
Case 25: Canadian Department of Informatics	National Information Department	E-mail			▨	Organisation structure; decentralisation; managerial style & roles; autonomy & control; role plays.

Table 0.1   The Structure of This Book

The table also provides other useful information:

- The second column indicates the organisational setting involved. Cases 11 and 12, for instance, relate to insurance companies, while case 13 involves a merchant bank.

- The third column shows the technology involved in the case study. Cases 11 and 25, for instance, both involve electronic mail systems. Some of the technologies under review are small-scale, cheap, or stand-alone (the three terms are not necessarily synonymous). Others are bigger in scope. These are usually expensive, and some are highly integrated. Some can also be regarded as state-of-the-art, at least from the technical point of view.

- The fourth column indicates the development phase covered by the case study. This ranges from early design, strategy and planning, through implementation and change, to the final phase of use and evaluation. These phases often overlap one another, but reference to this column will help readers to concentrate on the areas that interest them most. For example, cases 1–3, 7, 8, 11, 12, 15, 18 and 21–24 generally involve design, strategy and planning.

- The last column summarises the key issues and ideas involved in each case. Organisational culture, for instance, is of central importance to cases 1, 5, 7–9, 12, 14, 15, 18 and 20. However, we must emphasise that these key issues have been identified by the authors and editors; readers may wish to establish their own cross-referencing of important issues and ideas.

Both the casebook and the teacher's manual have subject indexes giving more detailed references to particular themes and topics of interest. As editors we have tried to ensure the book covers a wide range of topics, including the ergonomics of individual hardware and software pack-ages, job and work system design, management style and organisational structure, culture and politics. We have included such highly significant issues as equal opportunities and competitive advantage, while process issues include strategic choice, the management of change, and the role of users.

We do not expect readers to work through every case in the book. Instead we hope this brief introduction, and a study of Table 0.1 and the subject indexes, will allow teachers to select and develop useful material that will supplement their other activities.

USERS OF THIS BOOK

This book is aimed at a wide variety of users including teachers and students of IT, engineering, business studies, personnel management and industrial relations, organisational behaviour, organisational and occupational psychology, and industrial sociology. They may be on full-time, part-time, day-release or post-experience courses at universities, polytechnics, business schools or colleges of further education, and may be studying for Higher National Diplomas, undergraduate degrees, postgraduate degrees or professional qualifications. Certainly more and more people are studying (and trying to influence) the development and impact of IT. We hope these case studies will help some of them.

PEOPLE AND ORGANISATIONAL ISSUES RAISED BY INFORMATION TECHNOLOGY

The case studies in this book are designed to encourage students to explore some of the opportunities and problems that may accompany the introduction and development of information technology (IT) systems. Certainly all the cases illustrate the accepted principle that microelectronic technology does not predetermine the human, organisational and economic consequences of its application; rather its effects reflect managerial choices, which are inevitably influenced by existing organisational structures, processes and cultures.

The cases illustrate issues that have pervaded empirical research on IT in Europe and the United States over the past decade. These issues include:

- the nature of IT, and why it is potentially 'different' from earlier technologies;

- ergonomics and usability;

- management control, job design, deskilling and upskilling;

- organisational design;

- managing change and the role of users;

- employment, careers and skills.

The nature of IT

The essential difference between the new technology and its predecessors lies in its ability to process information. This ability depends on the silicon chip. Chips contain electronic circuitry that can be used to create a computer's central processing unit, or simply for information storage, ie *memory* (Francis, 1986, p2). As a result, microelectronic technology has four essential characteristics:

- information capture (the ability to collect data);

- information storage (the ability to retain data);

- information manipulation (the ability to process data);

– information distribution (the ability to transmit data electronically).

Mechanical technologies could only supplement or substitute for the physical capabilities of their users. New technologies can either substitute for, or complement people's mental capabilities. In theory, this is most clearly shown in the development of software systems using artificial intelligence (so-called *expert systems*). In practice applications of this kind remain rare and problematic.

The usefulness of microelectronic systems is further enhanced by developments in telecommunications technology, including the use of lasers, optical fibres, speech synthesisers, infra-red sensing devices and so on. As Gill (1985, p4) put it:

> Thus the fusion of information *processing* (represented by the role of computer technology) and communications (increasingly dominated by telecommunications) has brought about a revolutionary change in the quality of information *flow*.

More information can be processed more efficiently and flexibly than ever before. It can also be transmitted and acted upon far more rapidly. Hence the emergence of the generic term 'IT'.

In addition, this new technology makes it possible to improve three main elements of the process:

– control;

– flexibility;

– integration.

Manufacturing offers a useful illustration. In manufacturing industries, IT can be used to *control* production processes in two ways (Wall and Kemp, 1987, p4):

– *Indirectly*, to store, manipulate and analyse data (as with general office applications) to support and control production management. Example applications might include production planning and scheduling.

– *Directly*, to control machinery. Examples include CNC, DNC, AGVs (automatic guided vehicles) and robotics.

Whether managers choose to centralise or decentralise, these abilities extend their opportunities for control in two main ways (Child, 1984a):

– by providing faster, more comprehensive and accurate information about operations, particularly when data is taken directly from sensors and monitoring devices;

– by unifying individual or segmented control systems, allowing a comprehensive, holistic assessment of performance.

These opportunities raise a number of important questions for management:

- Who is to control the 'controlling' software?
- What implications will this have for reallocating tasks and responsibilities, and for redesigning and redefining jobs?
- Who is to be responsible for the database, and who will have access to it? What accountabilities will they have?

The answers to these questions will affect organisation and job design, skill structures, recruitment and selection, pay, and union demarcation and membership.

Such issues are further highlighted by the second characteristic: the programmable *flexibility* of the equipment. This allows 'flexible specialisation' (Piore and Sabel, 1984) in the pursuit of competitive advantage. Flexible specialisation is a strategy based on flexible, multi-use equipment, skilled and adaptable workers, and competition through innovation (Child, 1987, p107). This strategy is one way of coping with the high levels of interdependence and technical uncertainty that can be produced by such advanced systems. These systems must be tightly coupled together to achieve the full potential offered by integration, and as the flow of operations accelerates, operators must be far more ready to cope with unforeseen or non-routine variations that cannot readily be controlled by computer (Cummings and Blumberg, 1987, pp47–48).

This brings us to the third characteristic: *integration*. At present, direct and indirect IT applications in manufacturing are usually so-called *stand-alone* technologies. In theory, and increasingly in practice, these stand-alone systems can be integrated into a comprehensive production system. As an example, the direct applications in a flexible manufacturing system can be combined with indirect applications to create computer integrated manufacture (CIM) – 'the factory of the future' (Voss, 1984; see also Wall and Kemp, 1987, p5, for a summary description). IT's potential for integration, both within and between organisations, means reconsidering boundaries, accountabilities, and the appropriate basis of control in the context of strategic decisions about market position and the bases of competitive advantage.

Finally, IT offers many attractive, if conventional, benefits. It is (relatively) cheap. It is compact, reliable and accurate. It offers high operating speeds coupled with low energy consumption. These benefits are not confined to new technologies, but few conventional technologies can offer such an attractive combination.

Ergonomics and usability

The ergonomic aspects of technology and the work environment have attracted considerable study, and in many countries they are also subject to the law. In the UK, for example, employers are bound by the regulations of the Offices, Shops and Railway Premises Act 1963 and the Health and Safety at Work Act 1975. In the USA, regulations derive from the Fair Labor Standards Act 1983 and the Occupational Safety and Health Act 1970.

These regulations cover the working environment (including temperature, lighting, humidity, air quality and noise), equipment and its siting (including displays and controls) and physical hazards (eg electric shock and explosions). Most of the relevant legislation predates IT, which is thus not specifically addressed. Even so, IT products are subject to the same regulations.

The rapid growth of the IT market has encouraged considerable research and development, notably in the design of computer keyboards and visual display units (VDUs) (see, for example, the reviews by: Dainoff and Dainoff, 1987; Grandjean, 1987; Oborne, 1985). One outcome has been an attempt to develop industry-wide standards of good design in such areas as character height and luminance, keyboard angles and keytop surfaces (see Cakir, Hart and Stewart, 1978; Clegg et al, 1989). It is clear that international standards will be agreed over the next few years in many of these areas, certainly within the European Economic Community, and later perhaps worldwide.

Research is also continuing into the potential risks of long-term exposure to VDUs. It has been suggested that they can cause facial rashes, cataracts, abnormal pregnancies, muscular injuries and eye strain. For these and other reasons many trade unions have negotiated working practices that limit continuous use of VDUs. To date, however, there is no clear evidence that they emit dangerous levels of radiation (see Health and Safety Executive, 1983; Pearce, 1984).

In parallel with this work on computer hardware the last decade has seen a rapidly growing interest in the design of software interfaces. Early interfaces were often very difficult to use; today the idea of a so-called *user-friendly* interface is common currency. This is partly because computers are no longer the domain of the specialist programmer for whom, perhaps, the interface was less problematic. As computers become more widely used by non-specialists, interest in their usability has grown.

There is worldwide interest in these issues, and researchers argue that most interfaces are difficult both to learn and to use. Frustratingly, however, those concerned with usability are less powerful than those concerned with marketing and new product development, and are also lagging some way behind them.

At present there are many debatable issues in this field. How can end users become involved in system design? If a system has reached the prototype stage, is it too late to change it? Can users be involved in generic as well as in tailor-made systems? Is it possible to generate user-defined standards of good practice, or are these simply a matter of common sense? How can standards be linked to empirical research and current theory? Should work in this area be problem-driven or theory-driven? And what is the appropriate level of analysis for such work? (See, for example, Frese, 1987; Helander, 1988; Card, Moran and Newell, 1983; Carroll and Campbell, 1989; Shneiderman, 1986; Suchman, 1987.)

There is one growing area within this field that mirrors evolution within traditional hardware ergonomics: the search for guidelines, reflecting good practice, that can later be formulated into standards (see, for example, Smith and Mosier, 1986; Ravden and Johnson, 1989; Ulich, 1987). But much remains to be done, especially in the field of usability, and at present the gap between research and practice seems large.

Management control, job design, deskilling and upskilling

We have seen that managerial choice can affect the impact of IT on a wide range of issues, but it is generally recognised that this choice is itself affected by three important considerations:

- decisions about market positioning and the bases of competitive advantage;

- perceptions of the skills of existing employees and potential recruits;

- (above all) the political interests and relative power of all those potentially affected by the technology.

These considerations will mould management's approach to the three pervasive issues of control, flexibility and integration. Nowhere is this more evident than in the research findings and debates about management control, job design, deskilling and upskilling.

For instance, much debate has arisen from Braverman's (1974) Marxist proposition that IT inevitably deskills jobs. Braverman suggests that management, being the instrument of capital, exploits IT's potential for enhanced direct control over labour to extract the maximum surplus value at the point of production. (For general discussions see Braverman, 1974; Wood, 1982; Armstrong, 1988.)

Clearly, however, the benefits that management seeks from IT do not point to a consistent and monolithic deskilling strategy. Research admittedly suggests that improved direct control through deskilling is often a clear management objective (see, for example, Noble, 1979;

Buchanan and Boddy, 1983; Wilkinson, 1983; Child et al, 1984). But other objectives (perhaps involving enhanced control) are often to the fore. These might include the reduction of lead times from design to production and manufacture, the reduction of inventory and work in progress, and improved engineering and design analysis. These in turn should lead to better products, improved quality assurance and consistency, increased flexibility of production, faster and more accurate text processing and reduced material costs (Bessant, 1983; Buchanan and Boddy, 1983; Kemp et al, 1984; Voss, 1984).

It seems that motives for innovation vary according to the functional and hierarchical differences within management. Senior management, for instance, tends to concern itself with strategic objectives such as company image and competitiveness, while middle management is more concerned with controlling work flow. However, it has also been suggested that there may be a diversity of objectives within each group (Buchanan and Boddy, 1983; Mueller et al, 1986). And as McLoughlin and Clark (1988) point out, even where management consciously pursues control objectives, they may not be specifically concerned with controlling labour. They may simply wish to reduce the risks and uncertainties involved when human beings intervene in the control of work operations. Bessant (1983) even suggests there is rarely *any* defined motive on the part of management. Instead, he suggests, a range of factors are used to justify investment in IT, and labour considerations weigh no more heavily than any other factor.

Rose and Jones (1985) suggest that in this context the idea of management having a conscious strategy of control is unhelpful. They point out that the strategies adopted by management are likely to vary according to differences in the interrelationships between trade union positions, product markets, and by existing control systems. Commentators such as Hyman (1988) consider that management strategy often lacks coherence and consistency. They argue that managements in general are often faced with contradictory pressures and constraints, and are likely to respond with opportunistic and unstable policies. Perhaps Kelly (1985) makes the most useful comment in reference to managerial motives and practices in the redesign of work, when he argues that the labour process is only a part of the picture. It is important to examine the full circuit of industrial capital, including the purchase of labour, power in labour markets, exploitation and extraction of surplus value in the labour process, and the realisation of surplus value in product markets.

Whatever their intention, however, the debate continues as to whether management IT strategies actually *do* result in impoverished, deskilled jobs. This issue is all the more problematic because there is no clear definition of 'skill' in this context. Rothwell (1984, p128) points out that the perception of a new job as more or less skilled depends very much on the viewpoint of the observer (see also Scarbrough, 1984):

> An engineering maintenance craftsman may acquire more 'vertical' skills by adding 'electrical', yet have a narrower range of 'horizontal' skills if these are only performed within one particular department.

Wilson (1988) illustrates this by showing how the introduction of CNC simultaneously reduced some skills in the machinist's job while developing others. Clark et al (1988) report similar skill changes among maintenance technicians involved in the move from electromechanical Strowger telephone exchanges to electronic TXE4 exchanges. Although manual dexterity and other physical skills declined, mental skills were enhanced, and the work developed a much greater abstract content.

It is also difficult to recognise and evaluate the 'tacit skills' associated with new or redesigned jobs (Jones, 1983; Manwaring and Wood, 1985). Another problem is that management may impose new skills on workers, but resist acknowledging their existence if training is very short or informal, and if unions are not involved. As Rainbird (1988, p176) states, "The unions' ability to claim new skills and to obtain formal recognition for them will be fundamental to the redefinition of skilled work." Issues of gender and equal opportunity are obviously relevant here (Cockburn, 1983).

Despite the complexity of this area, it is possible to make some tentative generalisations about the effect of IT on management control, job design and deskilling. First, as already stated, IT may restrict managerial choice but is not in itself deterministic. The way in which it is used, and the jobs and work practices resulting from this use, are dictated by management choices and employee reaction to those choices. Secondly, management can choose to retain or enhance skills, or they can choose to increase direct control at the expense of skill. This choice is likely to be made on the basis of:

- the amount of non-programmable skill and judgement the task requires;

- the risks and costs of human error if equipment breaks down (Child, 1984b).

Where both factors are important, management will tend to aim for flexibility by retaining and enhancing skills. Non-programmable skills are usually needed when the work involves uncertain or unpredictable situations and, to a lesser extent, complex tasks. In manufacturing, such unpredictability is associated with short product life-cycle, small batch size, frequent batch changes, a high incidence of new work and variability in materials or physical conditions (Jones, 1982). In the service sector, non-programmable skills are associated with the perceived need to keep an element of personal service.

Risks and costs of human error become particularly important where life or security could be threatened (Child, 1984b). When the task is largely programmable and risks are small, a management strategy involving greater control is likely to lead to deskilling.

The ability of employees to resist deskilling and greater management control will depend in part on management's perception of the tasks they are performing. It will also depend on:

– the employees' use of ideological defences to retain occupational control;

– the employees' position in the labour market;

– the employees' position in the decision-making structure of the organisation.

These factors tend to be mutually reinforcing either positively (placing employees in a strong negotiating position) or negatively.

Organisational design

If IT applications are to achieve their full potential, most commentators believe an appropriate interface between new technology and the existing organisation is vital (see, for example, Bhattacharyya, 1985; Ingersoll Engineers, 1985). Organisational design, like management control and job design, is affected by the three key issues of control, integration and flexibility.

Again the consensus is that consideration of these issues is affected by choices made about the markets where the organisation is expected to compete. More and more organisations are facing intense international competition. In this market the pattern of demand may be unpredictable, while the products or services on offer may be growing more and more sophisticated. Both factors can create the need for continual adjustments and problem solving, and this demands close integration of a wide range of management functions.

Organisational design can be used to improve integration in several different ways:

– Tasks can be merged that were previously performed by separate people or departments by, for example:

  • allowing a designer to create drafts with CAD rather than using a draughtsperson.

– Different roles can be coupled more closely by, for example:

- creating multi-disciplinary teams;
- matrix organisation;
- forming 'companies within companies'.

This integration need not take place under one roof. By using common databases it may be possible for staff in different locations to work as an integrated team.

IT may provide opportunities for greater centralisation, or for more effective decentralisation. Centralisation is improved when full, up-to-date information can be passed directly to senior management. There is, of course, a risk that this information will be too complex, or that there will simply be too much of it; this risk can be avoided by using programs that can integrate large amounts of data from different sources and draw key analyses from them. Furthermore, this choice would be facilitated if new technologies were used to simplify management structures and to reduce the span of control that is required of senior management.

Decentralisation strategies can also benefit from new technology. Each unit within the organisation can be linked through a common computer network. This allows a free exchange of information and makes it easier to monitor the resulting decisions. Entering proposed decisions into the network could encourage local initiative and discourage intervention from the centre, especially when local units can benefit from better analytical facilities and better information (Child, 1984a, pp218–219). The case for centralised decision-making has always rested, in part at least, on efficiency. With fewer people involved there are fewer bureaucratic delays, committee stages, etc. The case for decentralisation, by contrast, rests on its flexibility. Decisions are left to the people on the spot, who can respond immediately to changing circumstances.

Management, in choosing whether to centralise or decentralise, in the light of its competitive strategy, ought to be thinking about such task contingencies as variability of production, the number of different environments that will be served, and their complexity. It is equally important to look at interdependences within the processing system. Where there is reciprocal interdependence, centralisation is not appropriate; management of this variable and uncertain situation is best left to decentralised, multi-functional teams. Where interdependence is pooled, centralisation is unnecessary, and probably demotivating. Even so, it offers clear benefits where the processing system is characterised by sequential interdependence (Thompson, 1967); here it can supplement existing centralised planning. Some multi-divisional firms achieve a compromise. The control possibilities of IT simultaneously allow both a decentralisation of operating decisions to local level, but enhanced centralisation of control at the centre by making local operating conditions and performance immediately visible to management.

Another related issue concerns IT's effect on management structure, managerial roles, and the size of the managerial overhead. Does it encourage elaboration or simplification? Some would argue that both trends are possible, notably in relation to AMT. Management of production and product support is simplified; management of systems development, programming, information security and training becomes more complex. There can be similar contrasts in the role of the supervisor. Sometimes the 'man-managing' supervisor is replaced by a trouble-shooting, computer-based systems manager. But where computer operations are imposing greater standardisation, combined with deskilling and demanning, the motivational skills of man-management may be at a premium to counteract their potentially alienating effects, exacerbated by worker isolation.

There are three ways in which IT can reduce managerial overheads. Staff reductions may be possible:

- at administrative and clerical levels, by using office automation;
- at supervisory and middle-management levels, by exploiting the enhanced control and integration offered by IT;
- in EDP departments, by increasing the use of personal micro-computers and networked terminals.

Senior management may well be looking for reductions of this kind in the interests of a lean and simple management structure, but implementing them is another matter. Such schemes can often be frustrated by delays, dilution and resistance from middle management.

Clearly, then, IT can shrink the management hierarchy and change its structure. In large organisations these processes may be reinforced by a growing tendency to subcontract to smaller organisations. Subcontracting in this context involves two interrelated strategies: 'just-in-time' (JIT) and 'flexible organisation' (see Morgan, 1988; Atkinson, 1984; Atkinson and Meager, 1986a/b; Handy, 1984). Both strategies hinge on the control, flexibility and integration provided by IT systems. They also depend on the relative costs of managing production or services within the hierarchy or buying them in the marketplace (Williamson, 1975). Both JIT and flexible organisation embody ideas of networking structures and both have tremendous implications for job and organisational design.

JIT, in theory at least, links manufacturers, suppliers and retailers into a single, integrated system, where goods and services are delivered just a few hours before they are needed. JIT encourages the different organisations involved to see themselves as part of a single network, and manage their relations in this wider context. It also encourages employees to see themselves as both producers and customers.

Flexible organisation involves dividing employees into increasingly peripheral and therefore numerically flexible groups, clustered around a small stable core of full-time, functionally flexible career employees, which conducts the organisation's firm-specific continuous activities. The philosophy is simple: overheads should be justified in terms of the direct contribution made by products or services, and services that do not make a direct contribution should be bought in the marketplace. Whether employees qualify to be part of the 'core' or in the periphery of employment may depend on such factors as (Child, 1987, p127):

- Are the employees required:

  a) only periodically?

  b) all the time?

- Is their contribution:

  a) relatively self-contained (and therefore measurable)?

  b) in need of close integration with contributions made by others (and therefore not easily measurable)?

- Can it be provided:

  a) easily and cost-effectively from the marketplace?

  b) only from within the organisation (eg if it requires in-house expertise)?

Tasks that fulfil the options marked (a) are likely to be contracted out, reducing the size of the core group. The use of IT to increase the amount of work that executives do at home is also relevant. If IT is used for skill enhancement and to create 'flexible specialisation', the core group is likely to grow larger.

In theory, the idea of flexible organisation meshes well with the JIT ideas about networking organisations. Similarly, it may be dovetailed with existing multi-divisional structures. An operating division can be formed from small, semi-autonomous units, each with its own core and peripheral groups. These units are integrated not geographically, but by imaginative use of IT. The operating divisions, in their turn, may be coordinated by the use of corporate performance controls implemented through a high-level IT network.

Alternatively, multi-divisional companies can reduce employment levels to the point where IT will allow simpler management structures. Decentralisation may also be possible, even if it appears to be a federal alliance between semi-autonomous profit centres.

Managing change and the role of users

Research into the introduction of new information technologies almost always characterises that change as technology-centred (see, for example, Blackler and Brown, 1986; Clegg and Kemp, 1986). In effect this means that changes in strategy within the organisation are usually driven by technology. 'Automate or liquidate' and 'Automate or bust' were common slogans in the UK in the early 1980s. The people and organisational issues covered in this book do not normally command large resources. Often they are not discovered until changes have already been implemented, and are then regarded as 'operational difficulties'. For the planners and developers of high-technology systems, people often represent a source of error and unpredictability. If these unreliable users cannot be designed out altogether, they are given the 'left-over' tasks. This results in fragmented jobs that offer little fulfilment or motivation. Within this approach, end-users have little say in the design of the new system, its operation, or the training required to use it. In effect, IT has been appropriated by the technologists (see Clegg and Symon, 1989). Many researchers and commentators believe that Taylorist assumptions about the design and management of work remain prevalent (see Taylor, 1911).

Not surprisingly, this approach appears to be ineffective, and fails to capitalise on the benefits of IT. In 1988 the consultants A T Kearney published a report on computer-aided manufacturing in the UK which showed that the average shortfall between expectation and performance was a colossal 30% – and that the principal reasons for the shortfall were people and organisational issues.

In the last few years a strong set of 'countervailing' approaches have emerged. Although these remain in the minority, they do provide alternatives to the technology-centred viewpoint. In sociotechnical design theory, for instance, participation has been a central tenet for a number of years (see Cherns, 1976). Similar ideas have been applied to the new information technologies by several researchers, perhaps most notably by Bjørn-Andersen and Hedberg (1977) and Ehn et al (1983) in Scandinavia, and by Mumford (1983) in the UK.

Hirschheim (1985) presents several arguments for participation in the design and implementation of new technologies. Some are concerned with benefits to the individual (eg the intrinsic satisfaction of such involvement) and some with benefits to the system (eg improved technical quality and functionality). The issues cannot always be separated: for example, it can be shown that participation promotes commitment to the new system, and this in turn increases system usage.

Unfortunately some of the work in this field has been more concerned with general advocacy than with actual practice, and there remains a need for detailed and specific research. Spinas, Ackermann and Ulich (1988) make useful distinctions between the forms of participation (direct or indirect), the degree of participation (information-sharing or influence), the topics covered, and the stages at which participation takes place (eg during analysis, design or implementation). Their work was concerned with software development, an area in which user-centred design (see Norman and Draper, 1986), has become increasingly important over the last few years.

In software development, participation has largely focused on the design of user interfaces. The intention has been to make them both easier to learn and easier to use. To support this work there has been a rapid growth in research and development on the human–computer interface in Europe, the USA and Japan, including significant work on user modelling and rapid prototyping (Nickerson, 1986; Monk, 1985; Christie, 1985; Gardiner and Christie, 1987).

While the effort to improve user participation continues, much of this effort has focused on the interface itself. Moreover, it is usually applied late in the design cycle, when a prototype is already available. There have, however, been some exceptions. The European Strategic Programme for Research and Development into Information Technology (ESPRIT) has supported an enormous international project (HUFIT) intended to incorporate human concerns into the design of office-based systems at a far earlier stage. The intention is to consider such factors as ergonomics, human–computer interfaces and job design at the same time as user requirements are specified (see Phillips and Galer, 1986). ESPRIT also supported a smaller project concerned with human factors in a manufacturing context (see Clegg et al, 1988).

Meanwhile technical developments continue. A recent trend has been the development of structured design methodologies such as the structured systems analysis and design method (SSADM). These techniques, intended to help software teams integrate their design efforts, are now mandatory in organisations such as the British Civil Service. Further work is in progress to incorporate user and organisational needs into such methodologies in the form of *portfolios* (or *kitbags*) of appropriate techniques (see, for example, Civil Service College, 1987).

At the same time work on promoting 'human-centred technologies' is growing, notably in the social science communities of Europe and the USA. To date this has mainly focused on manufacturing organisations (Cooley, 1987; Rosenbrock, 1987; Brodner, 1987; Martin, Ulich and Warnecke, 1987). Once again, user participation is a central element in these projects (Clegg and Symon, 1989).

Despite these developments, participation remains a difficult area. It is still rare for end users to have real influence over the design and implementation of information technology. When participation is attempted it is often restricted to the human–computer interface, ignoring such fundamental issues as the design of users' jobs, the allocation of system functions, and the wider organisational concerns. This is partly because it is difficult to do and to manage simultaneously, and partly because participation will raise political and educational issues in any organisation. It is not always simple to decide who the user is, and it will become less so as systems grow larger and more integrated. Who, for instance, are the users of a CADCAM system? Are they the designers, the draughtspeople, the methods engineers, the programmers, the machinists, the project managers, the stress engineers, the quality inspectors, the supervisors or the managers? The answer, of course, is 'all of them', but how can they all participate?

In a deliberately polemical piece, Clegg (1989, p401) has argued that the IT industry currently conveys a number of strong images, which may be widely held and which can be summarised as follows:

- "Technology is more important than people."

- "People do not have a significant role in advanced systems."

- "We should trust in the technology and the technologists."

- "We should leave IT to the experts."

Employment, careers and skills

In the early 1980s it was popular to imagine that IT would substantially reduce the number of jobs within a firm, and that the remaining 'core' jobs would demand high technical or professional skills. The remaining deskilled jobs would be far fewer, and no longer considered part of the core (see, for example, Jenkins and Sherman, 1979; Handy, 1984). The evidence, however, shows the dangers of such popular generalisations. IT does not necessarily create massive job losses. Some traditional skills will remain important, even if new skills are also required.

Beginning with the idea of job losses, it is obviously possible for new technology to create job losses by enhancing productivity by:

- improving process efficiency;

- changing product design, including component reduction.

However, productivity gains at plant level will not automatically produce job losses. The extent of such losses will depend on the extent to which theoretical utilisation levels can be achieved, and the extent of any associated job specialisation or fragmentation. It seems a substantial learning process has to take place within the organisation before it achieves planned utilisation rates. Inevitably this moderates the potential impact on jobs.

Besides, unless the work is highly specialised or fragmented (eg as in spot welding) the new technology may speed up only one part of a larger job. It is also possible that technically feasible job losses may be impractical, for instance if ATMS allows 'half a person' to be saved at each of a bank's widely dispersed branches (Willman and Cowan, 1984). To achieve any potential labour savings management must rationalise unit design, and combine the introduction of new technology with a Tayloristic approach to work that produces high indirect costs of its own.

New technology may also produce a greater demand for the company's products or services. This, too, will work against job losses at the organisational level. In any case, reduction of the workforce may not be a prime management objective. Major cost savings from IT are mostly in other areas. EPOS, for instance, generates cost savings in inventory control and by its ability to pick out the fastest-selling and most profitable lines.

In summary, at organisational as at national level, it is difficult empirically to separate the effects of IT on employment from those of the general economic climate. IT can create jobs (by helping organisations to grow) or destroy them (by making them less labour-intensive). In recession, it is almost impossible to tease out the differential effects on employment of IT and depressed demand. In growth, it is difficult to identify either how many extra jobs are being generated through IT-facilitated organisational growth, or how many fewer jobs than might have resulted from economic growth, have failed to materialise through the labour saving potential of IT.

However, it is possible to identify a new labour market created by IT: the information sector. This includes:

- hardware suppliers such as IBM, DEC, Hewlett-Packard, Honeywell Bull;

- software houses;

- satellite industries such as computer games.

The effects of IT on skill levels once again depend on management choices (eg skill enhancement or deskilling), and the extent to which technical, supervisory and management roles are redesigned to require new skills. However, this is not always a simple matter of cause and effect. Employers are more likely to opt for skill enhancement if they believe there is a strong base of existing skills in the workforce. If they lack this confidence, they are likely to opt for deskilling. In any case, traditional skills will not necessarily be displaced: they often provide the basis for using new skills more effectively. Even so, it is accepted that some skills must be enhanced to make the best use of IT's potential. Managers in both manufacturing and service sectors must:

- understand the basic principles and applications of relevant IT;

- understand the systems thinking required to use it most effectively, and the consequent blurring of traditional boundaries between jobs and functions (eg Senker, 1984a; Bjørn-Andersen 1984; Morgan 1988);

- develop skills in interactive dialogue with IT systems.

Senior management in particular must have sufficient grasp of IT to work actively with engineering and systems specialists in coordinating investment strategies (Senker, 1984b).

In manufacturing, plant operation skills will increasingly involve software writing and electronic interfacing with hardware. Traditional skills (eg maintenance and advanced machining) will not be displaced automatically, and certainly not when the organisation is at the beginning of a learning curve. However, there will be a far greater requirement for technical and software skills. These may be needed on the shop floor or in specialist staff groups, according to the management strategies discussed above. Skill enhancement at any level seems to produce the need for a change of emphasis. The focus shifts from time served to standards attained, and training becomes broader-based. The aim is to produce multi-role or multi-skilled craftsmen, with greater analytical skills and greater ability to evaluate or use information for diagnostic purposes (Cross, 1985; see also Willman and Winch, 1985). Certain new roles emerging at technician and professional levels will call for systems thinking (eg CAD systems managers, front-line systems managers and manufacturing professionals).

The influence of IT on employees' careers obviously depends on:

- job and organisational design;

- employment and training.

It is arguable that the demand for specialist EDP skills, coupled with the deskilling of erstwhile generalists, is leading to more fragmented internal labour markets. It could also be argued that career paths are broadening because of the demand for cross-functional integrative generalists. However, to the extent that deskilling occurs and employees are pushed into the periphery of the 'flexible organisation'. The prediction is that careers are likely to be characterised by breaks in full-time employment (redundancies and lay-offs, part-time employment, government-assisted work experience schemes, short-term contracts and even job sharing). The core group may experience a truncated period of continuous employment. Entry will be delayed by prolonged education and training. Continuous learning and change may well lead to premature 'burn-out' and an early departure, especially as appraisal systems become more stringent in the fight to cut down non-contributory overheads. All employees are likely to face high levels of job change and even changes in career direction through, for example:

- demands for flexibility in the internal labour market;
- the networking of former core employees in the primary external labour market;
- the conversion of deskilled employees to casual workers in the secondary external labour market.

While employees may well work fewer hours in the course of a lifetime, the intensity of their work is likely to increase. Child (1987, p28), citing Massey and Meegan (1982), suggests that the use of contracting out and networking is likely to reinforce management control: payment is for work actually done, or for specified hours on a specified job, which reduces the porosity between productive labour and paid (but unproductive) labour.

Management faces many new challenges:

- management of change;
- designing IT to meet user requirements;
- job design;
- organisational design;
- employment, training and development issues.

By incorporating IT into its products and processes, a company can win itself a competitive edge. Product quality can be improved, and so can the company's response to unpredictable consumer demand. However, this is also likely to reduce product (and service) life-cycles dramatically. How can management ensure that core employees learn the skills they will need to move rapidly from research and development into effective production and marketing, and to generate an acceptable return on capital within a decreasing payback period (Morgan, 1988, p99). How can employees who are used to low-risk bureaucratic structures and hierarchical values adapt to the demands of autonomy? Can they learn the necessary entrepreneurial skills? Will they be prepared to experiment, and to commit themselves to learning and creativity (Argyris and Schon, 1978)?

Investment in IT is a response to these market-driven demands, but it also helps to create them; and these demands underlie current calls to change the traditional view of specialist personnel management. These managers are no longer 'guardians' of employees and organisational issues. Instead they are in the front line of a wider, strategic view of human resource management.

REFERENCES

Argyris C, Schon D, *Organisational Learning*, Addison-Wesley, 1978

Armstrong P, Labour and monopoly capital, in Hyman R, Streeck W, eds, *New Technology and Industrial Relations*, Blackwell, 1988, pp143–159

Atkinson J, Manpower strategies for flexible organisations, *Personnel Management*, 1984, vol 16, no 8, pp28–31

Atkinson J, Meager N, *New Forms of Work Organisation* (IMS Report No 121), Institute of Manpower Studies, 1986a

Atkinson J, Meager N, Is flexibility just a flash in the pan?, *Personnel Management*, 1986b, vol 18, no 9, pp26–29

Bessant J, *Microprocessors in Production Processes*, Policy Studies Institute, 1982

Bessant J, Management and manufacturing innovation: The case of information technology, in Winch G, ed, *Information Technology in Manufacturing Processes: Case Studies in Technological Change*, Rossendale, 1983

Bhattacharyya S K, *State-of-the-art and Future Directions* (Presentation to the TCC Workshop on advanced engineering technology in the UK mechanical engineering industries), TCC, 1985

Bjørn-Andersen N, Management use of new office technology, in Otway H, Peltu M, eds, *The Management Challenge of New Office Technology*, Butterworths, 1984

Bjørn-Andersen N, Hedberg B, Designing information systems in an organisational perspective, *Prescriptive Models of Organisations* (vol 5), North Holland, 1977

Blackler F, Brown C, Alternative models to guide the design and introduction of the new information technologies into work organisations, *Journal of Occupational Psychology*, 1986, vol 59, pp287–314

Braverman H, *Labor and Monopoly Capital*, Monthly Review Press, 1974

Brodner P, ed, *Skill-based Automated Manufacturing*, Pergamon, 1987

Buchanan D, Boddy D, *Organisations in the Computer Age*, Gower, 1983

Cakir A, Hart D J, Stewart T F M, *Visual Display Terminals: A Manual Covering Ergonomics, Workplace Design, Health and Safety, and Task Organisation*, John Wiley, 1978

Card S K, Moran T P, Newell A, *The Psychology of Human–Computer Interaction*, Erlbaum, 1983

Carroll J M, Campbell R L, Artifacts as psychological theories: The case of human–computer interaction, *Behaviour and Information Technology*, 1989, vol 8, no 4, pp247–256

Cherns A, The principles of sociotechnical design, *Human Relations*, 1976, vol 29, pp783–792

Child J, New technology and developments in management organisation, *Omega*, 1984a, vol 12, pp211–223

Child J, *Organisation*, Harper and Row, 1984b

Child J, Organisational design for advanced manufacturing technology, in Wall T D, Clegg C W, Kemp N J, eds, *The Human Side of Advanced Manufacturing Technology*, John Wiley, 1987, pp101–133

Child J, Loveridge R, Harvey J, Spencer A, Microelectronics and the quality of employment in services, in P Marstrand, ed, *New Technology and the Future of Work*, Frances Pinter, 1984, pp163–190

Christie B, ed, *Human Factors of Information Technology in the Office*, John Wiley, 1985

Civil Service College, *Business Analysis and COMPACT* (internal report available from Civil Service College, London), 1987

Clark J, McLoughlin I, Rose H, King R, *The Process of Technological Change*, Cambridge University Press, 1988

Clegg C W, The dark side of IT: A personal comment, *Behaviour and Information Technology*, 1989, vol 8, no 5, pp399–402

Clegg C W, Kemp N J, Information technology: Personnel, where are you?, *Personnel Review*, 1986, vol 15, no 1, pp8–15

Clegg C W, Ravden S J, Corbett J M, Johnson G I, Allocating functions in computer-integrated manufacturing: A review and a new method, *Behaviour and Information Technology*, 1988, vol 8, no 3, 1988, pp175–190

Clegg C W, Symon G J, A review of human-centred manufacturing technology and a framework for its design and evaluation, *International Review of Ergonomics*, 1989, vol 3, pp15–47

Clegg C W, Warr P B et al, *People and Computers: How to Evaluate your Company's New Technology*, Ellis Horwood, 1989

Cockburn C, *Brothers: Male Dominance and Technological Change*, Pluto Press, 1983

Cooley M, *Architect or Bee?*, Hogarth Press, 1987

Cross M, *Towards the Flexible Craftsman*, TCC, 1985

Cummings T, Blumberg M, Advanced manufacturing technology and work design, in Wall T D, Clegg C W, Kemp N J, eds, *The Human Side of Advanced Manufacturing Technology*, John Wiley, 1987, pp37–60

Dainoff M J, Dainoff M H, *A Manager's Guide to Ergonomics in the Electronic Office*, John Wiley, 1987

Ehn P, Kyng M, Sundblad Y, The Utopia Project, in Briefs V, Ciborra C,

Scheider L, eds, *Systems Design For, With and By the Users*, North Holland, 1983

Francis A, *New Technology at Work*, Clarendon Press, 1986

Frese M, Human–computer interaction in the office, in Cooper C L, Robertson I T, eds, *International Review of Industrial and Organisational Psychology*, John Wiley, 1987

Gardiner M M, Christie B, eds, *Applying Cognitive Psychology to User-interface Design*, John Wiley, 1987

Gill C, *Work, Unemployment and New Technology*, Polity, 1985

Grandjean E, *Ergonomics in Computerised Offices*, Taylor and Francis, 1987

Handy C, *The Future of Work*, Blackwell, 1984

Health and Safety Executive, *Visual Display Units*, HMSO, 1983

Helander M, ed, *Handbook of Human–Computer Interaction*, North Holland, 1988

Hirschhcim R, *Office Automation: A Social and Organisational Perspective*, John Wiley, 1985

Hyman R, Flexible specialisation: Miracle or myth?, in Hyman R, Streeck W, eds, *New Technology and Industrial Relations*, Blackwell, 1988

Ingersoll Engineers, *Integrated Manufacture*, IFS Publications, 1985

Jenkins C, Sherman B, *The Collapse of Work*, Eyre Methuen, 1979

Jones B, Destruction or redistribution of engineering skills? The case of numerical control, in Wood S, ed, *The Degradation of Work?*, Hutchinson, 1982, pp179–200

Jones B, *Skills, Tacit Knowledge and Automation of Metalworking Production* (paper given to the University of Aston Management Centre), November 1983

Kearney A T, *Computer-integrated Manufacturing: Competitive Advantage or Technological Dead End?* (report published by A T Kearney Ltd), 1988

Kelly J, Management's redesign of work, in Knights D et al, eds, *Job Redesign: Critical Perspectives on the Labour Process*, Gower, 1985

Kemp N J, Clegg C W, Wall T D, *Human Aspects of Computer-aided Manufacturing* (paper presented to the IEE International Conference on Computer-aided Manufacturing, University of Warwick), December 1984

McLoughlin I, Clark J, *Technological Change at Work*, Open University, 1988

Manwaring T, Wood S, The ghost in the labour process, in Knights D et al, eds, *Job Redesign: Critical Perspectives on the Labour Process*, Gower, 1985

Martin T, Ulich E, Warnecke H J, Appropriate automation for flexible manufacturing, in Iserman R, ed, *Automation Control World Congress*, Pergamon, 1987

Massey D, Megan R, *The Anatomy of Job Loss*, Methuen, 1982

Monk A, ed, *Fundamentals of Human–Computer Interaction*, Academic Press, 1985

Morgan G, *Riding the Waves of Change: Developing Managerial Competences for a Turbulent World*, Jossey-Bass, 1988

Mueller W S, Clegg C W, Wall T D et al, Pluralist beliefs about new technology within a manufacturing organisation, *New Technology, Work and Employment*, 1986, vol 1, pp127–139

Mumford E, *Designing Human Systems*, MBS Publications, 1983

Nickerson R S, *Using Computers: The Human Factors of Information Systems*, MIT Press, 1986

Noble D, Social choice in machine design: The case of automatically controlled machine tools, in Zimbalist A, ed, *Case Studies on the Labor Process*, Monthly Review Press, 1979

Norman D, Draper S, eds, *User-centred System Design*, Erlbaum, 1986

Oborne D, *Computers at Work*, John Wiley, 1985

Pearce B, *Health Hazards of VDTs?*, John Wiley, 1984

Phillips K E, Galer M D, *The Development of Computer Human Factors Classification and Collection of Human Factors Knowledge* (interim report available from HUSAT Research Centre, Loughborough University of Technology), 1986

Piore M, Sabel C, *The Second Industrial Divide*, Basic Books, 1984

Rainbird H, New technology, training and union strategies, in Hyman R, Streeck W, eds, *New Technology and Industrial Relations*, Blackwell, 1988, pp174–85

Ravden S J, Johnson G I, *Evaluating the Usability of Human–Computer Interfaces: A Practical Method*, Ellis Horwood, 1989

Rose M, Jones B, Management strategy and trade union responses in work reorganisation schemes at establishment level, in Knights D et al, eds, *Job Redesign: Critical Perspectives on the Labour Process*, Gower, 1985

Rosenbrock H, *Technology and Society* (paper given as Cockcroft Lecture, Manchester Technology Association), 1987

Rothwell S G, Company employment policies and new technology in manufacturing and service sectors, in Warner M, ed, *Microprocessors, Manpower and Society*, Gower, 1984

Scarbrough H, Maintenance workers and new technology, *Industrial Relations Journal*, 1984, vol 15, no 4, pp9–16

Senker P, Engineering skills in the robot age, in Mastrand P, ed, *New Technology and the Future of Work and Skills*, Frances Pinter, 1984a

Senker P, Implications of CAD/CAM for management, *Omega*, 1984b, vol 12, pp225–231

Shneiderman B, *Designing the User Interface: Strategies for Effective Human–Computer Interaction*, Addison-Wesley, 1986

Smith S L, Mosier J N, *Guidelines for User-system Interface Software* (Technical Report ESD-TR-86-278, MTR 10090), Mitre Corporation, 1986

Spinas P, Ackermann D, Ulich E, User participation in software development: Results of case studies, in Bullinger H J, Protonatorios E N, Bouwhuis D, Reim F, eds, *Eurinfo '88*, North Holland, 1988

Suchman L, *Plans and Situated Actions*, Cambridge University Press, 1987

Taylor F, *Principles of Scientific Management*, Harper, 1911

Thompson J D, *Organisations in Action*, McGraw Hill, 1967

Ulich E, Individual differences in human–computer interaction: Concepts and research findings, in Salvendy G, ed, *Cognitive Engineering in the Design of Human–Computer International Expert Systems*, Elsevier, 1987

Voss C A, *Management and the New Manufacturing Technologies* (unpublished paper, Australian Graduate School of Management, Kensington, New South Wales), 1984

Wall T D, Kemp N J, The nature and implications of advanced manufacturing technology: Introduction, in Wall T D, Clegg C W, Kemp N J, eds, *The Human Side of Advanced Manufacturing Technology*, John Wiley, 1987, pp1–4

Wilkinson B, *The Shopfloor Politics of New Technology*, Heinemann, 1983

Williamson O E, *Markets and Hierarchies: Analysis and Antitrust Implications*, Free Press, 1975

Willman P, Cowan R, New technology in banking: The impact of autotellers on staff numbers, in Warner M, ed, *Microprocessors, Manpower and Society*, Gower, 1984

Willman P, Winch G, *Innovation and Management Control: Labour Relations at BL Cars*, Cambridge University Press, 1985

Wilson F, Computer numerical control and constraints, in Knights D, Willmott H, eds, *New Technology and the Labour Process*, Macmillan, 1988, pp66–90.

Wood S, ed, *The Degradation of Work?*, Hutchinson, 1982

Section I
Manufacturing Sector

1 Manufacturing change at Belma Joints

Chris Hendry

BACKGROUND AND SETTING

Belma Joints is a subsidiary of a UK-based international engineering group. It is one of a number of companies within the group making transmission products for the motor industry. In the 1960s and 70s it benefitted from the switch to front-wheel drive vehicles, where it had originated a unique product, the constant velocity (CV) joint. In the 1970s, in order to supply car manufacturers on a global basis, the group acquired other subsidiaries in Germany and France. These subsidiaries had developed their own version of the CV joint. Plants were also opened in North America. As a result, Belma's cost structure relative to these new plants began to deteriorate. Towards the end of the decade the company came under increasing price (and quality) pressure from its major customers, themselves seriously threatened by Japanese manufacturers. Belma's patents expired in the late 1980s, and this, combined with the risk of losing one or more of its three principal customers, threatened its long-term survival. Moreover, the collapse of the UK markets for trucks and agricultural vehicles put its other major product line, propeller shafts, in serious jeopardy.

Initially, management improved productivity by closing three peripheral plants and concentrating production on one site. Next, propeller shaft production was transferred to another company within the group. Belma's own facilities were entirely devoted to CV joints, where there were prospects for continued growth. During the rationalisation process between 1979–83 the number of employees was reduced from nearly 3700 to just over 2000. Nevertheless, by concentrating redundancies elsewhere the company maintained good relations with the workforce on the main site. The process produced a significant improvement in profitability (see Table 1.1).

In 1982 the company secured its medium-term future with a series of five-year sales agreements. These agreements were made on the basis of immediate and ongoing price concessions. To fund these, management set about modernising the plant to reduce operating costs and achieve

| | (£'000) | | | |
	1980	1981	1982	1983
Sales	66,299	65,997	62,279	77,875
Profit before tax	(754)	772	(2,467)	8,228
Profit after tax and extraord. items	(3,503)	135	(2,645)	4,498
CV Joint Operations Only				
Sales	37,828	46,588	44,362	65,165
(plus royalty income)	n/a	n/a	3,300	n/a
Operating profit	(368)	(1,210)	(3,590)	5,592
Fixed assets			16,409	14,812
Working capital			10,302	14,900

Table 1.1   Belma Joints Financial Results (1980–1983)

more reliable standards of quality. Meanwhile the group's managing director for automotive products had taken senior management and production engineers from the CV joint companies to study Japanese manufacturing systems. He then instructed each company to develop an engineering strategy and a modernisation plan that would enable them to compete into the 1990s.

PLANT MODERNISATION

In late 1983 Belma Joints engaged consultants to help develop a manufacturing strategy. The proposals that emerged early in 1984 were governed by three objectives:

- the need to reduce product costs;

- the need to cut working capital (in view of the state of group finances);

- the need to improve product quality.

The targets laid down for return on sales and capital included a 50% reduction in direct and line-related indirect labour (eg setters, inspectors and labourers) and a 25% reduction in overheads (notably in tooling, maintenance supervision and quality control). This called for a total reduction in the labour force of around 800 – or 40% of all employees (see Table 1.2). Table 1.3 shows the financial savings envisaged.

1984			1989/90
Superintendents/ Supervisors	2	24	Section Managers
Production Foremen	30	0	⎰ Team Leaders
Chargehands	2	218	⎱ Tech. Operatives
Direct Operators	837	182	
Setters–Operators/ Toolsetters	220	21	
Labourers	91	24	
Others	6	49	
Inspectors	101	37	
Mechanical maintenance	71	56	
Electrical maintenance	28	28	
Maintenance labourers	28	0	
Toolroom	63	51	
	1529	730	

Table 1.2   Some Projected Changes in Occupational Categories in Works and Production from New Technology at Belma Joints

The existing plant comprised some 1400 machines. Of these, half were more than 15 years old, and a third were more than 20 years old. These machines ranged from stand-alone, manually loaded equipment to modern computer numerically controlled (CNC) machine tools featuring limited automation of materials transfer. It was clearly time for a radical

In financial terms, the following savings were envisaged:
Projected Savings

	Before		After	
	£m	% of total	£m	% of total
Materials	22.74	38%	20.92	44%
Direct (and line-related indiret) labour	9.52	16%	4.76	10%
Overheads	27.10	46%	21.68	46%
	59.36		**47.36**	

Table 1.3   Projected Savings

redesign of these facilities. This involved a substantially reduced number of machine tools, and improved layout. By 1980, moreover, the CNC and robot technologies were mature and reliable. As the consultants noted:

> The basis for achieving the substantial cost reduction required is a significant investment in flexible automation, including state-of-the-art machine tool and materials handling technology.

As we have seen, the company's main objectives were to cut direct and indirect manning and reduce work in progress. At the same time, product volumes at Belma were high. With 33 types of CV joint, and three major customers, output was running at around six million joints per annum. This led the company to favour a form of just-in-time (JIT) manufacture involving an integrated flexible flowline system rather than the more usual flexible manufacturing system (FMS). A series of machine cells, each dedicated to part of the task, was linked by a pallet conveyor system. The main (bell) line produced the bell-shaped outer housing of the CV joint. This line comprised seven CNC machine cells with one, two or three machines in each cell to achieve a balanced line. Each cell carried out operations such as turning, grinding, induction hardening, and thread and spline rolling. Robots transferred individual components to and from machine operations along the 100-metre line. Three less complex lines produced other parts for final assembly.

The lines incorporated some innovative (and untried) technology, including laser crack detection designed by Belma's own engineers.

However, the whole concept depended on putting together equipment from Italy, Germany, Sweden, Japan and the USA; initially very little was available in the UK. The plan was that three similar groups of lines would eventually be set up, replacing the old technology for everything except reworking and short runs.

The new, integrated lines were intended to run continuously at a rate of 240 pieces an hour, despite reduced manning levels. This meant that operators would have to take all 'first level' decisions at the point of production. 'First level' decisions included basic fault-finding and maintenance, as well as validating and editing programs. To ensure flexibility, the operators would function as a team backed by a small 'central resource' of specialist maintenance engineers. This called for what the company described as 'technical operatives' with knowledge of machining, programming, hydraulics, electrics and electronics. Demarcations between electrical and mechanical trades would have to be removed as operatives became multi-skilled.

At this stage the management and their consultants were also considering the creation of 'team leaders'. These team leaders, recruited from the technical operatives, would take the role of foremen/chargehands under section managers. The idea was consonant with the high degree of initiative expected from the group as a whole, and from individual operatives. In essence, jobs and work organisation were modelled on ideas of 'responsible autonomy', with minimal specification of tasks and minimal supervision. As the managing director, Tom Guest, put it:

> We wrote all the nice words in the plan about the Japanese style of management and operator involvement, while trying to get away from the idea of 'operators'.

The personnel director, on the other hand, saw the actual design of jobs and work organisation as a logical and pragmatic result of choosing this type of technology:

> The start point was "We're going to have few people. What are we going to do?" . . . They've got to be multi-skilled . . . They've got to be flexible.

However, it was not quite so easy for Belma's production engineers to work out actual manning levels until more detailed work had been done. Their estimates for the two shifts envisaged in the first phase continued to vary between 24 and 36 until late in the day.

THE EXTENT OF CHANGE

The total investment in new plant was costed at £28 million – almost twice the value of Belma's existing assets. This figure included radical improvements in manufacturing support services, design and development, notably the purchase of a computer-aided design and computer-aided manufacturing (CADCAM) system. Quality control, for instance, would be improved by automatic inspection systems on the line, and handling defects would be eliminated by flow-line automation. In general its role would move more towards quality assurance. In plant maintenance, the emphasis would change from a fire-fighting operation ('panic maintenance') to preventative maintenance. With the machine population halved, and standard items of plant such as robots and Siemens controls, maintenance of this kind would be considerably easier, but operators would need to have more formal disciplines, and knowledge of electronics would have to be more widespread. Tooling, similarly, would benefit from greater standardisation of machines. Materials handling would benefit from the endless-loop conveyor built into the bell line, from automatic guided vehicles (AGVs), and from the rationalised plant layout.

The production engineering function, however, was critical to the investment programme. The feasibility analysis included a review of strengths and weaknesses in the company's human resources. The consultants noted that production engineering needed 'urgent strengthening', and supervision was also considered weak. One of the first steps, in 1984, was to recruit a new managing director. As he commented:

> We've had to uprate and update the knowledge and experience of the department as a whole, because no engineer in this company has hands-on experience of new technology.

In fact Belma Joints was one of the few West Midlands firms to maintain its apprentice training programme during the recession. The new managing director was strongly committed to apprenticeships and to training, and the training school was equipped with the latest robotics and CNC equipment. Traditionally half the annual intake of 12–16 apprentices went into production as quality engineers, setters, and occasionally tooling operatives; the others went into engineering and design. Anticipating 'new tech', the company had raised its intake standards some 18 months earlier, and started to sponsor apprentices onto engineering degree courses at university. By 1984, when the planning of the new lines began, six out of sixteen apprentices were being sponsored in this way every year.

In 1984, however, there was an immediate need for more formally qualified engineers. Over the next two years about 15 new engineers were recruited in a department of 50. At the same time five staff with skills limited to 'tool-proving' activity were redeployed (not always willingly) into production supervision, setting and maintenance. Meanwhile the company lost 12 engineers whose training and experience in leading edge technology had made their skills more marketable.

The company's ability to manage the technical demands of the project was limited, manning reductions would be considerable, and considerable retraining was also necessary. It therefore seemed desirable to phase the investment. As Tom Guest put it: "£30 million would have killed us off, we would have failed." Belma were also aware of the example given by Lucas, who had opened a new plant on a greenfield site at Telford, recruiting an entirely new workforce away from all their old traditions and working practices. Belma never formally asked the unions to guarantee that they would accept changes in work practices as a condition of getting group approval for the investment. Even so, the unions were aware of the alternatives:

> With new tech we lose five jobs and gain one. If we hadn't got an agreement to put new tech in here, it would probably have been done elsewhere, and we would have lost all five jobs. At least there is some security, and the workforce is better equipped with skills for the future if we do fail. At some point in the future, we'll level out with new technology and then maybe start recruiting again. But that's maybe in the 1990s.

In mid-1984, a steering group chaired by the personnel director was set up. Its tasks were:

- to oversee the project;

- to identify implications for each function (eg that in a JIT system the buying department needed to give more attention to delivery in its negotiations);

- to create 'ownership' across the company.

This last objective would help to challenge functional boundaries, especially between staff and works, setting the wider climate for change.

In May 1984 the company began training staff in statistical process control (SPC). This, too, was a valuable climate-setting activity, but also part of Belma's policy of improving quality. At this time the company was still negotiating the terms for new technology, and the capital expenditure had still to be approved. Works (machine operators and supervisors) and staff (quality and production engineers) all attended the initial training sessions together, helping to break down barriers between them. The SPC course also made everyone conscious of the need to raise standards generally. The managing director's presence on every course helped to emphasise this:

> He'd only spoken to me once before, and he'd said "Move!" He turned up and he started chatting. He actually said, "Have you got anything you want to say?" And people started to get involved.

SPC was the first formal training that semi-skilled people on the shop floor had received for many years. It revealed deficiencies in basic numeracy and literacy, and encouraged people (with the company's support) to seek help with this. This was a valuable precursor to training for 'new tech'. It also helped to create a new climate for training and education throughout the company. For instance, it stimulated a request for open learning facilities and basic CNC training, which the company helped to arrange at the local technical college.

IMPLEMENTING CHANGE

New technology affected almost everyone in the company. Even so, the most visible impact was on the shop floor. It was they who had to bear the brunt of redundancies, new skills and changes in terms and conditions.

The company was dominated by one union, the Metal Mechanics (then part of TASS), with 70% membership of the workforce. The AEU had 20%, while EETPU and T&G had a handful each. The bulk of the Metal Mechanics' members were machine operators on piecework, but union representation was not strictly split along skill lines. In particular, the ten shop stewards elected to the Joint Industrial Council (JIC) acted as a cohesive group under the leadership of Mike Thomas, a highly respected and capable convenor. Belma's well-developed system of joint consultation created an open, cooperative and pragmatic relationship between management and the union, and a willingness to face change. In nine years only one day's work had been lost through strike action (and that in a national day of protest). As one member put it:

> Everything gets sorted out here. The industrial relations are brilliant – basically because we don't have inter-union problems, and because of the JIC. We don't stop work while we're sorting a problem out. We might get angry. They'll be ranting and raving up there, but we'll still be working . . .

> We have a convenor who's a very good manager. While he looks after our interests, he also scolds us and wouldn't let us go further than is for our own good . . .

Similarly, according to personnel director Peter Walters:

> We discuss everything and anything. Management set the object- ives, but then we, decide jointly on the means. The style is to make a lot of noise, and settle. Mike Thomas is essentially looking for solutions to problems. The biggest rows are not about pay issues, but where he feels a lack of consultation that puts him on the spot when he hasn't a ready answer to his members.

On top of this there was a strong family culture (literally, in that

	Age Profile (1984)				
	Total	Staff		Works	
		M	F	M	F
16–20	68	7	4	55	2
21–25	119	30	6	81	2
26–30	198	37	6	155	–
31–35	147	25	5	115	2
36–40	191	35	6	145	5
41–45	247	42	4	195	6
46–50	254	29	4	211	10
51–55	299	38	6	248	7
56–60	211	19	6	185	1
61–65	55	10	–	45	–
	1789	272	47	1435	35

Table 1.4

"everyone has an aunt or uncle here"), with traditions of long service (see Table 1.4).

The machine operators had high status within the workforce. This was reflected in a system of piecework that provided them with between £180 and £200 a week in 1984. With their bonus running at 50% of earnings, they earned up to £20 more than those on the 'skilled' rate (setters, electricians, fitters, foremen and toolroom staff) and more than many production engineers at that time. A favourite phrase was "the pieceworker is king". The company acknowledged this imbalance, but accepted the union view (as the personnel director put it) that:

> The pieceworkers are your motivated people – your skilled, your indirects, are not motivated. Equally, in the old days, we couldn't afford to lose our best workers as foremen, so the foreman's job was not looked up to. He was a service to the production man.

The consultants, however, saw the piecework system and other elements like it as "complex and dated", while the compressed grading structure that determined other rates made it difficult to recruit staff. The consultants favoured merit payments as technical operatives gained new skills, but while the company wanted a small bonus element (up to 15%) it felt this would be divisive. It was also open to question whether piecework would be practicable on the new lines. Mike Thomas remained convinced that incentives were essential to keep men motivated.

The Metal Mechanics, as the pieceworkers' union, also had considerable leverage in the allocation of jobs through the principle of service. Traditionally machine operators started as labourers. Later they moved into machining, receiving basic training from their colleagues. When a well-paid job fell vacant, the union manoeuvred the longest-serving applicant into the vacancy so that his eventual pension would be enhanced. The company had decided to break with this tradition. The union, while recognising this decision, were concerned about possible management favouritism in selecting people for new jobs, and the problems this might create in selling the new proposals.

The same morality influenced their attitude to the payment of those trained in new technology. As Peter Walters commented:

> We feel they are worth more. But the union doesn't, because, as they say, you spent some of our money (meaning the company as a whole) in training these people. So while you've been training them, we've all had to work harder to support them. So it's wrong if they come out with a better package than what we've got. You mustn't be divisive, so pay them the skilled rate.

Similarly, the union sought a training rate £40 below what the top pieceworker could earn (and £20 below the skilled rate). It also supported the idea of clawing back training costs from any trainee who left within an unreasonable period; this period was written into trainees' contracts. For many, these policies meant a step backwards to begin with. However, the pay for technical operatives later increased to parity with top pieceworkers.

Agreement on new technology was signalled when an area within the factory was fenced off and set aside to receive the new plant (the 'slab'). In the autumn of 1985 the newly-trained technical operatives began installing the plant. This reinforced their 'ownership' of the lines, a process that had started when they visited suppliers (mostly abroad) to become familiar with the equipment. It also kept them occupied during delays in the delivery.

By late 1986, nine months after start-up, the lines had reached only 80% efficiency, and management were applying pressure to reduce the number and length of shutdowns which they thought unnecessary. The production manager attributed these shutdowns to the high proportion of ex-'indirect' employees (75%) selected for the first phase. The managing director was more inclined to blame their training:

> I wouldn't take shopfloor people off for six to nine months' training again. They've lost the work ethic. We've trained them in everything else except achievement and there is no impatience to get things done. They switch the line off for hours, and they've lost sight of what it's all about. You can almost hear them saying,

"Break down! Break down! I want to use the skills I've got." I've actually got the convenor saying to me, "We've got to watch this multi-skill thing, because it's too interesting for them."

To correct this problem, management introduced more directive supervision. This combined an old-style chargehand for the whole area with more technically-oriented supervisors (from outside production) working closely with the line. However, technical operatives and maintenance staff saw the problem as a lack of management understanding:

Where they went completely wrong was they educated us, then they said, "We'll get you a couple of managers." If I'm going to change my attitudes, then they've got to change theirs, and they should be part of a team . . .

Glorified machine operators is what we are. I've done a lot of training, five and a half years in all. At the end of the day I didn't expect to be a glorified pieceworker.

THE FUTURE

As everyone gains experience with the lines, and phases two and three come in, this balance could well change again. The technical operatives themselves have already changed their views about the idea of team leaders. The company avoided writing job descriptions for technical operatives because it expected and hoped that they would push out the boundaries of their jobs. Maintenance staff, for example, welcomed the idea that technical operatives might take over fringe areas of their work (which they themselves regarded as chores), and even basic fault-finding routines. From the beginning the technical operatives have also carried out weekly preventative maintenance on Saturday mornings. As a maintenance engineer put it:

It will grow as much as the technical operatives will allow it or want it to. It depends how interested they are in going deeper. There are no defined limits as to how far they are expected to go. It's massively flexible as to what's expected.

Early on, they also wrote the programs for CNC grinding, and have continued to modify and edit all programs. As Peter Walters noted:

The difference between an engineer and shop floor has now shrunk. What they're doing on the slab, in the old days maybe would have been done by an engineering technician. They're starting to blur the lines. I'd like to think over the next few years that the people writing the programs will be as much on the shop floor as in offices. Some of those lads are quite capable of doing that.

On the other hand, through CADCAM, there is the potential to write and directly communicate all CNC programs to the line through DNC hard-wired links, and to modify them directly. This system was installed in mid-1985; the company prefers to call it 'computer-aided engineering', which is regarded as a better description of the way it is used. However, because time was needed to train staff and build a database, Belma did not expect to link the system fully to the shop floor until the end of the decade. For the time being, the priority was to solve fundamental problems involved in completing the reinvestment, and raising the technical standards of engineers. As the engineering director said:

> The technology is still developing, and there is an argument frankly for letting someone else be the guinea pig. Let them solve the problems. I've got enough problems just getting the lines in.

CASE STUDY TASKS

Although the new lines were the showpiece, the changes proposed would affect most people in the company. The consultants foresaw "an equivalent step change in people policies" emanating from the step change in technology. A number of people could be expected to play key roles in such a process. You, however, as the personnel director, have a central role. You must anticipate problems that are likely to be encountered, plan your human resources strategy, and adapt it during the implementation process.

An effective approach to the questions that follow is to consider them in groups of two or three, and then return for a class discussion on each in turn. There is also a video (produced by Granada TV's *Jobwatch* programme) that can be used in conjunction with the discussion.

1 What considerations would influence you in:

   a the decision to phase the investment?

   b the choice of a 'brownfield' site, within the present factory, for the investment?

2 How would you manage the industrial relations process, and what would you be looking for in new agreements?

3 How would you go about selecting and retraining, bearing in mind the job requirements and the impact of the changes on the workforce as a whole?

4 What are the likely knock-on effects of the changes in production workers' skills?

ESSENTIAL READING

Jones B, Work and flexible automation in Britain: A review of developments and possibilities, *Work, Employment and Society*, 1988, vol 2, no 4, pp451–486

Wilkinson B, *The Shopfloor Politics of New Technology*, Heinemann, 1983

ADDITIONAL READING

Andrews K R, *The Concept of Corporate Strategy* (rev ed), Irwin, 1980

Hendry C, Pettigrew A, Multi-skilling in the round, *Personnel Management*, April 1987, pp36–43

Jones B, Scott P, Flexible manufacturing systems in Britain and the USA, *New Technology, Work and Employment*, vol 2, no 1, 1987, pp27–36

Scott P, Automated machining systems and the role of engineering craft skills, in Bullinger H J, ed, *Proceedings of the Second International Conference on Human Factors in Manufacturing*, IFS Publications, 1985, pp121–130

2 Implementation of a CADCAM system: The management of change at EML

Gillian Symon and Chris Clegg

INTRODUCTION

"This is a moaning minnies' charter!" The engineering director had clearly had enough of the feedback he and his colleagues were receiving. The other three (Bob and Dave from corporate engineering and John from management services) sat quietly while he warmed to his theme:

> You see, we work in the real world. I've been trying to get CADCAM in here for ten years. Ten years! And I've had to lie, cheat and connive to do it. I'm not complaining. That's what I'm paid so well to do. Don't get me wrong. I agree with every word you've said. But those quotes you read back to us could have been laid at every new implementation I've ever done. Ever! Those guys sat here have managed the best implementation this company has ever seen. Bar none! And we've got almost no resources to do it.

> All right, so it isn't perfect. But what is? The system is in. It's happening, and we'll cope. It takes strong characters to get things done in this company, or you don't survive. Politics, that's what it's all about here. Lying to get a three-year payback on a £3 million investment that is impossible but that accountants insist on. Cajoling to carry people with you when they don't want to change. Persuading the guys in manufacturing that we're not after their empire. Wearing down the MD, whose first response to every investment is that we can't afford it. That's what my world is like. So don't tell me about end users and what their worries are!

The researchers were half-way through their second feedback session, this time to the senior managers. Unfortunately, only the four people who were responsible for the introduction of the new system had turned up, and they were proving defensive. No one from manufacturing had come, nor any key users from the product groups. It was turning into something of a rough ride. The researchers continued to defend their position:

> You're talking as if we're selling you some problems you haven't

49

really got. That it's only people taking advantage of the opportunity to complain. But we're not convinced that the new system *will* actually perform as you want. The evidence from elsewhere is that new IT systems are almost always a disappointment, operating well below what people expect. And this is often because the change isn't well managed. In fact your own people, who we met this morning, agree with what we say. Almost all the people we've interviewed over the past months said there's a real danger that the new CADCAM will fail, just like your last large IT investment – and everyone says *that* failed because no one took account of the users!

And so the meeting went on, with the researchers unhappily cast in the role of academic idealists failing to understand the daily politics of life in an engineering company. In fact it had gone much better in the morning, when they had fed back their report on how the CADCAM implementation was being managed to more junior members of the company. These were the people much more directly involved, most of whom would be users of the system in one way or another. All of them had been interviewed about the change. The turnout then had been excellent, with people from manufacturing methods, corporate engineering, management services, and designers from the different product groups. There had been queries about one or two points, but a lot of agreement that the change needed managing differently. Above all, these users complained of lack of resources and lack of direction and information. They were particularly interested in what the senior managers would have to say later that day!

The researchers had originally agreed the terms of reference for their study in Engineering and Manufacturing Ltd (EML) with Bob, the chief designer in corporate engineering. The objectives of their study were to examine and help optimise the impact of the new CADCAM from an organisational rather than a technical perspective. The company had been very open, and the researchers had been allowed to interview whomever they wished. Altogether they had spoken to 35 key people from different levels and different functions in the company. This is what they found . . .

THE ORGANISATIONAL SETTING

The first time the researchers went to visit EML, in the north of England, they were immediately struck by the sense of tradition pervading the company. Many of the 2000 employees have been at EML for 20 years or more, and over this time they have developed a very strong sense of pride in their achievements and abilities, and a belief in expertise and established methods.

EML have built up a reputation with their customers for reliability and innovation in the field of light engineering. This reputation is standing them in good stead in the highly competitive market of the late 1980s. This is also particularly important given that their products, aerospace parts, are subject to strict internal and external rules for design and manufacture. These rules have led to a company-wide emphasis on achieving high standards in design and production. They have a (relatively) firm governmental client base, but also attract contracts from a variety of multinationals.

Right from their first interview with the chief designer, Bob, the researchers got the impression that EML is good at coping with and solving problems when they arise, but is rarely proactive (eg in planning ahead to *prevent* problems). After a recent management training programme, Bob had been surprised to discover "how little we know about business" and "our lack of an overall view".

The researchers' first problem was trying to understand the organisational structure at EML! Due to expansion plans (yet to come to fruition) they have adopted a new organisational structure (see Figure 2.1) which, like their products, is very complex. The basic organisation is by product group, but overall it could be termed a partial matrix structure. Two of the four product groups share a manufacturing resource which is managed as an independent product group. Each product group has its own designers. The designers within the product groups are responsible for the design of a product that it will meet the customer specification and win the order; manufacturing are responsible for making that product on time and within budget, and to a standard that will be accepted by the customer.

Alongside this structure is the corporate function, acting as resource and support for the product groups. Included here are marketing, personnel and public relations. Due to the company's specialised products, and the high demand for quality, there is also a separate engineering and quality section within corporate; this is usually known as corporate engineering. Corporate engineering has particular responsibility for maintaining engineering standards in design. Their function is to audit both the design process and the product design. Bob the chief designer, Ron the chief auditor and Dave the chief draughtsman operate from this function. Management of EML's computer systems is under the remit of management services. They are usually responsible for IT purchases in order to maintain compatibility between systems.

On the whole, the product groups operate quite independently ("almost like different firms"), but this has led to problems of coordination and integration, particularly between the different design groups and manufacturing. Lack of communication has led to difficulties between these two functions over the years, yet they are probably the departments most dependent on one another.

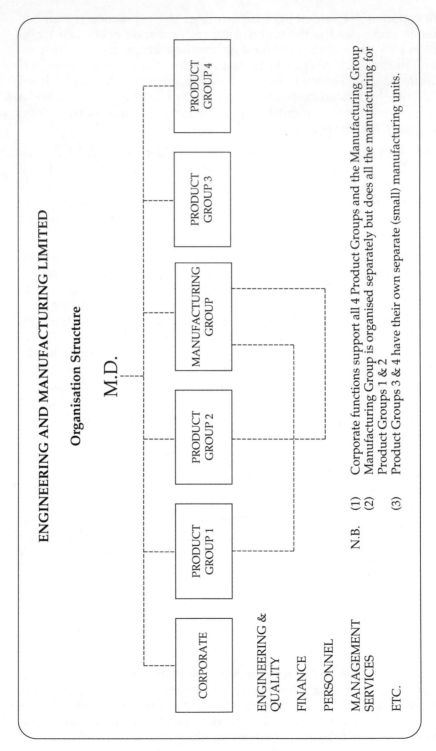

Figure 2.1

THE PRODUCTION CYCLE

Having established what the organisation looked like, the researchers' next step was to find out how the production of an aerospace part is actually achieved. And they had thought the organisational structure was complex!

Each time a customer specification is received, the proposed design goes through a predetermined set of stages. The first 'design schema' (a comparatively rough drawing) is prepared by designers in the product group and sent to the customer. If accepted, the designer then prepares a detailed drawing. This process involves several feedback mechanisms both to check that manufacturing can make the product and to check that the design is up to standard and quality. At each feedback stage it is 'signed off' by the relevant person. There are strict controls on changing drawings, and each change has to be clearly recorded, verified and signed off.

Once the drawing is finished it is passed on to manufacturing (the manufacturing department also accepts drawings from external sources). This is when the drawing is transformed into the actual part. First, the production process has to be scheduled: the right parts have to be available in stores, the machines on the shop floor have to be booked in advance, etc. This is carried out by production planners on a factory-wide basis, and then in more detail by methods engineers (MEs) at the level of individual machines. Their main concern is to use the shop floor capability efficiently, and to produce the part on time.

Some manufacturing processes can be carried out by automatic computer numerically controlled (CNC) machines, and the code to control these machines has to be written by specialist NC programmers in methods engineering. They do this by translating the dimensions of a part drawing into code which controls the operations performed by the machine. Once a part is finally made, it has to be tested to very stringent specifications. Only after it has passed these tests is it released to the customer. In order to maintain engineering and manufacturing standards, the developing product is checked at least three times during the production cycle by the design audit function (with corporate engineering). Both legally and commercially, they cannot afford to make any mistakes.

WORK DEMANDS IN DESIGN AND MANUFACTURING

By this time the researchers were beginning to get a flavour of what it is like to work at EML. In particular, they were beginning to appreciate the differences between design and manufacturing. Consequently they were especially interested in the survey Bob had recently carried out across the product design groups. He had discovered that 40% of design effort is expended on meeting the customer specification (designing for performance) and 20% on considering ease of manufacture. The rest of their effort is split between such tasks as achieving reliability and meeting the delivery date.

Although each drawing is checked by manufacturing long before it reaches production, this process can be cursory, and changes in the design over time can negate it. Furthermore, this checking process usually consists of simply deciding whether or not the part can be made, not whether it could be designed differently so it could be made more easily, or whether it can be made within budget. Sometimes designs are modified *after* they have gone into production. At the end of the line manufacturing often find themselves having to make up time lost earlier in the production cycle so that the parts will be delivered to the customer on time.

EML AND NEW TECHNOLOGY

So what did EML feel about new technology? How did the implementation of their CADCAM system compare with that of other systems?

It soon became clear that an earlier attempt to implement a company-wide management information system had not been entirely successful. It was difficult to use (one designer described it as "a bit anti-people") and there was little inter-departmental consultation at the time. It was designed entirely by management services ("Management services give you the best system, but not necessarily what you want") and a general lack of user training led to mistakes and lost time in use. However, this is regarded – with resignation – as the EML way: "The minimum are trained and the rest pick it up, probably by experimenting."

However, EML have a variety of other systems, including production scheduling systems, CNC machines and NC programming facilities – and no one seemed to be having any difficulties with those.

Overall, then, most employees in EML are familiar with new technology, and the company has experienced little resistance to technological change over recent years. On the whole, however, most of the technological investment has been manufacturing-based rather than office-based; perhaps this is where the production cycle can most easily be automated and speeded up.

THE CADCAM SYSTEM

The first thing the researchers wanted to know was why EML wanted a CADCAM system at all. It was a pretty big investment – their biggest in new technology so far. It was going to cost them £3 million just to buy the system and train their people – and that did *not* include any frills, such as support facilities! How could they justify spending that kind of money?

The main feature of a CADCAM system (computer-aided design joined to computer-aided manufacturing) system is that the whole production process can be carried out using the same system, from designing the part to specifying the NC program. In this case, the designs could be created on screen and then transmitted automatically from a terminal in one of the product groups to another in manufacturing. Methods engineers in manufacturing could then look at the design to work out what planning and scheduling would be needed. (It is unlikely they would actually be able to alter the design.) The NC programmers in the methods area could use the same equipment to draw cutting paths for the machine tools directly onto the design, and this information could then be translated into NC code automatically for the CNC machines on the shop floor. The major benefits, in organisational terms, were envisaged as being:

– a shorter production cycle;

– increased accuracy in both design and manufacturing.

As CADCAM explicitly links design and manufacture, it was hoped that the new system would improve communication, so solving some of the problems of integration between departments.

Although EML's customers generally saw them as reliable, the company thought that they could improve their image still further by using advanced technology. They had begun to experience problems, as some clients insisted on communicating on disk rather than on paper. Designs on disk from external sources were a particular problem for manufacturing. The use of CADCAM might also attract more contracts, and better qualified staff. In the highly competitive market where EML now found themselves, CADCAM might be just the thing to convince their customers that they were moving with the times. It would also, in all probability, allow them to bring forward their delivery dates. However, these advantages had to be weighed against the potential costs of the ensuing disruption, and a proper balance had to be kept between maintaining reliability and improving efficiency.

That was the 'official' perception – but emphases varied. For the designers, the major benefit of CADCAM was in the reduced time necessary to produce a design. Editing drawings would also be much quicker. After the initial 'rough' drawing had been approved, it would be a much simpler process to prepare all the detailed drawings: now, instead of copying out the drawing again, parts of the original rough could be blown up on screen, and the details could be filled in immediately.

Furthermore, completed drawings (eg for repeat production) would be much more accessible on a database than they were in the drawing library. However, the designers were adamant that they would not be forced into using the system – drawing boards would still be available, though they would gradually be phased out.

Within manufacturing, the introduction of CADCAM was seen as a step towards CIM (computer-integrated manufacturing). They hoped that their different systems would eventually be linked, cutting down on paperwork and speeding up the production process. As far as the NC programmers were concerned, the more routine parts of their task would be considerably reduced. They would be able to work straight on to the screen, on top of the final drawing, rather than copying a paper drawing on to the screen first. This would cut down on errors in the translation process from drawing to NC code, as well as speeding up programming considerably.

Another advantage that manufacturing could see was in 'design for manufacturability'. In fact, as far as the manufacturing engineering manager was concerned, this should be the major reason for the introduction of CADCAM. Constraints should be built into the CADCAM database which would 'force' designers into designing for manufacturing capability, for example using a restricted range of readily available tooling. Furthermore, because the 'drawings' would be more easily accessible through the computer system, manufacturing would be able to check the designs for manufacturability much earlier in the design cycle.

For their part, corporate engineering saw CADCAM as a means of standardising working practices (based on their own engineering standards manuals) and improving data management. Their particular concern was for the database and the control system. The database would hold the drawing data, and encapsulate the engineering standards (currently contained in several manuals). These manuals specified everything from the standard layout for a drawing (including spaces for signatures, relevant headings, etc) to recommended manufacturers of screws that would be bought in. With a database to provide all this information automatically all designs, no matter who created them, would look exactly the same and match the same high standards. The control system would constrain the design process so that drawings could only be made and processed in predetermined ways:

- A drawing would only be passed on to the next stage if the relevant signatures had been stored on the database.

- Users would have to know the appropriate password to log on, and have the appropriate ID to be allowed to make changes to drawings.

- A drawing would not be released to manufacturing until all relevant signatures had been received.
- It would be easier to track each drawing, as all changes would be recorded.

In summary, the system would control and monitor access to the designs. Theoretically, this would be the same as the manual method – except that a computerised method would make it impossible to bypass any of the rules. Computer terminals could make access easy, so controls would have to be strict. In this way, corporate engineering could be confident that standards were being maintained, and the possibility of error reduced. For those very reasons, the people in charge of the implementation felt it was essential for the control system to be designed and finalised before users had the opportunity to use it in designing and manufacturing a major product.

Corporate engineering wanted to make sure that this changeover to a computerised method of working was simply a change of medium rather than a change in work roles. This was partly because they had to ensure the standards of the old manual system were retained, and partly to maintain continuity and promote ease of learning. As a result, much energy had already been devoted to designing an electronic pad linked to the operating system so that users could 'sign off' drawings with an actual signature, just as they had always done.

Corporate engineering had been given the responsibility of choosing a suitable CADCAM system to match EML's particular needs. The choice was largely influenced by the engineering capabilities of the system, and this reflected the considerations of the decision-makers and the complexity of EML's products. It was therefore technically very advanced – and very expensive!

THE IMPLEMENTATION PROCESS

The project management team included three representatives from corporate engineering (including Bob, the chief designer, and Dave, the chief draughtsman), one from management services, and one from manufacturing. They had decided to install the system in three phases. The first phase involved the installation of eleven terminals, finishing with the full complement of 55 three years into the project.

The project team were meeting at least once a month, but the day-to-day management was the particular concern of two employees. One, Colin from corporate engineering, was full-time; the other, Tim from management services, was part-time. As with any other EML project, progress was recorded on the project management system so that critical paths could be identified and schedules maintained.

The initial implementation proposal to the directors had included a training budget. The project team were keen that everyone who would use the system received adequate training. They realised the importance of operating the system properly to achieve performance targets. To this end the team intended to appoint a full-time trainer, as well as sending an initial group for training by the system manufacturers. In fact they had someone in mind from an early stage: one of the designers, who was already familiar with CAD.

The first people to use the Phase 1 terminals included:

- a designer from each product group;

- a designer from corporate engineering (to concentrate on inputting standards);

- two NC programmers from manufacturing.

This meant each stakeholder group within the company had a representative initial user, so all relevant sections within the company could have some feeling of involvement in the CADCAM implementation.

THE PROBLEM

Having got this far, the project team were beginning to run into difficulties. They were hoping that the researchers might be able to offer advice on some of the non-technical issues – especially on where the terminals should be installed.

Would it be best to put them all together, or in clusters throughout the company? There would certainly not be enough terminals for people to have one each; at best each terminal would be shared by three regular users, so wherever they were put, some kind of rota system for their use would need to be established. Space was another problem. Empty rooms were already at a premium, and the terminals would need complex wiring and proper ventilation. Obviously the new system would lead to better communication between groups, but what other human and organisational factors might they need to consider?

Colin found that more and more of his time became occupied with technical problems; the actual management of the implementation process had become a lesser consideration. These technical problems included:

- designing the database and control system;

- integrating the system with others already in operation, and in particular the management information system.

Eventually the team realised that Colin would need specialist help, and a technical expert was brought in.

The full-time trainer that the team had been 'grooming' for the post was offered a promotion within his own product group, and no longer wanted to train CAD users. The project team felt that his manager did not want to lose him. It is generally accepted in EML that the more people a manager has under him, the greater the influence he wields and the better his prospects of promotion.

In the meantime Colin had shed some of his technical responsibilities, and had now moved on to carrying out training so the project could remain on schedule. He still had little time for managing the project.

One problem they did *not* have was user participation (which made this experience very different from their earlier experience with the management information system). End users were already working on the system, and it was definitely the corporate engineers' 'baby' – they, rather than management services, had full responsibility.

PARTICIPANTS' DIAGNOSIS OF CADCAM IMPLEMENTATION

These were some of the problems perceived by the project team. The researchers were interested to find out how other people in the company perceived the implementation process up until then, and whether they thought there were any problems with it. The general reaction was immediately apparent: many people had no idea what was going on! Even those who thought it unlikely that they would ever use the terminals said they would be glad to know more about CADCAM. People who were actually going to use the system *would* be trained on it, but was that really enough – even for them?

The designers

Most of the designers from corporate engineering were not unduly worried. They knew they would use the system eventually, and expected to be told all they needed to know at the appropriate time. There was certainly no feeling of anxiety. Colleagues who had already been trained on the system appeared to be enthusiastic about it, and since the terminals had been set up in one of the design offices, everyone was quite familiar with them. In fact the designers were rather excited about the new system – it was their 'toy'. It was often called 'the new CAD system' rather than CADCAM. Designers from the different product groups were less knowledgeable about the system, apart from the select few who were already using it. They were interested in knowing more, but were not worried about possible outcomes.

The manufacturing function

Over the road in manufacturing, however, perceptions were rather different. Many people thought they *should* know more, and the whole system was regarded as being 'owned' by corporate engineering. Furthermore, as the potential trainer was initially going to be one of the designers, there was a suspicion that proper training would only be available for the designers, and not for the methods engineers.

The issue of possible deskilling within methods engineering remained undecided. The methods engineer's core skill is his knowledge of the metal-cutting process: from now on this would simply become a matter of drawing cutting paths on to the screen. Was this a precursor to more fundamental changes? Morale was already fairly low in manufacturing (there was talk of intensifying trade union activity) and CADCAM could be perceived as threatening – by those who knew about it! However, as one systems programmer put it, people in manufacturing "had got used to losing out". There was a general feeling that they always "got the short straw", and senior management levels were more concerned with design and corporate functions than with actual production.

In general many more concerns were expressed in manufacturing than in design, from all levels and on a variety of topics. When it came to operating the system, the programmers already spent many hours at their terminals – would they now spend *all* their working time at a VDU? What implications did this have for their health?

The manufacturing engineering manager was annoyed that none of the three senior managers in manufacturing had been called to a project team meeting for the last three months. Others were also worried about this. The feeling was that because manufacturing were not closely involved in the project, they would finish up with the functions that the designers *thought* they should have.

On a broader front, one of the manufacturing managers felt that wholesale changes in project management methods were necessary, and that CADCAM was only one factor. It should speed up the production cycle, but it would be most effective if time could be saved on the most critical projects. Decisions as to whether or not a project was critical were generally made from an engineering rather than a manufacturing perspective. Throughout the project management process, more consideration was given to engineering than to manufacturing aspects. In his view the whole process had been badly planned, and needed 'some direction'. This, however, was a normal state of affairs at EML; management never gave themselves enough time to plan, and always ended up 'fire-fighting' later.

In general

EML's traditional approach to management – cost-cutting and fire-fighting – was a byword among employees in several departments. More than one remarked that the company was run so tightly, and there was so much work to do, that no one could afford time off to learn new techniques or go on courses. "Everyone has too much to do, so we work on whatever is shouted for the loudest."

The special programmes manager (from corporate engineering) had drawn up the initial proposal for the system, and subsequently been moved on to another project. He expressed concern. He felt that the implementation process had not been properly managed, and would probably remain disorganised. He predicted that there would be little concern for the support infrastructure once the system was fully implemented: user support (eg manuals and help functions) was considered too expensive, and there was no obvious financial payback from it. Once the system was fully implemented the only likely evaluation would be of its financial performance.

In fact, he felt that EML simply had the wrong idea about what was happening. This was more than the arrival of some new technology; it was a major opportunity for real change. The system was much more than a change in the medium of work – it involved a fundamental change in EML's *methods* of working. "This is a major opportunity for us, and we should grasp it with both hands."

By this time the researchers felt they had gathered enough information, and the project team – Bob especially – were keen to know what they had found. They duly wrote a report which described their findings so far, related them to experiences elsewhere, and made recommendations for managing the introduction of CADCAM in the immediate future.

What would EML's reaction be? They were soon to find out . . .!

CASE STUDY TASKS

We have provided two alternative sets of tasks. The first involves a set of questions that can be attempted either individually or on a group basis. The second requires the specific application of Soft Systems Methodology (see Checkland, 1981). It may be interesting for different groups to undertake alternative tasks, and then to see what different answers emerge.

Task 1

Imagine yourself in the researchers' position. Your task is to produce a set of recommendations which will help to guide the human and organisational aspects of the implementation process. Answering the questions below should help you to formulate your recommendations.

1 What are the major human and organisational issues?

2 How would you characterise the relationship between design and manufacturing, and how could CADCAM help?

3 How would you characterise EML's approach to the implementation?

4 You were called in particularly to consider where the terminals should be sited. What are the costs and benefits of the two possible choices: centralised and clustered?

5 What recommendations would you make to guide the rest of the implementation process?

6 What impact would your recommendations have on the different groups involved?

Task 2

To answer the following questions, you need to be familiar with Checkland's 'Soft Systems' Methodology. Think of the case study as the 'mess' with which you are dealing. Use the soft systems approach to break down the situation and re-state it from another perspective. The tasks below should guide you through your application of the methodology.

1 Illustrate the relationships between groups, and the key actors in the implementation process, by means of a 'rich picture'. Remember to include both factual data and subjective interpretation.

2 From the above 'rich picture', what root definition is driving the implementation process? (Consider the espoused costs and benefits as outlined in the project proposal to the board of directors, and the problems perceived as critical by the project team.)

3 You are now in a position to formulate an alternative root definition, based on the most appropriate of your relevant systems. The CATWOE classification may be helpful here.

4 Draw a conceptual model of the activities necessary to achieve the root definition as it now stands. This can now be compared with the rich picture to identify similarities and differences between the activities in the real world and your ideal activities.

5 As a result of the comparison between your conceptual model and the rich picture, what are your recommendations for change?

6 What should EML now do to fulfil these recommendations?

ESSENTIAL READING

Blackler F, Brown C, Alternative models to guide the design and introduction of the new information technologies into work organisations, *Journal of Occupational Psychology*, 1986, vol 59, pp287–314

Briefs U, Ciborra C, Schneider L, eds, *Systems Design For, With and By the Users*, North Holland, 1983

Checkland P, *Systems Thinking, Systems Practice*, John Wiley, 1981

Clegg C W, Appropriate technology for manufacturing: Some management issues, *Applied Ergonomics*, 1988, vol 19, pp25–34

BACKGROUND READING

Cherns A, The principles of sociotechnical design, *Human Relations*, 1976, vol 29, pp783–792

Clegg C W, Symon G, A review of human-centred manufacturing technology and a framework for its design and evaluation, *International Reviews of Ergonomics*, 1989, vol 3, pp15–47

3 Computer-aided design at Kandu

Arthur Francis

INTRODUCTION

Kandu plc is a large multidivisional company. Its main line of business is the production of specialised components for another major industry. Kandu is a market leader for this type of product in the UK and also has a sizeable international presence. Until the late 1970s it enjoyed what was almost a monopoly position in the UK. However, the growth of international competition generally and the recession in the UK from 1979 to 1980 eroded its market dominance to some extent. Kandu lost some market share and, in common with many British engineering firms, shed nearly half its employees during this period. Much of the reduction in its labour force resulted from productivity improvements which brought the company more closely into line with its international competitors. Since the early 1980s the company seems to have stabilised its market position, and it now appears to be internationally competitive. By the late 1980s its employees numbered about 20,000 worldwide; it had an annual turnover of about a billion pounds in 1988, and made profits of slightly under £100 million.

So specialised is Kandu's main product range that the company has to design most of its own production machinery. It also builds the prototypes of these machines, though production of repeat orders is contracted out. The design and development of these highly specialised machines is a major task for the company, as is the design of the product itself. (Indeed, the product is so specialised and the company itself so dominant in this market that it cannot be described in any detail here. To do so would identify the company, who wish to remain anonymous.)

Until 1978 machine and product design were divided between three locations in the southeast of England. The company then decided to centralise research, design, and development activity. The three locations were closed down, and a purpose-built prestige facility was set up on a greenfield site just outside Ravebury, a small market town along the M4 corridor. The facility comprises design offices, research laboratories, development workshops and an engineering workshop. It is here that prototype production machines are assembled from parts which are mostly bought in from outside suppliers. Here, also, products are designed for production in Kandu's various production facilities worldwide. About 600 people are currently employed here. Most of them are technician- or graduate-level technical personnel. There are no recognised unions.

THE DESIGN PROCESS

Designing production machines for use within the company, and designing the products which Kandu sells, are two rather different activities. The former involves three processes:

- conceptual design;
- layout design;
- detailing.

Conceptual design involves working out how the machine will work, laying down broad principles of operation and making rough sketches. These concepts are then passed to other designers for the next stage.

Layout design involves refining the sketches into precise drawings of the entire machine, indicating the relationship between its various components.

Detailing is the production of drawings of individual components in such detail that they specify quite precisely how that component is to be manufactured. It is these detailed drawings that are used by machinists on the shop floor. Traditionally, designers/draughtspeople in drawing offices have progressed during their careers from detailing to layouts, and then to conceptual design.

Kandu's products are single components of complex shape. Product design at Kandu is the process of establishing that shape, though to do this aesthetic considerations must be combined with rather complex engineering considerations to do with stress analysis and the behaviour of various types of material. Unlike the design of production machines, this work is not divided into stages. Product design is done by one person, who may seek advice from technical experts about particular features of the product design.

COMPUTER-AIDED DESIGN (CAD) TECHNOLOGY

Computers aid design in a number of ways. In general the pencil and drawing board are replaced by a VDU and some combination of keyboard, joystick, and mouse. Instead of drawing onto paper the designers input their design to a computer by 'drawing' on the screen. The advantages to a designer are similar to those that word processors offer hand or typewriters. Mistakes are easier to correct. New designs with stong similarities to previous work can be drawn very quickly, simply by altering the relevant characteristics. And even when the designer has relatively little skill, the output always looks presentable. A further advantage of CAD is that given the right equipment the output can be used to prepare the instructions for computer-controlled machine tools. However, unlike most word processing packages, CAD systems are usually very complex, and take a significant time to learn. Designers need to use them very frequently in order to become competent and speedy.

An important distinction between various types of CAD package is the number of dimensions they can handle. Many can only work effectively in two dimensions – in other words, they can only be used to draw flat surfaces. As engineering drawings are always on flat pieces of paper, two-dimensional CAD systems can adequately replace conventional drawing in this respect. However, many objects have a complex three-dimensional shape which cannot adequately be captured on a 2-D drawing (eg a car body, a turbine blade, or Kandu's own product). The traditional solution is for engineers to make 3-D models of the object, usually in clay or wood. The component is then produced on special machine tools. These have a device which trails a feeler over the wooden model and copies from that. Some CAD systems which can handle complex 3-D surfaces will also produce instructions which can be fed directly into computer controlled machine tools. Such systems offer a number of advantages over traditional methods of design and manufacture. Cutting out model-building eliminates an important source of inaccuracy and error, and reduces lead times in manufacturing. At Kandu most of the design for production machines requires only 2-D facilities, but a 3-D facility is essential for product design.

Computers can also aid the designer by enabling complex mathematical analysis to be performed. In the past, engineering was often characterised by a 'cut and try' approach. Components were designed, the metal was cut, and then the component was tested. If it broke, then designers went back to the drawing board. Advances in engineering science now enable much more analysis to be done at the design stage (eg to check the component's performance under stress or under particular dynamic conditions). Much of this analysis requires powerful computing resources to crunch the numbers involved. The most advanced engineering design now requires, therefore, that designers have access to computer resources both for numerical analysis and for graphical purposes. Sometimes numerical and graphical operations can be carried out with a single, integrated computer installation. Often this is impossible.

One final point completes the picture and sheds some light on the situation at Kandu. In the engineering industry computers are increasingly being used for materials, resources and production planning. Kandu is looking for some kind of interface between the computer systems used for this work and computers used for design.

CAD AT KANDU

Kandu were one of the early users of computer-aided design (CAD). It bought and installed its first CAD equipment very soon after moving to Ravebury, in 1980.

This was an early date for a UK company to install CAD. Part of the reason for this early move seems to have been Kandu's self-image as "a company working with technology, and so seeing CAD as a technology we ought to have". The move to their very impressive new facility also helped trigger the decision to invest in CAD: CAD fitted the image of the new facility, and the sale of the other three sites in the south-east generated substantial cash. Indeed, as early as 1977 a committee had been set up to investigate CAD possibilities for the company, and had engaged in lengthy deliberations. However, the decision to purchase CAD was effectively taken by just one person, a senior engineer who has now left the company for higher things elsewhere. He was an enthusiast for the technology, having seen it at work in the automobile industry in the USA, and had "a direct line to the MD". He used the move to Ravebury as an opportunity to get the managing director's agreement to purchase. The decision was made to go for CAD in 1979, and the equipment arrived in 1980.

The essential technical advantage which Kandu found attractive at this early stage was CAD's potential for improving drawing office productivity. By 1980 the company had just come through the down-sizing operation mentioned earlier, and management were still looking for further ways of reducing manpower. CAD was seen as one way of achieving this.

In fact, like most other CAD users at that time, Kandu found that claims of immediately improved productivity were greatly exaggerated. CAD vendors at that time were telling potential customers that it could increase productivity (and so, by implication, reduce staff levels) by at least 30%. Perhaps unsurprisingly, this was precisely the figure required to justify the necessary capital investment to the company's financial directors, based on the labour costs then current in UK drawing offices! With the benefit of hindsight, the company now claims that the chief benefits of their early entry into CAD were seen in the learning curve. Naturally, CAD operators learned about the system, but this was not the only learning process, or even the primary one. Kandu also learned a great deal about CAD suppliers, the bugs that CAD systems were likely to have, and what to look for when buying and installing such systems. Kandu has also found that the specific efficiency advantage of CAD is seen less in reduced staff levels than in its ability to reduce lead times. In other words, what matters most to the company now is getting new designs to the market as quickly as possible.

As an example of the competitive edge offered by faster lead times, take the case of a customer who is developing a new or improved machine that incorporates a Kandu product. This customer will only be able to specify the requirement for this product at a fairly late stage in the development process. If others are competing with Kandu to supply that product, the supplier giving the earliest reliable delivery date is the one most likely to get the order. CAD now enables Kandu to produce product designs in hours rather than days; and the direct numerical control links with its machining operation allow prototypes to be machined directly from the CAD output. Moreover, if the customer requires any alterations, they can be incorporated just as quickly. Once again there is a parallel with word processing, where authors can make quite substantial alterations to their texts without retyping the entire document.

WHAT CAD IS USED FOR AT KANDU

The 1980 system, though state-of-the-art at that time, was slow and not very powerful. It comprised six workstations. At first these were scattered throughout the Ravebury facility so that the whole site had access to them. This was found to be unsatisfactory for two reasons:

- knowledge could not be shared by users who were in different locations;

- the equipment was suitable only for a limited number of tasks.

Because operators could not share their knowledge their progress up the learning curve was slow. CAD packages are complex, and there are many tricks or wrinkles that can be learned to get the best out of them. If terminals are close together operators can share this knowledge. This helps everyone to learn more quickly, and is particularly useful when new operators are introduced to the system. Because the terminals were spread throughout the facility draughtspeople became discouraged when they used CAD. If they found a problem with the package that they could not easily solve for themselves, there was no one more experienced available to ask for help. Instead they would then give up, and go back to the drawing board.

At this stage in its development the chief limitations of the CAD equipment were its lack of speed and its inflexibility. It was really only suitable for two- rather than three-dimensional work, and for detailing work as opposed to conceptual work or layout design. This meant that CAD was wasted in most areas of the facility, and useful only to those doing routine design work. As a result the engineering design manager met no opposition as he gradually acquired all six workstations for the office where the production machines were designed. Soon all six were in use for detail design work.

In 1985 improvements were made to this system. More capacity was added to the central computer processing unit, and the software was upgraded. At the same time an additional, different, CAD system was purchased. This comprised five highly intelligent and very fast work-stations that could cope with software from a variety of suppliers. Its power and speed made the system suitable for designing Kandu's products, with their highly complex surface geometry, so it was located in the product design office. This system has more recently been linked into the site's central computer facility so it can interface with the stress analysis packages used in the design process. It is also directly linked to the computer-controlled machine tools in the machine workshop.

In 1988 the company invested in a dozen of the more powerful personal computers (PCs) on the market. These were used to run graphic design software which matched and communicated with the original 1980 system. Some of these machines were put in the product design office. Others were put in the production machine design office, where they were used for layout work.

WHO USES CAD?

When CAD was first introduced at Ravebury, management decided to experiment with its use. They selected 18 people for training, deliber-ately choosing them to represent as wide a cross-section of potential CAD operators as possible. They included highly experienced staff and new recruits, graduates and technicians, people from product and from machine design, layout designers and detailers. All ages were repres-ented. It was not, they now assert, a good idea. With only six workstations between 18 trainees no one spent very much time at the screen. Because the system was at an early stage of development it was rather difficult to use, and none of the trainees were able to become fluent with it. Finally, the trainees had been selected by management, and not all were willing learners. In fact some of the designers were extremely reluctant to use the system, and kept going back to their drawing boards. Kandu report that those over 35 years of age were among the most reluctant. The combination of slow speed and operator unwillingness was unfortunate. As one manager put it, "They didn't like it and we couldn't afford it."

When the six workstations were brought together into the production machine design office they were used only by detailers, all of whom were young. Most detailers are young: this job is the first rung on the ladder of design expertise. Even so, their youth and the kind of work they were doing made CAD an ideal solution at this time. However, Kandu then changed its policy about detailing. Rather than doing it in-house, the company decided to farm out the detailing to the subcontractors who manufacture many of the components for the production machines. This policy change was to deal with a shortage of detail design staff within Kandu. These subcontractors now work from the layout drawings, so today CAD is primarily used for production machine layout design, and for the design of Kandu's specialised products.

Layout work for machine design is now done partly on the drawing boards and partly on either the original 1980 equipment or the new PCs. Only those who actively want to use CAD are doing so, and the dozen CAD designers each have exclusive use of his or her own workstation. Designers have a free choice about whether or not to use CAD, but all the users in the machine design section are 34 years of age or younger. None of the highly experienced older designers are currently using the system.

All product design work is now CAD-based, using the powerful 3-D system. As in the machine design area, each CAD workstation is used by a single designer. They are a motley group. None is older than 38, but graduates and those from an apprentice background work side by side. One is working on the development of a complex three-dimensional drafting package, two are working on the design of complex components and two are drafting simpler products. There is no relationship between educational background and qualification and the complexity of the work being done; willingness, interest and the ability to use computer technology are the only criteria for allocation to the CAD workstations. Indeed, the most complex work is being done by someone who was an apprentice on the company's HNC programme. Although he was not the best designer, he did show the greatest aptitude for computers. He then went on to get an Open University degree in science and computer studies.

THE PROBLEM

The engineering design manager has identified a number of problems with the current organisation of work in the design offices. At present each designer has a personal workstation and uses it for a single, specific purpose. He regards this as too inflexible. Designers are not getting enough breadth of experience and the utilisation of the expensive workstations (each of which costs between £15,000 and £20,000) is low. He is also concerned about the growing gap between the older, non-CAD using designers and the younger CAD users. Many of the older designers have come up from the shop floor, and have a lifetime of experience in the industry. Many of the younger designers, though adept at using the CAD systems, are very recent graduates with almost no practical experience.

He is also unsure how to respond to pressures from his technical director to improve lead times, and productivity, by investing yet more capital in a further expansion of CAD. Should he see this as an opportunity or an unwelcome and unrealistic pressure? If he does agree to buy more CAD equipment, how should he use it?

CASE STUDY TASK

The engineering design manager has decided to set up a working party to examine these problems. He has decided the terms of reference of the working party but has yet to choose its members.

The terms of reference are:

- To consider the proposal that the design function should take a further substantial step forward in CAD use, and replace all drawing boards with CAD equipment.

- If this proposal is accepted, what form of work organisation should be used? For example, should tasks continue to be allocated as at present with specific people always doing conceptual design, others doing layout work, and detailing contracted out? Should the rigid division between production machine design and product design be retained, or should more flexibility be introduced? More flexibility would:

  • allow the company to switch designers as work pressures change;

  • create a more experienced workforce.

- However, the present division of labour allows designers to develop a high degree of specialisation. Should all the designers have their own machines, or should facilities be shared? If they are to be shared, how might this be organised, what problems are likely to arise, and how might they be overcome? Shift-working would increase the utilisation of this expensive equipment but might not be welcomed by the designers. Should the company try this?

- If CAD is to be increased incrementally, what changes in work organisation will be needed to meet the problems already identified (low machine utilisation and inflexibility)? Should a system be introduced to share CAD facilities between all the designers, so that each of them uses CAD at least some of the time? Should the present division of labour between conceptual, layout, and detailing work and between machine design and product design be retained? Should it be replaced by a more flexible form of work allocation? If so, how much flexibility should be sought?

You are members of this working party and you have been asked to produce a report covering the terms of reference already quoted. You should also recommend the extent to which the workforce itself is to be involved in discussing these issues. There are various interested groups among the designers, and each is likely to have different preferences (eg CAD users and non-CAD users, senior designers, junior designers, production machine designers, product designers, etc). Which, if any, should be represented, and why?

ESSENTIAL READING

Boddy D, Buchanan D A, *Managing New Technology*, Blackwell, 1986, chapter 5

Cummings T, Blumberg M, Advanced manufacturing technology and work design, in Wall T D, Clegg C W, Kemp N J (eds) *The Human Side of Advanced Manufacturing*, John Wiley, 1987.

ADDITIONAL READING

Primrose P L, Creamer G D, Leonard R, Identifying and quantifying the 'company-wide' benefits of CAD within the structure of a comprehensive investment programme, in Rhodes E, Wield D (eds), *Implementing New Technologies*, Blackwell, 1985

Senker P, Implications of CADCAM for management, in Rhodes E, Wield D (eds), *Implementing New Technologies*, Blackwell, 1985

4 Work organisation for CNC drilling machines: Paragon Electronics plc

Toby Wall and Robin Martin

Paragon Electronics plc is a computer manufacturing company. We are concerned here with its printed circuit board (PCB) plant, which produces single and multi-layer boards for assembly into micro- and mainframe computers. The plant makes over 800 different types of board, in batch sizes ranging from one to several hundred, and has an average weekly output of 10,000 units. Most of the 400 shop floor jobs on site are classified as semi-skilled, and just over half are filled by women. Virtually all shop floor employees are represented by one trade union, which is committed to the introduction of advanced manufacturing technology within the plant. Support staff (eg engineers, programmers and supervisors) belong to one of four other trade unions. There is competition between unions over the role of their members in operating the new computer-based technology.

The production of PCBs involves a series of very different operations. These include photography, chemical etching, bonding, drilling, metal plating, component insertion, soldering and testing processes. These processes employ various automatic and semi-automatic technologies, but manual techniques are also used. Corresponding to this diversity, the plant is organised into separate areas, with boards routed through each according to type. These areas have a very high degree of functional interdependence: performance in one area affects the flow and difficulty of work in the next. At every stage of production, quality is of prime importance. A typical PCB comprises hundreds of components and several thousand connections, and a fault in any one of these means it will not work.

Manufacturing requirements in the plant are constantly changing. Frequent modifications to components, improvements in product design, and the move towards computer-integrated manufacturing (CIM) result in the regular introduction of minor (and sometimes major) changes in task procedures and work practices.

BACKGROUND TO THE CASE

You are interested in the human implications of new technology.

75

Because Paragon Electronics wish to develop CIM in the plant as a whole, they have asked for your advice on the associated job and organisational design issues. You have defined your role as a 'disinterested party', and this has been accepted both by management and trade unions. A few months after starting fieldwork you are asked to take on an additional task. Management and shop floor alike feel that current work practices in the drilling area are causing a problem. You are asked for your explanation of the nature and causes of this problem, and your suggestions on achieving an immediate improvement, bearing in mind likely longer-term developments within the plant.

THE DRILLING FUNCTION

The drilling area prepares 'bare boards' for the insertion of electronic components. The raw materials range from thin single sheets of copper (the basis for single-layer boards) to thick bonded laminates (the foundation for more complex multi-layer boards). Preparation consists of drilling intricate patterns of holes; there may be several thousand in a single board. The patterns vary according to the board type, and each involves a range of differently sized holes, some so small they are barely visible. Great drilling accuracy is required: the size and position of each hole has to correspond exactly to the parameters of the component it will house, and to the point in the microcircuitry where a contact has to be made.

THE TECHNOLOGY

Drilling is carried out on computer numerically controlled (CNC) machines. There are nine in the area. Each machine has four parallel drill heads above a moving table. This table holds the boards; it also holds the 'pods' used to house additional drill bits. The drill heads can only move vertically. They are lowered to drill a hole, or to return one drill bit to its pod and pick up another. The table moves horizontally to position the boards under the drill heads as required, or to exchange a drill bit. The sequence of drill head and table movements is controlled by a computer program loaded in the form of a paper tape. There are plans to replace the tape system with control through microcomputers. These in turn will be linked to a host computer which will store all the control programs required for the different boards, as well as providing a scheduling aid. This system is due to come on line in 18 months' time.

The drilling machines are a relatively straightforward application of CNC technology, and although several years old they are highly reliable. However, there is one significant operational weakness connected with the automatic changeover of drill bits. Periodically the drill heads fail either to release a bit or to pick up its replacement.

Accordingly, eight of the machines are programmed to halt whenever drill bits are exchanged. This makes it easier to check, and if necessary correct, their operation. For technical reasons, however, the ninth machine could not be programmed in the same way and runs continuously. Attempts to introduce pauses created operating problems elsewhere in the drilling cycle. As a result operators themselves must stop this last machine at the critical points in its cycle.

OPERATOR TASKS

The operation of the drilling machines can be broken down into six main tasks:

- loading the bare boards on to the table;

- placing drill bits into 'pods' on the table and (since often more bits are required than pods are available) changing drill bits during the production cycle;

- loading the relevant computer program;

- monitoring the drilling process and rectifying errors by hand, eg removing or inserting drills not properly exchanged, replacing broken bits, removing swarf;

- unloading completed boards;

- inspecting the drilling boards visually.

WORK ORGANISATION

To meet production requirements, the drilling area operates 24 hours a day, five days a week, with occasional weekend working. There are three permanent shifts, each staffed by six people. The morning shift consists of three men and three women. The afternoon and night shifts are staffed by women and men respectively.

The nine CNC machines all have essentially the same technical specification. Nevertheless, work within each shift is organised in such a way that individual operators face very different work demands. There are three salient job differences.

Firstly, three employees are required to operate two machines simultaneously (*double-minding*), whereas the other three operate only one (*single-minding*) – the result of a compromise reached some two years ago. At that time management had intended to introduce double-minding as standard practice, but trade union representatives opposed the idea.

Secondly, one pair of double-minded machines is used exclusively for drilling very expensive multi-layer boards. This is because the relevant programs have been developed only for this pair of machines. Since this allows output requirements to be met, production planning see no need to adapt the programs to other machines. The effect, however, is to create one job with particularly high cost responsibility. With two machines, each with four drilling heads, the operator is processing eight boards at a time. Each board is worth several hundred pounds. An operator who fails to notice an operating fault, selects the wrong size of bit, or who causes or fails to prevent a range of other possible problems, may be responsible for up to four thousand pounds' worth of lost production.

Finally, as mentioned earlier, one (single-minded) machine is programmed to run continuously, whereas all the other machines pause at critical points in their drilling cycles.

As a result, task allocation, production planning and technological factors combine to produce four distinct types of work across the six jobs in the drilling area:

- one case of double-minding machines used to drill expensive boards;

- two cases of double-minding machines drilling cheap boards;

- two cases of single-minding machines processing cheap boards;

- one case of single-minding machines drilling cheap boards under the unique condition of a continuous operating cycle.

These job conditions, along with the general layout of the area, are depicted in Figure 4.1.

To maximise flexibility within the drilling area, employees are trained to operate all nine CNC machines. They are paid at the same basic rate, although night shift employees receive an additional premium to compensate for unsocial hours. To balance the uneven demands from the four types of work, operators within each shift rotate jobs on a weekly basis. Each shift has a different supervisor, shared with a neighbouring area. As a result, operators are not closely monitored. Instead, the supervisor chases up incoming work and allocates batches for drilling by adjusting the master production schedule to local circumstances. Work allocation involves placing batches of boards for drilling on the operators' work benches and collecting them when they have been drilled. Of course the supervisors have many other responsibilities as well. It is their job to maintain quality awareness, and they are also the main channel of communication between shop floor and management.

THE PROBLEMS

In objective terms, little seems to be amiss in the drilling area. Boards are

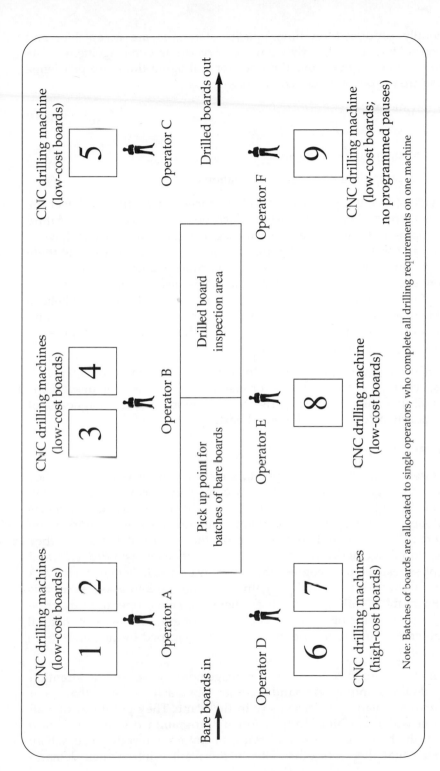

Figure 4.1 The Drilling Area

Note: Batches of boards are allocated to single operators, who complete all drilling requirements on one machine

generally produced on time, quality standards are acceptable, and operators turn up regularly for work. Nevertheless management, trade union representatives and the operators all agree there are problems. These are variously described in terms of:

– low morale;

– stress;

– uncooperative attitudes;

– poor shop floor–management relations.

Managers, contemplating technical advances within the area, feel the atmosphere of 'an uneasy truce' does not augur well for its future development. Indeed, one senior manager suggests that he may have to "get rid of troublemakers" before any progress can be made. The trade union convenor considers that a disproportionate amount of her time is taken up dealing with ostensibly trivial issues arising from drilling operators. For their part, the operators feel stressed. They do not believe that management appreciates or even recognises the effort they put into their work, and they do not consider that their trade union represent-atives are providing adequate support.

The natural starting point seems to be an examination of the operators' perspective. You set about this through informal on-the-job discussions with all involved. These give rise to three more specific 'diagnoses' of the underlying causes, as described next.

DOUBLE-MINDING

An issue raised by all the operators concerns double-minding. They report that a week of operating two machines leaves them feeling 'drained', and they consider themselves to be under strain. The effects of double-minding, it seems, colour their experience of work more generally. When asked to elaborate on the nature of the stress they describe a range of symptoms including anxiety feelings, headaches and sleeplessness. Some recognise the experience as a challenge as well as a strain. Others describe only negative reactions. When asked what it is about double-minding that causes them problems, operators describe the issue in terms of a relentless demand for attention – eg of 'natural breathers' arising from one machine being usurped by demands from the other.

To the trade union convenor and management, however, the attention that double-minding demands is not obviously greater than that required for many jobs elsewhere in the plant. They point out that all but one of the machines in question are programmed to halt at critical points in their cycles, thus allowing operators a respite. You satisfy yourself that there are other jobs in the plant – jobs which demand similar or even greater attention – but where operators do not feel themselves to be under stress.

However, further enquiries reveal that double-minding is only practised in the drilling area; and although the practice has been established for almost two years, it remains a sore point. As mentioned earlier, operators were supported by their trade union when they resisted the original management proposal. At the time they feared unacceptably high work demands and job losses. After several months of negotiation, they reluctantly accepted a partial introduction of double-minding, but only with the proviso that individual operators would not be required to mind two machines all the time. The current practice, where operators rotate between single- and double-minding, reflects this history.

WORK SCHEDULING

A second important issue relates to work scheduling practices. All operators accept the overall production schedule, and the automatic allocation of expensive boards to a designated pair of machines (machines 6 and 7 – see Figure 4.1). However, operators consider that the distribution of work between the remaining machines is less than ideal. It is a matter of optimising the match between the drilling requirements for different boards and the specification of the machines.

Some technical detail serves to illustrate the practical complexity of this issue. Alternative board types require the use of varying numbers of differently sized drill bits. The appropriate bits are placed in the pods on the table. From here the drill head automatically picks up and replaces the bits that are needed at different points in the program. However, many boards require more drill bits than the pods can accommodate. To deal with this problem the drilling cycle is broken down into sub-cycles, each using different sets of drill bits.

It is also the case that different machines have different numbers of pods. In general the most efficient solution is to load the board types that demand the largest number of bits onto the machines with the largest number of pods, or those where the number of bits required is a whole multiple of the number of pods available. This minimises the number of sub-cycles (and the number of times pods must be restocked) in the overall drilling program, speeding up production. However, this does not always occur in practice. The supervisors are not fully aware of the relevant board and machine specifications. Operators often find themselves on machines with few pods, but drilling boards that require many bit changes, and thus have to accommodate several sub-cycles. At the same time, other operators may be on machines with more pods processing boards requiring fewer drill bit changes, leaving some pods unused.

Many other factors affect the optimum allocation of boards to machines, such as:

- batch size;
- the mix of board types to be drilled;
- urgent deadlines.

There is, however, a more general point. To optimise work scheduling, board requirements must be closely matched with the capabilities of individual machines. This requires detailed knowledge; and the drilling operators believe they have this knowledge. They see present practice as inefficient and thus frustrating.

COMMUNICATIONS

Underlying both these issues is a problem with communications that is less clearly defined, but equally strongly felt. Managers and operators report a lack of trust on both sides, and supervisors feel caught in the middle. Elsewhere in the plant various avenues are open for direct dialogue between managers and shop floor employees (eg quality circles and periodic meetings). There are no similar avenues in the drilling area. Managers are rarely seen on the shop floor, and the only channel of communication is through the (shared) supervisors. Operators feel divorced from management.

From the operators' point of view, this problem is largely a legacy of the double-minding issue. They feel that double-minding was presented to them virtually as a *fait accompli*: managers had developed the idea without consultation, and introduced it in such a way as to limit operators' room for manoeuvre.

Because the company has a stated policy of upgrading technology throughout the plant, operators fear that history will repeat itself. They believe management has private plans for drilling which, as before, will be announced only at the last possible moment. Rumours to this effect are rife. Asked to comment on this issue, managers point out that they are continually monitoring technological and other developments to identify ways of improving production, but do not yet have any concrete plans for changes in the drilling area. However, given the negative attitudes of the operators, they are reluctant to discuss some of the possibilities with them for fear of an 'overreaction'. The problem, it seems, is a vicious circle of mistrust.

CASE STUDY TASKS

This case requires you to combine a research orientation with a consultative role, and the tasks below reflect this dual perspective. Tasks 1 and 2 concern the methodology you might use to identify causes of strain in the department. Most books on research design should be of use for this purpose, and Cook and Campbell (1979) is of particular relevance. Tasks 3 to 6 cover matters on which you are to offer practical advice.

1 How could you exploit existing differences in job requirements and practices in the drilling area to determine whether double-minding is a cause of strain?

2 How could you make use of your access to other areas in the plant to reinforce your investigation of the drilling area?

3 Assuming you find that double-minding is not a cause of strain except where it also involves drilling expensive boards, what work-design or technological change(s) would you recommend?

4 What recommendations would you make for improving work scheduling, bearing in mind the planned replacement of paper tape control with a microcomputer-based system incorporating a scheduling aid?

5 What changes would you suggest to help overcome the communication problem?

6 What recommendations would you make about how to refine and implement the suggested changes?

ESSENTIAL READING

Boddy D, Buchanan D A, *Managing New Technology*, Blackwell, 1986, chapter 5

Wall T D, New technology and job design, in Warr P B, ed, *Psychology at Work*, Penguin, 1987, chapter 13

ADDITIONAL READING

Cherns A, The principles of sociotechnical design, *Human Relations*, 1976, vol 29, pp783–792

Clegg C W, Wall T D, Managing factory automation, in Blackler F, Oborne D, eds, *Information Technology and People*, British Psychological Society, 1987, chapter 3

Cook T D, Campbell D T, *Quasi-experimentation*, Rand McNally, 1979

Daniel W, *Workplace IR and Technical Change*, Francis Pinter, 1987

Sinclair M, Ergonomic aspects of the automated factory, *Ergonomics*, 1986, vol 29, pp1507–1523

Wall T D, Martin R, Job and work design, in Cooper C L, Robertson I T, eds, *International Review of Industrial and Organisational Psychology*, John Wiley, 1987

5 Oliver Tools: A problem of job design

Bernard Burnes and Mike Fitter

ORGANISATIONAL SETTING

Oliver Tools is a manufacturer of high-quality hand tools such as screwdrivers, hammers and wood planes. It is the largest overseas division of an American-owned multinational company, and operates on four sites in the north of England. Each site is controlled by its own general manager, who reports directly to the British Board of Directors.

The present case study is based in the largest of the four sites: the Laurel Plant, which has 800 employees.

In recent years Oliver Tools has suffered severely from declining markets and increased competition. In 1984 the four factories employed 2000 and had a turnover of £30 million. However, in the subsequent two years this dropped to £20 million, with employment falling to its present level of 1200. Despite this, Oliver Tools has never made a loss, and in 1988 announced a profit of £3.8 million.

The main reason for its profitable position is the swift action taken by the parent company to reduce costs and increase profit margins. This resulted from a reorganisation of the American and European operations involving both a rationalisation of product lines and the transfer of some products from Britain to other countries and vice versa.

In Britain this was accompanied by a £3 million investment programme between 1984 and 1988. The objective was to move from being a low-technology, labour-intensive company to becoming a high-quality, low-cost company by introducing modern technology and methods.

It was made clear to Oliver Tools that their future viability depended upon the outcome of this process of replacing labour with capital. Although the company has not made any official estimate, the trade unions believe that this process accounted for some 200 of the 800 jobs that were lost during the period.

Nevertheless, management–worker relations in the company are very friendly, albeit paternalistic, and grievances are dealt with by a wide range of joint management–worker committees.

The unions have tended to accept the redundancies as inevitable, and their main concern has been to protect the pay and conditions of those who remain.

One final point to note: the shopfloor trade unions are dominated by skilled male workers, despite the fact that these account for only about 10% of the membership.

BACKGROUND TO THE CASE

In 1984, at the beginning of the period of change, a computer numerically controlled (CNC) milling machine was installed in the Laurel Plant. Though this was part of the drive for modernisation, the main incentive for the purchase of the CNC was to overcome problems of poor quality. Nevertheless, it is considerably more productive than existing equipment, allowing work previously done by six setter–operators to be performed by just one operator.

CNC machine tools are computer-controlled devices for cutting and shaping pieces of cast or rolled metal. The three most common types of CNC are: turning lathes – machines for producing circular components; milling machines – for removing material from flat surfaces; and machining centres – similar to (but far more complex than) milling machines.

CNC has become popular because for the first time it allows the automation of small-batch production of engineering components. This is significant because small-to-medium batches are involved in 75% of all machining operations, and in 40% of all operations employed in manufacturing. Traditionally, batch production has been carried out on two types of machine tool:

- *Conventional machine tools* controlled manually by a skilled or semi-skilled machinist. These machines have the advantage of being very flexible, but they are slow and the resulting quality is variable. It is also difficult to machine complex shapes on them, and they often need expensive jigs (to guide the tool) and fixtures (to hold the work). For these reasons, they tend to be used on small batches.

- *Automatic and semiautomatic machine tools*, which are controlled by some form of preset mechanical or electromechanical arrangement. They have the advantage of being fast and consistent, but they are inflexible in that they are limited to performing a narrow range of machining operations. They are also slow to set up, and are only economic on larger batches of components.

In the past, the cost advantage for small batches has been with conventional machine tools, and for larger batches with automatic machines. The intermediate ranges have been done on either, depending on the complexity of the products involved. With CNC, this has changed: its proponents argue that batches between 5 and 300–400 can be more economically produced on CNC; this is especially true where complex components are involved.

The Plane Department, where the first CNC was installed, employs 90 workers. It is split into three separate sections, each with its own supervisor. The supervisors are responsible to the production manager, who in turn reports to the general manager.

The operations carried out in the Plane Department are the milling, drilling and tapping of wood plane bodies. Each section concentrates on a different range of planes. Despite the introduction of CNC, these operations are still mainly performed on a variety of conventional and semiautomatic machines, which only have a limited range of functions.

There are three basic machine-related jobs in the department: the setting-up of semiautomatic and conventional machines; the setting and operation of semiautomatic machines; and the operation of conventional machines.

Setters are classed as skilled workers, while setter-operators and operators are classed as semi-skilled. However, the operators are the lowest-paid (though numerically the largest) of the three groups. This reflects the fact that their job, which consists mainly of loading and unloading machines, has a low skill content.

One further issue of note is that the setter and setter–operator grades are exclusively male preserves, while the operators' jobs are occupied solely by women. Though such a gender divide is not unusual in engineering companies, in this case (as the following will demonstrate) it appears to be more acute.

Firstly, the company has not one but two social clubs: a Men's Club and a Women's Club. Secondly, in the early 1980s the union tried, against the advice of management, to negotiate a higher percentage wage increase for male workers than female. This was eventually rejected by the union's members, of whom the women form a majority, when they were balloted on the offer. Thus the gender divide, which is fiercely guarded by male workers, could prove a major barrier to restructuring jobs in the company – though management has shown no inclination to do this in any case.

The plant is organised around scientific management principles, and is therefore characterised by a high division of labour on the shopfloor and a wide range of functional specialisms elsewhere.

The actual job grade of each employee is determined by a complex and rigid job evaluation system: there are some 46 different grades of shopfloor worker in the factory as a whole. Each worker has his or her own written job description.

All the operators and setter–operators are paid a bonus related to their own output. The main role of the supervisors, who were all previously setters, is to oversee the work of the employees on their sections. They previously had a degree of responsibility for work scheduling, but since the introduction of a computer-aided production-management system this aspect of their work has declined.

Any technical problems which arise are referred by supervisors to the company's methods engineers, with whom they have a close working relationship. They in turn consult the supervisors over proposed changes or the introduction of new equipment.

Nevertheless, it is the methods engineers who are responsible for selecting and introducing new equipment, and also for determining how it will be used (job design). However, in the case of the CNC this latter function was taken out of their hands and decided by the general manager.

The result was that the CNC was operated by a female operator, but was set up and programmed by a male setter. In addition, a methods engineer was made responsible for overseeing the work of the setter.

The reason given by the general manager for his intervention was the pressure from head office to use new equipment in a manner which achieved the quickest return on investment. By replacing six setter–operators with one operator he achieved a two-year payback. Also, by making a setter responsible for setting and programming (instead of giving the latter task to a methods engineer, who might not always be readily available) he ensured that any problems which arose could be swiftly dealt with.

Despite the apparent logic of his explanation, in private he revealed that the real reason was to "buy off the trade union". At a time when the company was beginning to invest heavily in new equipment, he wished to reduce trade union fears – and potential hostility. By making a setter responsible for programming, he demonstrated that skilled shopfloor workers had nothing to fear and everything to gain from technology. This accounts for why he took the decision out of the hands of the methods engineers, who wanted to do the programming themselves.

As he anticipated, the union endorsed these arrangements for CNC, despite disquiet amongst setter–operators over job losses.

Therefore an existing operator was transferred to the CNC, where her job was to load and unload the machine. The speed of her work is controlled by the machine program; the cycle times range from 30 to 60 seconds.

One of the company's setters was given the necessary training, and his work was rearranged to allow him to set up and program the CNC. The remainder of his time is now spent setting semi-automatic and conventional machines.

THE PROBLEM

In 1986, two years after the first CNC was introduced, the company began to examine the case for a second CNC. As a result of this a wide range of dissatisfactions concerning the first CNC were brought to the surface.

The CNC operator complained that her job was boring, monotonous and strenuous. She found the work much worse than operating a conventional machine, nor was she paid any more money to compensate for this. Indeed, because she was paced by the machine, it was impossible for her to earn the same level of bonus as conventional operators, who could speed up their work if they wished. What is more, they could adjust the pace of their work to allow them to take longer breaks, whereas she could not.

As she said, "I'm working harder than anyone else and getting paid less money. Where's the justice in that?"

The setter, who in all other respects liked his job, also complained about pay. He felt that his enhanced skill level warranted a higher rate of pay. Though he had negotiated a small increase when he had taken the job, he felt this was inadequate.

The supervisors were also discontented with CNC. They felt that the setter was too powerful, and was thus undermining their authority. The main cause of this was their lack of knowledge of CNC. They did not know what the setter should do or how long it should take. There was no suggestion that he abused his position, but with this change coming on top of the decline in their scheduling responsibilities, they were naturally worried. As one of them said, "Our jobs might disappear if this goes on."

For similar reasons the methods engineers were also dissatisfied with the setter's role. They had originally wanted to program the CNC, but had been overruled by the general manager. Though in theory they were supposed to oversee the setter, in practice he resisted this, and their distance from the shopfloor meant they could not carry out their vaguely defined role. This led to a degree of resentment amongst them. As one commented, "It's bad practice to let shopfloor workers decide on production methods and speeds, and" – more importantly – "it's job erosion letting a setter do our job."

One might assume that the general manager at least would be happy, given that the CNC was seen as a technical and economic success. Far from it! He no longer felt the need to appease the union, as its power had been eroded both by the large number of redundancies in the company and by its ready acceptance of new technology. Instead, he believed that his original decision had created a situation where a shopfloor worker effectively controlled a key piece of equipment. If this continued with the introduction of more CNCs, then not only would labour control prove difficult, but he greatly feared that it might give them the power to hold the company to ransom.

He therefore wished to change the organisation of work around CNC, but there were two obstacles to this. Firstly, it would be a public admission that his original decision was wrong – never an easy thing to do. Secondly, and more problematically, the company's structure and practices are such that once a job grade and description are agreed it is very difficult to change them. The process for amending these is long; it involves a joint management–union committee, and there must be good reasons for doing so.

Nevertheless, the general manager was determined to change the organisation of work for future CNCs, if not the first one.

CNC AND JOB DESIGN

On a CNC machine tool, the whole cutting cycle is controlled by the computer, from the beginning of the cutting process on each component to its final completion; the process is automatic. However, though the CNC eliminates the need for human intervention while the machine is cutting, such intervention is required at five points during the production process:

- *Programming the machine*: each batch of components has to have a separate program. Therefore someone has to decide upon methods and tooling, select speeds and feeds, and calculate and write the program. The program is then usually encoded onto a punched-paper tape, which allows it to be fed into the CNC.

- *Setting up the machine*: this involves positioning the tools, and arranging jigs and fixtures if they are required.

- *Proving out (editing) the program*: programs are rarely 100% correct, and they need to be checked out (and if necessary amended) on the machine. This usually involves producing the first component of a batch or a test piece in order to check its accuracy.

- *Loading and unloading*: loading the raw material into the machine, and removing the finished component.

- *Quality control*: this involves inspecting the finished components for accuracy, and making adjustments during a production run to compensate for tool wear or material variability.

There is nothing inherent in the technology that determines who does these tasks. One person could do them all, or they could be split up amongst a number of people. All of them could be done by shopfloor personnel, or some could be done by staff specialists.

In practice there are at least five different models of work organisation around CNC:

- In the first model, a programmer – usually a member of staff such as a production or methods engineer – will prepare the tape; a setter will set up the machine and prove the tape; and an operator will run the machine, basically loading and unloading it.

- In the second model, a programmer can both prepare and prove the tape, leaving the operator to fulfil both the setting and operating roles.

- In the third model, a setter can prepare and prove the tape and set up the machine, leaving the operator to load and unload.

- In the fourth model, a programmer can prepare the tape, while the operator can prove it as well as setting up and operating the machine.

- In the fifth model, an operator can prepare and prove the tape, set up the machine and run it.

The first three models have a tendency to create boring and monotonous jobs for the operators. Little skill would be required, and the main function would be simply to load and unload the machine and to monitor its performance. The programmers and setters, on the other hand, would have more interesting and varied jobs.

The fourth model would eliminate the need for a setter and give that person's functions to the operator, whose job would become more skilled and interesting. The fifth model would be ideal from the operator's point of view in that it fulfils all the criteria of job design regarding variety, skill, autonomy and task completeness.

CASE STUDY TASKS

Imagine you are a consultant called in by the board of directors of Oliver Tools to advise on how changes in the design of jobs can improve productivity and quality. Your first task is to examine the operation of CNC.

You have interviewed all those involved, and are aware of their views and of the organisational constraints that are present. You have identified the following short- and long-term options, some of which (though not all) are mutually exclusive.

Short-term options

1 Continue as at present, but rotate the CNC operator's job between several of the staff.

2 Continue as at present, but pay the operator a fixed bonus in line with that earned by conventional operators.

3 Leave the first CNC as it is, but have any further CNCs operated by a setter–operator and programmed by a methods engineer.

4 Extend option 3 to include the first CNC.

5 Promote the setter to the post of methods engineer, and make him responsible for CNC programming.

6 Train the supervisors effectively to oversee the work of the CNC setter.

Long-term options

1 Eliminate the setter–operator grade, and use CNCs as at present.

2 Eliminate the operator and setter grades, and divide their tasks between the setter–operators and the methods engineers.

3 Merge the operator and setter–operator grades and tasks but leave the setters solely responsible for programming.

4 As option 3, but eliminate the setter grade and make the methods engineer responsible for programming.

5 Eliminate the supervising posts, and merge the three shopfloor groups to form an autonomous work group responsible for all CNC functions.

6 Extend option 5 to the entire factory, with concomitant changes to the bonus and job-evaluation systems and related practices.

SOME QUESTIONS

The questions and issues listed below reflect the factors involved, and a consideration of them will assist in formulating your recommendations:

1 In what ways can the job satisfaction and motivation of the CNC operator be improved, and what are the implications for existing company practices and other staff?

2 What will be the long-term job prospects for conventional machine operators, setter–operators and setters after the introduction of further CNCs?

3 Can the supervisors' concerns be resolved, or should the company change or even eliminate their role?

4 Consider the implications for shopfloor workers and the efficient, effective operation of CNC if the methods engineers are made responsible for programming.

5 How might the trade union unite its members given their differing and conflicting interests?

6 Do the existing gender and skill gaps on the shopfloor pose a major obstacle to redesigning jobs?

7 How will any changes affect:

a the company's bonus system?

b management control?

c the structure of (and practices in) the rest of the company?

d the introduction and operation of further forms of new technology?

8 What other options exist that have not been considered by the consultant, and what are their merits and demerits?

9 How should any recommendations for change be planned and implemented?

ROLE-PLAY EXERCISE

As a possible alternative to the questions above, this role-play exercise has been developed as a focus for discussing the case study.

The objective of the exercise is to give participants a sharper (and more experiential) understanding of the issues involved by taking on the role of someone in the case study.

The role-play exercise unfolds through a series of meetings at which the various actors put forward their views and aspirations. This culminates in the final meeting, at which the consultant puts his or her recommendations to a meeting of all the participants.

The motive for initiating the series of meetings is the proposal to introduce a second CNC.

The following roles are included in the exercise:

- CNC operator;
- setter–operator of a conventional machine;
- CNC setter;
- shop steward;
- supervisor;
- methods engineer;

- general manager;
- consultant.

The roles of each participant are as described in the text. Nevertheless, these may be embellished or altered as seen fit by those running the exercise.

Depending on numbers, more than one person can play each part (eg two supervisors) or new roles can be invented (eg head-office representative). However, past experience suggests that the best results are obtained when the women operators are not outnumbered by their male colleagues in union meetings, and when the roles of shop steward, general manager and consultant are played by strong characters.

The series of meetings through which the exercise unfolds are as follows:

- The general manager meets the methods engineer to discuss the need for a second CNC. They also discuss their respective concerns regarding the first CNC.

- The shop steward calls a union meeting to discuss rumours of a second CNC. Those involved are operators, setter–operators and setters.

- The supervisor meets the general manager to discuss the present situation with CNC and the prospects for the future.

- They are joined by the methods engineer, and discuss how to proceed.

- The shop steward meets with the general manager to verify the rumour of the second CNC and discuss the implications for his members.

- The shop steward, following his meeting with the general manager, reports back to another union meeting.

- The general manager, realising the difficulties which exist, asks the Board of Directors for the services of the consultant to review the situation. (It can be assumed that the consultant is fully conversant with the situation, and does not need a detailed briefing.)

- The shop steward joins the general manager and consultant to put his members' views.

- The consultant meets with all participants to put forward recommendations. General discussion follows.

It should be stressed that the main benefit of the role-play exercise is the understanding it can provide of the limitations on change posed both by the aspirations of the interested parties and by the structure and practices of the organisation. Participants should therefore not strive for an 'ideal' solution, but should instead concentrate on the benefits and drawbacks of a range of options.

ESSENTIAL READING

Burnes B, *New Technology in Context*, Gower, 1989

Child J, *Organisation*, Harper and Row, 1984

REFERENCES AND ADDITIONAL READING

Clegg C W, The derivation of job design, *Journal of Occupational Behaviour*, 1984, vol 5, pp 131–146

Davis L E, Taylor J C, eds, *Design of Jobs*, Goodyear, 1979

De Barr A G, *Numerically Controlled Machine Tools*, AUEW–TASS, 1978

Kelly J E, *Scientific Management, Job Redesign and Work Performance*, Academic Press, 1982

Knights D, Willmott H, eds, *New Technology and the Labour Process*, Macmillan, 1988

Sorge A, Hartmann G, Warner J, Nicholas I, *Microelectronics and Manpower in Manufacturing*, Gower, 1983

Wall T D, Burnes B, Clegg C W, Kemp N J, New technology, old jobs, *Work and People*, 1984, vol 10, no 2, pp15–21

6 The sexual division of labour: Brandwear Clothing Ltd

Carole Truman

ORGANISATIONAL SETTING

Brandwear Clothing is a large-scale clothing manufacturer, employing over 500 workers in an integrated multi-plant operation on two factory sites in and around the town of Burnley in the north of England. Over 80% of the workforce are women, and most are employed in semi-skilled machining jobs. Men's jobs have traditionally been located in the cutting room and dispatch, and in engineering functions.

Following a period of heavy redundancies in the 1970s, membership of the recognised trade union, the National Union of Tailor and Garment Workers, has been low, although in the last twelve months there has been a nationwide drive to recruit more women. The case study is set at a time when the factory management wants to increase output in order to fulfil new orders from a major high-street retailer.

BACKGROUND

Brandwear has always operated in a fiercely competitive market. Until the 1960s, however, that market was only really accessible to other UK manufacturers, who faced very similar costs and conditions to those of Brandwear. In the late 1960s foreign competitors began to flood the UK market with clothes that had been produced at far lower unit cost than UK manufacturers could ever hope to achieve in their existing operations. Things became worse during the recession of the late 1970s, and many factories in Burnley and elsewhere went out of business, making thousands of workers redundant. Brandwear was amongst those that survived, but was still forced to cut its workforce by almost 50% and review its operations.

During the first half of the 1980s, Brandwear was forced into crisis management from which there seemed to be little escape. Operations continued under a cloud of pessimism, and the future of the industry seemed to be in the balance. As one commentator put it:

Britain's textile and clothing industry is dying. There's no way

97

Britain can compete with cheap imports from low-waged countries, except perhaps by cutting wages further. There's no point in the unions trying to resist closures and job loss. And there's no point in the government putting money into a lame-duck industry like this.

The eventual saving grace of the clothing industry was the retail boom that was fuelled by the more expansionary economic policies from 1983 onwards. This led to the growth of the high-street fashion chainstores and a demand for fashion which provided long-awaited new orders. By the second half of the 1980s, UK clothing manufacture had divided into two sectors characterised largely by the markets which producers had begun to serve.

One sector consists of sweatshops and homeworkers making goods at prices which enable UK manufacturers to compete with those of foreign importers. Whilst the Clothing Wages Council set a minimum rate for machinists, an investigation by the Low Pay Unit estimated that over a third of these firms pay below the minimum legal rate. In addition to low wages, working conditions in this sector of the industry are commonly poor, and can be dangerous and unhealthy.

The other sector of the UK clothing industry contains those producers who have geared their production toward retailers such as Next, Principles and Richards, where the demand is for higher-quality or more fashion-oriented clothes. To serve this market a producer needs to have a good knowledge of fashion trends.

Under these circumstances, European manufacturers have an obvious advantage over Third World competitors. But there are particular implications for the way in which clothes for the fashion markets are produced in order to capitalise on this comparative advantage. Manufacturers have to be quick to respond to market changes, and new technology is seen to facilitate the 'flexible specialisation' that is required.

The use of sophisticated technology means that this sector of the industry is referred to as the *advanced sector*. Within this definition is the 'human factor' ethos that firms will compete on the basis of design and technology rather than sweated labour. In the advanced sector, new technology has had its impact, not only on the machines that operators use, but also on the systems used to assess pay and performance.

This is the sector in which Brandwear now operates. Len Archer, production manager at Brandwear, explained the company's present approach.

PRODUCTION MANAGEMENT AT BRANDWEAR

Once a cutter on the shop floor, Len Archer had worked as a foreman for many years before being promoted to his present position as production manager at Brandwear. From his office at the centre of the factory, he now mused over how the industry had changed during his working life:

> In the sixties, when I was a foreman, it would take you all afternoon to walk round the factory to see all the different lines from cutting to dispatch. I reckon you can see it all in less than an hour now. We've slimmed down a lot really, and a lot of it's been automated.

Mr Archer went on to explain how Brandwear had introduced new machines, which had automated many of the processes that had previously depended upon the skills of individual workers. He explained how the process of cutting the rolls of cloth had once required years of training, as one mistake would mean that yards and yards of cloth would be ruined and unfit for sewing.

> In those days the cutters were the elite, and each man deserved every penny he got because of the risks involved. A good cutter would size up the cloth and know just how to lay the pattern to get minimum wastage; there was no substitute for a man's experience. Once the cloth has been cut into garment pieces, things get less critical, because you're dealing with smaller pieces of cloth and smaller operations. Mind you, you'd never have got me working at the pace of those girls at the machines. But then, women are better at those fiddly jobs, aren't they?

As part of its modernisation programme, the factory had made a heavy investment in new machinery. Len reported that the expensive part of clothing production had always been the labour cost. The philosophy at Brandwear was now to deploy machines that minimised the company's reliance on manual labour, and which provided maximum flexibility. New technology had provided the key to achieving this.

> What we've done is to buy machines which don't take years to master. This way, the operatives can be moved round from one machine to another, depending on what orders we have coming through. I think they like it, because they don't get stuck on the same job, day in and day out. From our point of view, we'd like to automate everything, but there will never be a machine that will replace ten nimble fingers. This flexible system means that lines are easier to balance, and we don't get as many bottlenecks or hold-ups.

There have been several developments in the design and use of sewing machines, with the introduction of dedicated and programmable machines. The use of programmable machines has penetrated some of the most complex operations in clothing manufacture. Dedicated machines are designed to do a specific job. The trade press carries many examples of the range that is available – for example:

> The Adler model 821-1 is a machine designed to set cuffs to shirt sleeves. When using it the operator merely places a cuff and sleeve in the left or right clamping station, and the stitching is automatic. One operator can produce five sleeves a minute.

Whereas in the past skilled seamstresses were needed to produce garments, present technological innovations reduce the skill requirements to that of a machine operator. A change from sewing collars to cuffs no longer requires different skills, but merely demands a change in tempo on the part of the operator. Computer programs devised elsewhere by white-collar staff have now replaced the manual skills of machinists in local factories.

There are many examples of the old skills being superseded by new methods at all levels of factory production. Len Archer was particularly proud of the Gerber cutting machine, which proved to be far more productive than the old labour-intensive methods.

> These machines cost a fair bit, so it's only big operations like ours that have enough throughput to make them pay. But they really are marvellous. The operatives unroll the cloth. Once all the cloth has been laid out, layer upon layer, all the air is sucked out to keep it flat. The rest is down to the computer. A computer will help you with the pattern layout, so you can see at a glance exactly what percentage of cloth you're using and if it's possible to squeeze in an extra piece. Then all that information is fed to the cutting machine, which cuts the cloth automatically. The operatives just push a few buttons, then we all stand back and watch the technology take over. The workers love it, and we've even got a couple of women who are training up on it.

Automated sewing machines also reduce many of the risks associated with human error. Previously operators were required to adjust their machines to meet their own sewing styles. With programmable machines, this is no longer necessary, since once a sequence is begun it is completed automatically. As Len Archer remarked:

> Once the machinist starts sewing, the machine completes the sequence. If anything goes wrong, it has to be a fault on the part of the operator, because the machine is locked on course. We can put our new recruits onto jobs that would have taken months to learn in the past. And of course the women can easily move from one machine to another, so they don't get as bored. As these machines get more sophisticated, so they can do more of the job, but I don't think we'll ever see the day when things will be totally automated. And that's where we're having difficulties now: we could increase our output if we could get more recruits, but the youngsters don't

like factory work, even though it's so much more pleasant than in the past.

Part of Brandwear's modernisation process focused on the working environment. Better air conditioning and improved lighting replaced the dim, stuffy shopfloor of the past. Indeed, as Brandwear's good relationships with their major customers continued, regular factory inspections ensured that spring cleaning was a common event. Workers would lay bets as to which customer was expected depending upon the amount of effort which went into the clean-up. For example, if Barrett Brothers were due to visit, boxes would be cleared away and the floor swept. However, if certain areas received a fresh coat of paint and windows were polished, then everyone knew that Chambers and Smith were due for a visit.

CURRENT STAFFING PROBLEMS

Despite a move away from the old reality of factories as 'dark satanic mills', Brandwear was aware that as an employer it suffered from an image problem. As orders began to improve, there were problems with attracting trained or suitable staff. Indeed, it was known that some trained machinists had recently found employment in a new supermarket that had been opened nearby. The personnel officer, Mrs Green, explained the problem to the training adviser of the local council:

> We've tried everything to get women to come back to work for us, but we still have vacancies. We operate a twilight shift in the evenings, because we know that working mothers can often get help at home at that time of day. But whilst the twilight shift was once very popular, there isn't the interest there any more. I know that some have got jobs with the new supermarket, and they're not interested in the factory any more. But I still think they'd earn more money working here. And because we pay them according to how much they produce, they have control over what will be in their wage packet.

> We've introduced a new incentive payment system, which was tailor-made for us using ASD (average sewing data) measurements. Some of our top earners are doing really well; they work hard, so they deserve every penny they get. But the biggest advantage about the flexible manufacturing systems is that workers are no longer tied to one machine. The jobs are easier, so they can move round and get to grips with several operations. And ASD means we don't have to keep retiming the different jobs to work out the wages.

> We'd like to get more trainees, but it's a case of being able to provide the training that people want, and we clearly need help in that area.

TOWARDS A POSSIBLE SOLUTION

The local authority in which Brandwear is based recently launched an initiative to support local industry in order to boost employment opportunities in the area. Clearly, Brandwear's dilemma appeared to be the type of development problem that would qualify them for support from the local authority: a modern expanding company facing an acute skills shortage in an area where adult unemployment was still high. A new training scheme aimed at resolving this dilemma could be set up as a joint venture between Brandwear and the local authority. Also, a training scheme which offered multiple skills to employees seemed particularly attractive.

Mr Hood, senior economic adviser to the local authority, had the task of assessing whether Brandwear should receive a training grant. But first he had to consider the local authority's grant-allocation policy. He was convinced of the need for a training grant on Brandwear's part, but what sort of jobs would a training scheme lead to? Mr Hood therefore decided to talk to some of the shopfloor workers about their jobs.

Mr Hood recognised from the outset that Brandwear was fortunate to have survived the recession when so many other similar companies had been forced to close down. Brandwear had recovered, not by trimming margins to the bone, but by introducing new machinery and new working practices that enabled operators to work on more machines than had been the case in the past.

There were plenty of less reputable sweatshop operations in Mr Hood's area, so he was relieved to be negotiating with an established manufacturer such as Brandwear. But he also knew that if the local authority provided a training grant to Brandwear, the company would gain a clear advantage over other local firms. Would the money be better spent in offering incentives to sweatshop companies to encourage them to make improvements?

Another factor that Mr Hood had to consider was the local authority's equal-opportunities policy. This meant that it was crucially important to recognise which sectors of the community would benefit from the proposed training scheme. He knew that he had to think about the impact of the training scheme on women's jobs. Bearing all these factors in mind, Mr Hood set up a meeting with some of the present workers at Brandwear.

A questionnaire

The buzz of conversation ceased as Mr Hood introduced himself to the workers in the canteen. He explained that he wanted to ask the workers about the way their jobs had changed since the factory had become modernised and new technology had been introduced. Mr Hood explained that he was interested in finding out the effects of Brand-wear's multi-skilling operations which had been introduced with the new manufacturing systems. He told them that he would like them to write down their comments on the questionnaire he had designed. He assured them that anything they wrote would be treated in confidence, and that they could not be identified. After answering a few questions, he distributed the questionnaire to each of the workers.

Ten days later, Mr Hood returned to the factory to collect the completed questionnaires. He then went back to his office to look at the comments and analyse the results. Most respondents said that their job had changed since the new machines had been introduced. One comment revealed what this might mean to individual workers: "One girl now does the work of two. Women who were skilled machinists now just feed machinery."

However, although the output of individual workers might have increased, many of them appeared to have problems in maintaining their previous level of earnings:

> As an overlocker myself on the new machines, I have found much difference in performance. It took me ages to adapt to the change, handling the garments in a flat bed after using raised-bed machines for 12 years. My performance is still not what it used to be . . .

> I consider experience is being taken for granted when new work is introduced and minutes for such work are calculated. We are having to work at a more intense concentration and speed to achieve our weekly standard of earnings, which in the last few years have greatly decreased.

Workers also seemed to suffer from a lack of consultation by management about their workloads and working practices:

> There is a great lack of consultation. Work would be less tense if we were provided with detailed sheets stating machine requirements for each order . . .

> I feel pressurised and frustrated, mostly due to the pressure put on workers by the management, and a lack of communication and cooperation. If this could ever be solved, you would not need half your questions.

Mr Hood was interested in other aspects of multi-skilling. Did it, for example, increase variety and relieve boredom for the workers?

> We are put onto different jobs on piecework – often just small jobs like sewing the vents on leisurewear. There is no consideration of the method used to deliver the work to the proper place, and there aren't enough rollers to deliver work to the rail. So I have to take

> my work from a box, and this is not included in the minutes given
> for the job . . .
>
> During the last year I have noticed in myself and fellow workers a
> lack of interest and incentive towards these jobs. I put it down to a
> change of method of work. Having to do work in less time leads to
> pressure and bad quality . . .
>
> When you go home at night you cannot relax, because you are
> under so much pressure to get your work out and earn your units.
> I myself can go to bed at night and get up the next day, and not feel
> as if I've been to bed at all.

Mr Hood was also interested in the new ASD payment system that
Brandwear had introduced along with the new machinery. In other
industries, incentive schemes have been used as a means of improving
motivation amongst workers in repetitive jobs.

The clothing industry has a reputation of using timed payment systems
to push workers to the limits of what is humanly possible. ASD (average
sewing data) is a system of work study which takes short-run
production into account. When Brandwear introduced flexible manufacturing systems, ASD seemed an ideal choice of work measurement,
because it claimed to ensure that workers receive due allowance when
they experience frequent job transfers.

Mr Hood discovered, however, that women in the factory were
unhappy with ASD:

> ASD makes the timings very tight . . . although ASD is supposed to
> be fair, if you fall back in your first hour you cannot make it up in
> the next. Allowances are greatly minimised: two actions such as
> 'pick up with right hand' and 'put aside with left' are counted as
> only one action if they are done at the same time. Also, the ASD
> book has a recommended 18% allowance, but the girls are only
> given 11% when sitting and 15% when standing. There is a greatly
> minimised allowance for things like talking to the supervisor,
> changing spools, unpicking, etc . . .
>
> As a shop steward for about ten years, I have seen the change in
> stress on the shopfloor. Many of the girls find it hard to reach the
> targets set. ASD is not putting up the girls' wages, and most of
> them take home less. I am coming to the end of my sewing years,
> and the way the industry is pushing the workers, I am not sorry.
> But I feel sorry for the girls who are just starting. I hope your
> questionnaire will help the girls who follow on.

Mr Hood became concerned that the management's dream of multi-
skilling was not being shared by the workers in terms of the money they
took home in their pay packets. There also seemed to be some problems

with the workers' understanding of ASD itself. It is a sophisticated system which is computer-based, and according to one of the supervisors it is shrouded in technological mystique:

> ASD may be a very efficient way of timing for management, but it is a Shylock existence for the workers – giving management its pound of flesh. ASD is very much guarded, but I have got notes on it.

There were several areas of concern about the new technology in the factory that Mr Hood wanted to raise with management. As he continued to work through the responses to the questionnaire, Mr Hood began to get a much better picture of what, from the workers' point of view, was taking place.

Another issue that was raised in the questionnaire was that of health and safety at work. There were several comments about general workplace comforts:

> I have found since going back to work full-time that my health has deteriorated due to what I think is lack of fresh air. Working in a hot room is not healthy; it breeds germs. That is why people like myself continually lose time off work – not laziness as some would think. It is about time that management got together and did something about better air conditioning . . .

> The men get a smoke room, but the ladies do not. Our toilets are always smoky . . .

> The first aid should be much better than it is, and the canteen leaves a lot to be desired as the vegetables have too much water.

Mr Hood knew that it would never be possible to please all the people all the time, and that many of these comments could be seen as general workplace grouses. More disturbing, however, was the high level of accidents in the factory. Over of a quarter of the women said they had suffered an accident at work in the last 12 months, and the majority of these had experienced a needle going through their finger.

Indeed, one such accident occurred during his visit to the factory. A young woman was brought into the production manager's office with a needle in her thumb. Len Archer looked irritated as he arranged for a car to take the victim to the local hospital. He then explained that these accidents were a regular occurrence, but that he got annoyed because they could all be avoided:

> These new machines do everything for the operatives: once the pedal is pressed, the machine will complete its sewing sequence. If a girl gets her finger caught, it's because she has been stupid enough to leave it in the wrong place. Most of these accidents are

caused by stupidity, and we lose a lot of production because of them.

Mr Hood wondered if the simplicity of the new machines meant that workers were more likely to lose concentration than in the past when they were more involved with their work. Clearly, a lack of concentration on the part of individual workers could lead to more accidents.

Sex equality was another issue that concerned Mr Hood. He knew that in the past there had been a strict division between men's factory work and that done by women. For example, the best-paid jobs in the clothing industry were in cutting. Traditionally this had been a fiercely protected male domain, and had been thought of as highly skilled. On the other hand, sewing machinists tended to be women – unless of course bespoke tailoring skills were required, in which case male machinists might also be used. The difference in skill rating between men and women has always been a contentious issue in the clothing industry.

The division of labour at Brandwear had followed industry norms. The sewing machinists who answered the questionnaire were particularly vociferous:

> Equal pay has helped us *not at all*: our pay is still below that of cutters, who are equal skill . . .

> For the type of work we produce, we are grossly underpaid and conditions are disgusting. We more than show we are on a par with our cutters: we put *their* work right, and no one can do the same for us.

Mr Hood knew that women had been employed as cutters since the new computerised cutting machines had been introduced. His suspicion was that the reasons behind this were less to do with sex equality and more to do with the lack of attractiveness associated with the new cutting jobs.

Women were also concerned with the conditions of service and the lack of recognition they received even after a lifetime of work:

> The management should have a better attitude towards the workers. There is lack of training and promotion, and no staff status for working 17 years . . .

> After 28 years as a machinist I get no recognition for long service. I still make my own money, and never get paid if I take time off.

General conclusions

Mr Hood knew that he must consider the quality of long-term employment prospects for clothing workers. He then had to decide what to recommend to the local authority in terms of whether or not they should support Brandwear's proposed training scheme to help them recruit new workers.

He knew that if Brandwear received support, the local authority could attach certain preconditions which might improve the quality of jobs that were eventually created. Likewise, Mr Hood knew that Brandwear could easily look to workers abroad to supply the extra labour. If this happened, how long would it be before Brandwear followed the course of some of its competitors and signed contracts with production plants in Southeast Asia?

CASE STUDY TASKS

Imagine you are Mr Hood, and that you have to produce a report on jobs and skills, working conditions and training at Brandwear for the local authority. In writing this report you will need to address the following:

1 List the major issues you have identified during your research at Brandwear.

2 Is training the most important human resource management problem at Brandwear? If it is, then why? If not, then what are the most important problems, and why?

3 How do women's jobs differ from men's jobs in the clothing industry? Consider the issues identified in Questions 1 and 2, and the following in particular:

a how skill is defined;

b payment systems, equal pay and equal opportunities;

c how new technology has changed the design of jobs.

What practical steps would you take to address these issues?

4 How and why does management's view of new technology differ from that of the workforce? What do you think would be the view of the National Union of Tailor and Garment Workers?

ESSENTIAL READING

Cockburn C, *Machinery of Dominance: Women, Men and Technological Know-how*, Pluto Press, 1985, chapter 2

Dex S, *The Sexual Division of Work*, Wheatsheaf, 1985, chapters 2 and 7

Hyman R, Streeck W (eds), *Industrial Relations and New Technology*, Blackwell, 1988

FURTHER READING

Chapkis W, Enloe C, *Of Common Cloth: Women in the Global Textile Industry*, Transnational Institute, 1983

Coyle A, Sex and skill in the organisation of the clothing industry, in West J, ed, *Work, Women and the Labour Market*, Routledge and Kegan Paul, 1982

Lupton T, Bowey A M, *Wages and Salaries*, Gower, 1983, chapter 3

Morris J, *No More Peanuts: An Evaluation of Women's Work*, National Council for Civil Liberties, 1983

West J, ed, *Work, Women and the Labour Market*, Routledge and Kegan Paul, 1982, chapter 1

7 Developing a human resource management strategy: International Computers Ltd

Paul Sparrow

ORGANISATIONAL SETTING

At the time of writing International Computers Ltd (ICL) was a subsidiary of STC, and formed the largest part of its Communications and Information Systems Group. It was purchased by STC in 1984. ICL turned around a £49.8 million loss in 1981 to make a profit of £129 million in 1988 (a 16% increase on the previous year) on a turnover of £1,363 billion. ICL employs 21,000 people, and its manufacturing operations are unionised, the principal union at that time being ASTMS (now part of MSF).

The case study is set at a corporate level, and covers the period from 1983 to 1987. It is concerned with the management of change, both of business strategy and of human resource management, in an IT company. During the period in question, there was a major shift in the focus of ICL's business away from the manufacture and sale of mainframe computers towards the sale of total business solutions, such that by 1988 45% of ICL's business came from non-hardware areas.

BACKGROUND TO THE CASE

ICL was born in 1968 out of the merger between English Electric Computers (EEC) and International Computers and Tabulators (ICT). It was given £40 million of government support, and took six years to develop the 2900 Series of computers – a series that was incompatible with IBM computers and thereby retained ICL's independence.

At the time of the merger, IBM had advanced to a 50% market share in the UK. The UK government saw the amalgamation of British high-technology companies as the only way to stem the advance of American companies. As the government had been the largest customer of both EEC and ICT, there was little demand for an IBM operating system. EEC and ICT had invested heavily in the Series 4 and 1900 computers. Designers were characterised by a 'not invented here' syndrome. Therefore strategic alliances were ruled out, and ICL was left trying to cover the whole of IBM's territory.

The company began to move outside its traditional 'old empire' foreign markets in 1976, when it acquired Singer Business Machines. This acquisition also moved ICL for the first time away from sole reliance on large mainframe computers and towards smaller minicomputers. In the late 1970s, growth rates of 20% were achieved. The company, however, had a very high cost base, as it had maintained staff from all merged and acquired companies, and was operating in an environment of high UK inflation. Its strategy therefore depended upon being able to maintain high revenue growth rates. As long as its markets continued to grow, it was safe.

But its markets did not continue to grow. In 1979 the recession struck, and as revenues failed to grow sufficiently fast enough, the development funds began to fall behind what was needed. Some plant closures were made in 1979 with the loss of 900 jobs. By February 1980 it became apparent that results were getting worse, and the company was using up its available cash fast. It sold off its leases, and placed a ban on recruitment. These measures were too little too late, and by September ICL was faced with a £100 million shortfall in orders. There were only six months to go before bankruptcy, and the company took legal advice on when to cease trading.

Employee costs by now represented 50% of revenues, and the first public sign of impending disaster was when the job offers made to graduates were rescinded. Shortly afterwards, 2500 redundancies were announced and the government was approached. In March 1980 the government agreed to act as guarantor for a bank overdraft of £270 million. Only a couple of months later, the government invoked its power of guarantee by imposing three new directors. The new chairman, Chris Laidlaw, spent his time arguing and winning ICL's case in the City. The managing director, Robb Wilmot, spent his first few months formulating a new product strategy that was to change the shape of ICL, the way it did business, and the sorts of skills it needed.

The product strategy essentially entailed focusing on a limited number of niche markets, based on industrial sectors such as retail, health, financial services, etc. ICL would no longer attempt to compete with IBM across the board. It also decided to move into office computing, lessening its dependence on mainframe computers. The new computers were sold as a networked range of products supported by pre- and post-sales consultancy, software and maintenance services. ICL was to sell 'total business solutions'. To market its new range of products successfully, ICL needed very quickly to 'intercept' the new technologies and markets. It therefore pursued a new strategy of collaboration. The most immediate and significant of these collaborations was with Fujitsu, the Japanese microchip maker.

The ready availability of cheap components had meant that there were numerous companies producing hardware. Computer suppliers had found it increasingly difficult to differentiate their products on technology. Instead, they began to differentiate products once they had reached the market by focusing on applications software. The demand for software was reflected in an increasing emphasis on software in R & D budgets. In 1981 software was taking only 35% of R & D budgets in mainframe suppliers, but by 1985 this figure would rise to 55%. In focusing on applications software, computer suppliers could no longer continue to be 'all things to all people'. They had to focus on niche markets. The shift from hardware to total systems differentiation entailed a major skills reprofiling.

First, however, ICL entered a period of strict financial control, redundancy, restructuring and redefinition on the back of this product

System Type	Time March 1982	September 1984	% Change
Large and Medium	1280	1510	+18
Small	2850	4320	+50
Distributed	12500	43500	+248
Engineer Grade	**March 1982**	**September 1984**	**% Change**
Team Leaders and Support Engineers Systems	140	188	+26
Grades 1 & 2: Support Engineers	702	621	−12
Grade 3: Customer Engineers, Service Customer Engineers	1055	802	−24
Grade 4: Modification and Routine Maintenance Engineers	123	94	−24
New Grade: Service Representatives	—	193	—

Table 7.1 Skills Reprofiling in the Service Engineer Workforce. Figures for System Type represent the number of installed systems. Figures for Engineer Grade represent the number of engineers employed

strategy. By September 1981 another 9200 jobs were lost, and ASTMS (now part of MSF) had failed to gain support for a one-day protest strike. Payroll, however, now accounted for only 39% of sales revenue, and the financial crisis subsided.

The managing director had hoped that the new collaboration with Fujitsu, and the tighter quality levels, design-cycle times and perform-ance goals that this would entail, would 'recalibrate' the capabilities of his management and pace their skill development. However, although there was apparent buy-in to the strategy, progress was slow. To speed up the change process, and to sharpen its effect, he restructured the company around highly decentralised business units that were made responsible for their profits. Historically the product developers had designed very advanced and technically strong computers. But no one wanted to buy them, and marketing efforts had been poor. The new business units brought these two opposing camps together for the first time, and made them jointly responsible for achieving profit.

Once the two-stage reorganisation was complete, the ICL structure was designed in a diamond matrix. At the back end of the diamond came the manufacturing operations. These supported four main product-orientated business centres: mainframes, office systems, networks and industry systems. The organisation was spearheaded by two sales and marketing organisations: ICL (UK) Ltd and ICL International.

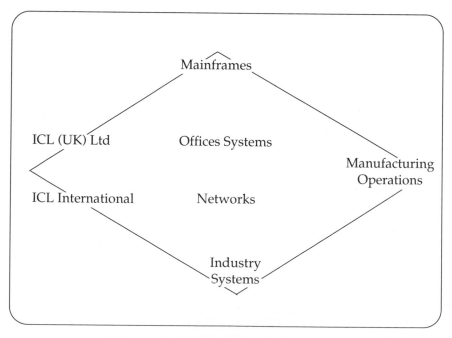

Figure 7.1 The ICL Corporate Structure

The restructuring

The first stage in this restructuring, however, was intended to make ICL a sharper, market-driven company by creating a series of small business centres. One manager explained the reasoning:

> Robb Wilmot said we can't have internal wars going on in product development and product marketing ... What we need is a crisp company ... Small companies within a big company with narrowed-down communication channels and the right focus ... They had a marketing focus on products, so that the marketing and development people had to work hand in hand for the good of the business centre. The first one was the Retail Business Centre ... There were going to be nice open-plan offices, but the first thing they did was to put great screens around themselves so you couldn't talk to them! But they settled down, and it didn't take long for the manager of the business centre to get the message across that we were in this to succeed or fail. It gradually got going very well.

The motivation for the restructuring had in fact been twofold. First, it quickened the pay-back on products. If the new business centres could not sell their joint offerings within 12 months, they were disbanded. Only those business centres that were able to work together effectively survived. Second, it created a manageable level of conflict. It exposed the common weaknesses and raised support for more lasting change.

By late 1982, however, commitment to the new product strategy was still poor. The company had been turned around financially, but the managing director was becoming frustrated. He recalled:

> I gradually realised the understanding was minimal ... The quality of the buy-in was poor. It lacked religion ... I lacked the levers to transfer my strategic insight into the hearts and minds of the organisation ... ICL's culture, based on functional organisation, was clearly misaligned with what I was trying to do ... During the financial crisis of 1981, people just did what they were told. It was war. But in 1982 I was facing a far more complex set of issues – a strategic crisis rather than a financial crisis. And I clearly hadn't got the organisation worked up to an adequate understanding of the nature of the strategic crisis ... Do you match strategy to what your organisation is capable of doing, or do you change your organisation so it is capable of executing the strategy? ... It suddenly dawned on me that the ICL culture was going to beat me if I let it ... What I had to do was build a culture that was about change itself.

Wilmot was perceptive enough to realise that the first flush of change was now over, and resistance was beginning to grow. An executive explained the nature of that resistance:

> When the company is on the precipice, it is quite easy to be fairly authoritarian, fairly directive and fairly autocratic in what you want to do, in terms of how you structure your organisation . . . But in a company operating in a crisis situation you can only do that for so long, because there comes a time when even if you are on the edge of a precipice people are going to say, "Stuff this, I'm going to jump off", and are just not prepared to tolerate this . . . His style of management after two or three years was creating a lot of internal conflict, because three years into his time with the company, he was wanting to change the organisation structure as quickly as during the crisis. This caused discontent, because by that time the company was being stabilised, products were ready to be launched, and trading relationships were starting to bear fruit. Things were turning round and people were starting to want to contribute.

Robb Wilmot initiated a major management education programme, which provided an understanding of the changing business environment, a new language about the strategy, and new marketing skills. The programme was cascaded down throughout the whole organisation, starting from the board of directors. The message was broken down into four increasingly sophisticated levels, each linked to individual career stages in the company. At that time profits were still fragile, and the £20 million required for the core programme (as it was called) represented 25% of the profits. It was a bold decision, but one that paid off. Gradually people began to appreciate the new strategy, and slowly the demand increased to attend the courses.

Against this background, the personnel function also experienced significant change. It was reduced in size, and many of the managers who had specialised in industrial relations left the company. A personnel manager later explained:

> We moved away in the 1980s from being an employee-relations-driven organisation, where the unions were predominantly the focus of everybody's attention on the personnel side . . . They were the drumbeat that we did everything by . . . Now we have managed to work with the unions to get rid of that . . . Consequently, the other side of the personnel function – the HRD side – is becoming far more critical, and far more attention has been paid to it in the last three to four years than at any time before.

By 1983, there was a new and dynamic personnel director, and a new group of managers with backgrounds in human resource development rather than industrial relations.

	1981	1982	1983	1984	1985	1986	1987
Turnover (£ million)	711	721	847	1124	1037	1194	1299
Operating profit (£ millions)	−49.8	+47	+61	+46	+71	+90	+110
Profitability (based on pre-tax profit)	Loss	3.3%	5.4%	2.9%	5.2%	6.8%	8.5%
Turnover per employee (£1000)	23	29	36.7	43	50.3	58.1	64.9
Borrowing as % of equity	Govt. Support	61%	27%	25%	29%	Surplus	Surplus

Table 7.2   ICL's turnaround from 1981–1987

THE PROBLEM

The new personnel director faced a major problem. In the late 1970s, ICL had been through a period of fairly turbulent industrial relations in the UK. There were common conditions of employment across the UK, with no local variation. The emphasis in personnel had been on centralised control, conformity and uniformity. But the perceived need for this centralised control had reduced under a number of influences:

- changes in the organisational structure of ICL;

- changes in the philosophy of how to run the company;

- political change in the country at large, leading to a reduction in union power.

The company had undergone a period of significant change that had entailed major redundancy, redefinition of the management task, restructuring around profit-accountable business centres, reprofiling of engineering skills, and management education. He now felt that ICL needed to implement a personnel strategy that would both stabilise the change and deliver on the product strategy.

ICL was integrating its product set and developing open systems. It was innovating increasingly on the basis of collaboration. It had altered the balance of its distribution channels, and had set up a network of traders to handle low-value, high-volume equipment. It had restructured around a series of industry focused niche markets, and was in the process of pushing this new market focus as deep into its organisation as possible. Finally, it had set the goal of making Europe its home base, with the intention of becoming a truly international organisation.

The personnel strategy had to develop five main skills:

- new technical skills;

- strategic marketing skills;

- knowledge of industry;

- collaboration and distribution management;

- management of change process skills.

The personnel director knew that the corner had been turned financially, now that borrowing was down to 27% of equity. The company was making a slender £61 million profit, and revenues were increasing by a healthy 17%. Nevertheless, it was clear that major adjustments needed to be made to the human resource management policies and practices.

He knew that ICL would have to make some more refinements to its structure to reflect the new industrial markets and to decentralise accountability even more. But he suspected that these refinements could wait until the implications of the recent restructuring had been digested. He knew that he would need actively to reskill and redeploy his resources, not only to meet both the short-term market and the technological skill needs, but also to achieve the longer-term effect of reinforcing competitive conscious behaviour. But perhaps most importantly, he knew that, in order to make sure these adjustments had a lasting effect on the organisation, he would have to ensure that ICL adapted the key processes that supported the business strategy:

- its commercial policies;

- its information systems;

- its internal human resource management processes, such as recruitment, training and rewards.

The personnel director stated his key need:

It is resourcing in the broadest sense ... We are talking about organisational capability, the ability of the company to adapt and build its organisation around its business strategy, and the ability to shift the organisation as the strategies move, which they inevitably do in this business.

The problem, quite simply, was how best to achieve the transformation.

CASE STUDY TASKS

Imagine you are the personnel director with overall responsibility for developing and implementing a human resource management strategy for ICL that will build on the recent change in direction. Suggest a critical path for this strategy, and outline the major personnel activities that would support it.

You should bear in mind that at the time ICL relied significantly on graduate recruitment to source new skills (traditionally recruited by separate business divisions from computer science backgrounds). It was operating in an environment of strict headcount control in the aftermath of the redundancies. Many of the skills it needed (in terms of new product knowledge, experience of its new niche markets, and software development) were not easily available in the labour market. Staff turnover levels were as much as 20% in some business divisions. There was also little flexibility in existing rewards arrangements. ICL was the only IT company in the UK to make a single pay award for all staff. The unions, however, were no longer the main focus of the personnel department's activities.

You should be prepared to answer the following questions:

1 How would you link your human resource strategy to the business needs?

2 How could you manage entry into the organisation to assist the reprofiling of skills?

3 What would be the basic question that your human resource strategy would address?

   a What changes, if any, would you make to rewards policies?

   b What would be the role of training and development?

4 What would be the major blocks to change that you would expect to experience?

5 What would be the implications of your strategy for the skills and competences of your personnel and training staff?

ESSENTIAL READING

Lawrence A, Lame duck takes to the wing, *Computing*, 28 April 1988, pp22–23

Sparrow P R, Recruitment and retention strategies in the computer industry: An HRM perspective, in *Recruiting and Retraining IT Personnel*, Intro UK Ltd, 1989

Sparrow P R, Pettigrew A, Strategic human resource management in the UK computer supplier industry, *Journal of Occupational Psychology*, 1988, vol 51, pp25–42

ADDITIONAL READING

Beer M, Spector B, Lawrence P, et al, *Human Resources Management: a General Manager's Perspective*, Free Press, 1985

Hendry C, Pettigrew A, Sparrow P R, Changing patterns of human resource management, *Personnel Management*, 1988, vol 20, no 11, pp37–41.

Kleingartner A, Anderson C, *Human Resource Management in High Technology Firms*, Lexington Books, 1987

Pettigrew A, Sparrow P R, Hendry C, The forces that trigger training, *Personnel Management*, 1988, vol 20, no 12, pp28–32

Storey J, ed, *New Perspectives on Human Resource Management*, Routledge and Kegan Paul, 1989

8 Information technology and JIT: Silica Tele Test

Patrick Dawson and Janette Webb

ORGANISATIONAL SETTING

The key issue which this study addresses is how information technology is able to accommodate and respond to qualitative innovations in the organisation of work. In this case we examine the use of computerised order processing and material requirement planning systems in conjunction with changes in management philosophy towards the use of just-in time (JIT) and minimum-inventory production.

The case study draws on material gathered from an empirical study of the management of innovation in a UK division of Silica Tele Test (STT), a US-owned multinational corporation. The company was founded in the USA in the 1930s, and employs approximately 82,000 people worldwide and 1100 at the UK division which is being examined here. Over the past decade, STT have experienced continual growth, with an increase in sales from $1 billion in 1976 to just over $8 billion in 1987. This has been achieved through a sustained commitment to the research and development of small-volume state-of-the-art products

The main business of the UK division set up in 1966 is to design and manufacture computer-based test equipment for the international telecommunications industry. In 1984 the product range was expanded to include the manufacture of mobile communications and cellular radio equipment. The company prides itself not only in being a manufacturer of state-of-the-art high-technology products, but also in making extensive use of IT products in its own production systems.

BACKGROUND TO THE CASE

Over the last decade there has been a continual decline in the lifespan of STT products. In response to this, STT have increasingly focused their attention on process as well as product innovations. This has involved a move from production for stock to production to order, and the use of just-in-time (JIT) and total-quality-control (TQC) principles alongside the existing computerised production scheduling, which provides a database and an analytic framework for order processing, material requirements and production planning.

The essence of JIT is that work is done only when it is needed. The aim is to make products to order rather than for stock. Inventory and work-in-progress are correspondingly reduced. Machine set-up times and methods are re-examined to allow changes of machine tools to be made quickly, thereby reducing overall cycle times. Customer orders are given to workers responsible for the final stages of production, who pull the necessary materials and subassemblies from workers upstream. The instructions may be communicated by means of a visual indicator (or kanban), which triggers the production of particular goods and parts. Materials are delivered in small lots, on demand, ideally to distributed stores at or near their point of use. The supplier base is reduced, and the purchasing firm works closely with suppliers to ensure that parts and subassemblies meet technical specifications and quality requirements.

The aim is to have no inspection of parts on arrival. The set of supporting conditions required to maintain such a system comprise:

- multi-skilling;

- flexible working and job rotation;

- simple payment systems;

- low turnover of key managers and workers;

- close involvement of managers and engineers on the shop floor;

- total-quality-control (TQC) groups to improve the production process.

The accompanying TQC methodology aims to reduce product errors to zero, and to create continuous improvements in the production process. Instead of 'working around errors', which tends to be the norm where there are high levels of work-in-progress, the workforce is expected to stop production and correct problems as they occur. All levels of staff are trained to assume responsibility for the quality of products.

Organisational activity is modelled in terms of customer–supplier relations. A workgroup with responsibility for a discrete stage of production is 'served' by staff who carried out the work immediately prior to their own tasks. This group becomes the supplier for a subsequent 'customer' (internal or external to the company).

All staff are trained to work in groups, using descriptive statistical tools to identify production problems and to develop solutions. Whilst JIT techniques can be used to identify problems (such as having large amounts of unfinished goods in manufacture), TQC methodology is needed to solve the problems identified.

The two main systems used for production planning are:

- order processing and tracking system (OPTS);

– material requirements planning (MRP).

These two systems in conjunction with the master schedule provide the map from which decisions are made on the routeing and rerouteing of material and subassemblies to meet customer orders.

At the centre of production planning is the *master schedule* (MS). This drives the production side of STT, and is determined by actual orders and order forecasts from marketing. At its simplest, the MS sets out the batch working of the production lines, and acts as a 'working Bible' for the production planner. Thus in STT there is an attempt to combine a master schedule based partly on forecasting, with a JIT system that aims to build products to order rather than to long-range forecasts.

The OPTS system is fully computerised, and has been designed by STT to keep track of new, ongoing and backlog orders. New orders are transmitted from all European sales offices to sales headquarters at Geneva, where the information is collated and then forwarded on magnetic tape to the various European divisions. The status of these orders is monitored and tracked through to the release of finished goods and the clearance of customer documents.

The MRP system automatically initiates material requirements orders at time-phased intervals to accommodate to the production plan. It provides detailed information on the demand for (and supply of) material parts and subassemblies required for manufacturing operations over some 60 weeks.

Prior to the adoption of a JIT system, MRP was also used to push materials into production, and to ensure that shortages did not occur. On the basis of the master schedule, anticipated material requirements would be identified and purchased in advance of actual production needs. Thus the buying of materials took place without the need for a customer order. Each month a new 60-week forecast is calculated to take account of monthly fluctuations in market activity.

Although the master schedule is regularly updated, STT production planners estimate that it could require a lead time of between 20 and 26 weeks to move from producing a batch of five of product X to a batch of ten. As the production planner noted:

> If we wanted to pull something in, it would be 20 weeks before we could do very much about it. It would only need one part to have a 20-week delivery time. You can get the other 99, but what's the point if you can't get the one?

Nevertheless, using the marketing forecast and data on past performance, the master schedule provides a reasonably accurate production plan. In practice, STT would hope to operate a four-week lead time from order processing to shipment of product. However, a sudden and unanticipated large order can pose difficult decisions for production management.

The main task of the production planner (PP) is to adjust the master schedule to accommodate to fluctuations in the level of product demand and materials supply. In the case of an unexpected rise or fall in product demand, changes have to be made to the schedule of manufacture, and to the organisation of the production lines.

While the computerised order-processing and material-requirements systems provide accurate information for the purpose of reformulating schedules, they also act to 'push' materials into production, and create congestion by instigating a high level of work-in-progress. Consequently it is often difficult to realign production to actual orders. The situation is exacerbated by the large number of suppliers (over 4000) which STT deal with in procuring their materials. As the material requirements manager explained:

> Materials is a filthy business to plan, to purchase for, to forecast and even to control. With all our computing power, if you're making ten a month and 5% of those might be option 8, then what do you do? Do you go and buy something, do you buy a half, or what? These are the sorts of practical problem we are faced with.

STT (UK) thus has a sophisticated computerised planning system that was initially supposed to give an advantage over competitors by guaranteeing the ability to anticipate demand for products more accurately than paper-based sales documentation, and by enabling orders to be met reliably, either from stock or within a predictable time period. The system was meant to solve the problem of tracking material requirements for a wide range of highly varied product options, while acting as a superior working memory for production planning and ensuring a reliable flow of appropriate materials to the assembly areas.

The system worked adequately until the late 1970s and early 1980s, when STT began to lose market share in the face of strong Japanese competition over price, quality and speed of production. In an attempt to create a system more responsive to customer orders, corporate management sought a solution from organisational restructuring rather than from further development of computerised production planning systems. In particular, they looked towards the use of JIT and TQC.

CORPORATE POLICY AND LOCAL RESTRUCTURING

The strategic innovation in production was initiated by the USA senior executive. The proposals were discussed with senior managers in Europe. In the case of STT (UK), the senior manager in charge of the new cellular radio equipment (henceforth referred to as TC), acted as a champion of change in facilitating the local implementation of a JIT production system.

Between 1984 and 1985, TC made a number of visits to America, and observed JIT techniques in a high-volume US plant, used at the top level of assembly and test, with batch production at lower levels. He also reported common moves towards 'demand-pull'/kanban systems in the US. The uniqueness of the plan for the STT production process was the attempt to apply JIT to a low-volume product. This challenged current wisdom on the need to build in batches to compensate for set-up times, thinking instead in terms of a building-to-order model of production. JIT concepts were used as a thinking tool for reconstructing the batch production process.

While TC became committed to the ideas of using JIT manufacturing, his peer groups of manufacturing managers at STT (UK) and other European divisions were not fully convinced. Production control, materials purchasing and stores began to get anxious about the consequences of straying from the conventional approach of computerised scheduling for production planning. Moreover, line managers were worried about how these changes would affect efficiency rates, which were based on maximising work-in-progress. Nevertheless, TC was able to allay their fears by pointing to the potential benefits of greater flexibility and higher quality that would result from reduced cycle times, reduced levels of scrap and lower inventories.

Over a two-year period from 1985 to 1987, TC set about orchestrating the introduction of a JIT system of production. The programme commenced with the manufacture of a new power meter product developed in the US. By choosing a product developed elsewhere, TC was able to introduce it in kit form for staff to assemble 'just in time'. This process of learning through the practical application of JIT TQC and concepts proved instrumental in establishing the norm that batch processing was not acceptable. Everyone was trained to think in terms of the finished product, by the device of asking repeatedly "How many X's were shipped today?", until the assembly workers and engineers concerned took it for granted that the main measure of their effectiveness was not just subassemblies and finished products, but 'shipped' products.

The initial rules of thumb for constructing working practice were:

- build to order;

- keep building cycles short and flexible;

- build to customer specifications;

- don't stock up on expensive components that are not immediately required.

Quality control was designed into the production process so that, as a surprised visiting manager from a US transfer team put it, "Manufacturing people feel responsible for quality directly to the customer, rather than trying to avoid the quality-assurance police."

In order to ensure the local ownership of this new work philosophy a transfer team was set up, with members on both sides of the Atlantic, and product teams spent time working on the relevant product in the US and in the UK. Moreover, the arrival of a mentor from the US was a key influence towards the acceptance of the production processes, in that he was able to put words to the JIT concepts, thus providing staff with labels to describe the techniques which they were already using.

The resulting work organisation was significantly different from that associated with conventional batch production at the factory. Physically, most lines were rearranged into U-shaped work areas. Assembly workers were organised into teams of 10–12, each with a supervisor, who was selected not so much for technical knowledge as for social skills. Supervisors were seen as a crucial link in workgroup acceptance of changes in individual tasks and responsibilities.

Responsibility for meeting daily production requirements was devolved to work teams, with supervisors allocating work within each team. Individual job content was changed to include a wider range of tasks, albeit at a similar level. Any assembly worker would be likely to work on a larger part of any given product, if not assembling the whole product. The workers at this level would now be expected to carry out the same operation no more than twice before switching to a slightly different operation, whereas previously they would probably have repeated one operation 10–20 times before switching.

Such changes, however, were not necessarily regarded by the workers as enhancing job satisfaction. On the contrary, the constant switching between product types was likely to be seen as a nuisance, requiring more effort and continual changing of tools.

On the other hand, perhaps the most significant development in work organisation was the attempt to introduce responsibility for quality at all levels and all stages. In effect, the assembly workers were required to act as their own industrial engineers, resolving problems that ranged from badly designed technical manuals through ill-fitting components to bottlenecks in production, and calling on the assistance of engineers and managers as necessary. This meant that, although the assembly tasks remained relatively routine, there was a considerable up-skilling in terms of the analysis of production problems.

Management sought to make explicit use of the formerly tacit knowledge of the workforce about the actual manufacturing techniques used to make product option X work. Such a revolution in the design of production jobs carried with it a further significant development: when the daily rate was met, the team stopped 'working', ie stopped building products. They would then carry out routine maintenance or work on a TQC project.

In terms of the UK experience of factory jobs, the changes were radical. They were introduced gradually through the creation of 'experimental' lines, with one team learning the new production processes for a small range of product options. The changes were heavily reinforced through TQC and working-in-groups training, and were still further reinforced through a payment system that rewarded participation in TQC activities.

By the beginning of 1987, steps were underway to move all products over to a JIT production system. The initial attempts had proved successful, and the senior executives were convinced that the adoption of these new techniques could result in an improvement in product quality while reducing costs (ie the opposite of the conventional equation of 'high quality = high cost'), increasing flexibility and improving customer relations through more reliable delivery schedules.

The local management of STT (UK) were given the task of the wholesale implementation of these changes in their five key manufacturing departments:

- production control;
- purchasing;
- stores;
- PCB assembly;
- the production lines.

A NEW APPROACH TO PRODUCTION CONTROL

Conventional production control operated a 'push' system, where material requirements were issued automatically via the master schedule to the assembly lines. Consequently, any changes to manufacture would result in surplus on-hand components being sent back to storage. As one line manager described:

It was not so much a continuous flow system as a continuous overflow system. Under this system the job of the manufacturing supervisor was to implement the master schedule and to ensure that there were no deviations to planned operations. Paradoxically, the system could be operating at efficiency rates of 95%, and yet bottlenecks as a result of a large number of unfinished products would be a more realistic indicator of an inefficient use of material and human resources. In short, this preplanned, inflexible system created a lot of work-in-progress and led to an uneven flow of finished products.

In adopting JIT techniques, production control introduced a 'blow-through' system by allocating one work order per run and then establishing a 'pull' system between the assembly lines and stores. Material requirements were now pulled by the daily needs of the various production lines, and supervisors were given the responsibility of changing planned operations on the master schedule in order to meet daily fluctuations in the supply and demand of resources. Thus at the start of each day all the supervisors met to discuss and plan the day's work.

It was no longer the master schedule which dictated the production plan. Instead the computerised information processing systems were used as a tool to facilitate operational decision-making at first-line supervisory level. It is now the line supervisor who initiates the pulling of materials from stores, and who monitors and evaluates the need to change preplanned schedules.

The devolution of day-to-day decision-making responsibilities was achieved through the application of TQC methodology. Within STT (UK), three personnel were given responsibility for providing training and support to staff, and between 1987 and 1988 a number of projects had been instigated and completed by TQC groups.

Since the reorganisation of the production lines considerable benefits have been documented, including:

- a reduction in make cycles from ten weeks to two weeks;

- a decrease of over 60% in scrap rates;

- an improvement in average delivery rates from 24 weeks to 6 weeks.

In addition, there has been a reduction in the number of assembly workers needed, and an increase in the use of subcontractors for lower-order components. As the production-services section manager pointed out:

> Well, I think it's part of JIT in that it gets rid of a bottleneck which we had at one time, and we don't need to hold the inventory for the bits and pieces that we want made. We just ask someone else to make it, and we pay them the overhead. Their overheads could well be cheaper than ours anyway. You often find that a lot of these companies can make things cheaper than us, when you add in all our overheads for bits and pieces.

Further attempts are currently being made to refine the material flow process and reduce make cycles. The main benefits of the new production control system are seen to be:

- greater staff flexibility, with improved understanding of daily needs and requirements;
- a significant reduction in the number of order transactions, and also in the amount of computer time required per week for production control;
- less firefighting, as controllers can spend a greater proportion of their time on prevention and improvement;
- reduced paperwork: in October 1986, for example, there were over 6400 work orders, but by September 1988 this number had been reduced to 2600.

Similar improvements in operating efficiency have also been recorded by materials handling. Before the implementation of the JIT management production system, central stores accommodated all material requirements for STT, and in response to the master schedule they would 'push' components into manufacture. In order to improve materials handling, central stores were reorganised:

- parts used infrequently were moved off-site to another storage facility;
- material common to a number of products was separated from unique material.

This resulted in a small central store, and in the creation of a unique stores area for each production line. The small central store now operates a 'pull' system with the production lines. These changes in the organisation of materials handling have brought about a reduction in the number of people in stores, and a vast saving in the average time required to put together the components for any product option (two days instead of the previous four weeks).

The official view in STT is that a combination of JIT principles and TQC methodology can bring about continuous improvements in the areas of product quality, production costs, speed of delivery to customers, and flexibility of work organisation. In short, the claim is that, while IT production planning tools can be used to monitor orders and their relationship to material procurement and supply, they should not be used to mastermind production. The use of JIT techniques exposes production bottlenecks and hidden inventory costs, and should therefore be used to manage daily production. Above all it is workgroups who solve the problems through the use of TQC techniques and methods.

THE PROBLEM

One of the unresolved problems in STT is that, with a wide range of product options, predicted demand for any given product is often very low – and the lower the forecast, the more volatile it becomes. In other words, a small discrepancy in a high-volume forecast is less problematic than where demand for a product is as low as one to four a month. So it is fairly easy for actual demand to double (or even triple) the forecast level of demand, requiring a quick response throughout the system. This rapid 'pulling-up' needs a work organisation that enables flexible production and a quick response on the part of material suppliers to meet short-term changes in the demand for components.

However, as has already been noted, lead times of up to 20 weeks are required for material suppliers of some component parts. So, for example, if production is running a batch of five for a given product and receive an unanticipated order for 50, then materials supply and product manufacture cannot respond immediately to this sudden increase in demand. Until STT can establish greater reliability of material supply, it is forced to operate on the basis of anticipated requirements as indicated by the computerised MRP system.

The conflict in operating philosophy does not stop at material procurement, but is also in evidence on the lines themselves. As one line manager commented:

> Well, I would still see it as a batch system heading towards a JIT, but not JIT as I understand JIT to be – mainly because we have too many products with too small volumes, so it doesn't really lend itself in lots of ways to *real* JIT!

Many staff expressed similar scepticism at the suggestion that they were operating a fully fledged JIT production system. One line manager suggested that the biggest change had been from running ten batches on a monthly basis to doing smaller batch runs on a weekly basis. While the assembly staff and test engineers are working a JIT system, the material input is controlled by the production managers and supervisors, who still operate according to a batch production system in line with the material requirements and master-scheduling information systems. Thus the computerised information systems still act as the working schedule for the supervisor.

Not surprisingly, the changes have also created some personnel problems. Although STT was generally evaluated by staff as a good employer, and operates a policy of no compulsory redundancies, a number of problems were recounted by sectional managers. For example:

> We had problems with our metal fabrication shop, in that we've been running that down over the past two to three years, and we've had to find jobs for the people somewhere else in the plant ... The same with our cable department: we had a lot of girls [sic]

who were experts in making cables and small transformers, and we don't really need them now, so we've retrained them to load PC boards.

In addition to staff relocation and training, the innovations in work organisation have also challenged the conventional discipline of clock time. The unease experienced by production workers during the change is a good indication of this. Many, for example, felt guilty about 'not working' when involved in TQC groups, and perturbed about 'stopping working' when they had built the daily complement of customer orders. Hence line managers recount the story of production workers secretly maintaining a store of work-in-progress, 'just in case' they were hit by unexpected problems in the following day's production.

The techniques clustered under the JIT heading by definition undermine certain taken-for-granted assumptions that production rates have to be steadily increased during normal working hours in order to meet delivery times more reliably. Concurrently, however, product build time was a central focus of change, and measures of its contraction were used as indicators of progress.

CASE STUDY TASKS

This case is intended to stimulate debate, so where applicable particip- ants should be encouraged to draw on their own experiences as well as the literature in formulating answers. Attention should be given to discussing the more general issues of innovation and change which the case raises, rather than merely focusing on the details of STT's particular experiences.

Students should be split into groups of three to six, and should be given 30 minutes to discuss and make notes on the questions listed below. Each group should be prepared to present their conclusions at a plenary session.

1 Outline the main advantages and disadvantages for STT in adopting a JIT/TQC production system.

2 Identify the problems of, and contradictions between, a computer- ised order-processing and production-planning system, based on quantitative data analysis, and an organisation strategy focused on production to order using JIT and TQC principles.

3 Describe the best course of action for STT to take in response to a large order for a traditionally small batch product.

4 Suggest how you would resolve the personnel issues arising from process innovation at STT.

5 Do you agree with the following statement?

A corporate culture which encourages employee commitment and participation may generate conflict and interdepartmental rivalry, whilst a corporate culture which discourages employee involvement may result in poor employee relations and resistance to change. There are no universal panaceas to the problem of managing change, but just luck and adhoc response to contingent circumstances.

Explain your answer by drawing on the case, on your own experience and on your knowledge of the literature.

ESSENTIAL READING

Dawson P, Webb J, New production arrangements: The totally flexible cage?, *Work, Employment and Society*, 1989, vol 3, no 2

Jewitt R H, MRP v JIT: Is there a conflict?, in Voss C, ed, *Proceedings of the Second International Conference on Just-in-time Manufacturing*, IFS Ltd, 1987, pp341–352

Turnbull P J, The limits to Japanisation: Just-in-time, labour relations and the UK automotive industry, *New Technology, Work and Employment*, 1988, vol 3, no 1

ADDITIONAL READING

Boddy D, McCalman J, Buchanan D, *The New Management Challenge: Information Systems for Improved Performance*, Croom Helm, 1988

Pettigrew A, ed, *The Management of Strategic Change*, Blackwell, 1987

Schonberger R J, World-class manufacturing with minimal capital investment, in Voss C, ed, *Proceedings of the Second International Conference on Just-in-time Manufacturing*, IFS Ltd, 1987, pp3–8

Woodward J, *Industrial Organization: Theory and Practice*, Oxford University Press, 1980

ACKNOWLEDGEMENTS

Many thanks to the staff of STT who helped in the collection of material for the case, and to the Faculty of Social Sciences, Edinburgh University, for their financial support towards the fieldwork.

9 Implementing integrated computer systems: Clever Control Ltd

John Bessant and Joanna Buckingham

ORGANISATIONAL SETTING

Clever Control Systems Ltd (CCL) is a medium-sized, non-unionised company employing 200 people. CCL is part of the Control International (CI) group of companies. Like all of the companies in the CI group, CCL was a spin-off development to exploit an emerging market niche. CCL are primarily involved in the design, manufacture and sale of electronic process control systems. The company has customers throughout the process industries sector.

The parent company, CI, have experienced considerable problems in controlling and coordinating management information across the group. In order to regain centralised control, CI has invested in an integrated manufacturing and information system, which is to be implemented at all the group company sites. Thus by insisting upon common hardware and software, CI imposed a groupwide standard set of procedures. The present case concerns the attempted implementation of the integrated system within one of the group companies – Clever Control Ltd.

BACKGROUND TO THE CASE

Reasons for implementing the system

In the late 1970s CI were floated on the Stock Exchange, thereby necessitating a legal requirement for improved accountability. Up to this point, each company within the CI group had been given considerable freedom in its style of operation. As a result, each of the companies had adopted its own individual measures of financial control, thereby creating incompatible cross-group figures and considerable administrative work for the CI head office. Following the flotation, these problems of incompatible financial data took on a new significance, and forced the group to reexamine its accounting approach.

Without consulting the group companies, CI head office adopted a 'quick fix' solution. This took the form of an integrated computer-aided production management (CAPM) system. This system, purchased in 1979, was seen as offering the group an integrated suite of software, which would enforce the uniform production of compatible financial information by imposing a common system on all the companies in the group. The CAPM system was also sold to the individual group companies as a means of overcoming production-control problems. The managing director commented:

> We went out looking for a piece of software that initially gave us compatibility of financial information across the group, and then we said, "Ah! Wouldn't it be good if we had a common manufacturing system!" So we got into all the right things for the wrong reasons.

In common with most manufacturers serving industrial markets, CCL faced the difficult challenge of responding flexibly to widely varying customer needs. Each electronic process control system, although having many common parts, has some unique features. Thus manufacturing within the company was undertaken in small batches. This in turn meant that keeping track of what is going on in the factory – the level of stocks, the status of particular orders, the flow of assemblies and components round the plant – was something of a nightmare with the original manual system. It was therefore thought that a CAPM system would allow the company to improve its control of the process of manufacture.

COMPUTER-AIDED PRODUCTION MANAGEMENT

CAPM systems range widely, from simple programs designed to run on a microcomputer and handle a local function such as stockroom records keeping, to complex systems designed for mainframe computers, which integrate information right across the business, from initial sales order processing right through to customer invoicing, from the procurement of raw materials through to the issuing of the final despatch note.

Although there is no such thing as a standard CAPM system, most are built up around a set of materials management programs (often called material requirements planning, or MRP), which analyse the forecast sales of the company's products and then break this information down into a calculation of what needs to be available in order to manufacture these orders. This calculation can generate both purchase orders (for items to be bought in from outside suppliers) and works orders (for components and assemblies which can be made in-house).

In the case of purchase orders, there are then subsidiary calculations for allowing sufficient time to place orders, for checking what is already held in stock (and therefore does not need ordering), for generating the necessary financial paperwork, and so on. In the case of works orders, the calculations include checking on available production capacity to produce these items, working out the sequence in which they should be made and when they will be available for further assembly into products, and again carrying out the necessary financial transactions for accounting control.

Since the entire basis of these calculations is a forecast rather than an exact level of demand, and since the situation in any one of the above areas changes (often radically) from day to day, the effectiveness of such MRP systems is only as good as the quality of information fed in and the frequency with which it can be updated. Systems are now available which introduce more information from a variety of different areas beyond that of materials management, and which allow for feedback and rapid updating. These are often referred to as systems for manufacturing resources planning, or (confusingly) MRP2.

Most systems currently available offer some variation on MRP2 principles, and are usually available in modular format, so that firms can add on modules as and when needed. So, for example, a firm might begin with a basic MRP suite of programs, and gradually build up towards full MRP2 by adding on modules covering functional areas in the production process.

Although the primary incentive for the implementation of CAPM in CI was to institute common financial data, the more usual advantage of such CAPM systems, provided they are implemented effectively, is that they introduce a much tighter level of control over all aspects of production management. They also permit savings in inventory (both of raw materials and of work-in-progress), better delivery performance and shorter manufacturing lead times. However, the problem with CAPM is that it is rarely implemented with complete success, and despite an often significant investment running into six figures, the resulting systems are often little better than their manual predecessors.

SYSTEMS IMPLEMENTATION: A COMMON PROBLEM

In common with many advanced applications of IT in manufacturing, CAPM is an integrated system. Rather than simply replacing a manual system with a computer in order to do what was always done a little better, such systems offer significant changes in the way information is handled and processed. But in order to get the best out of such systems, considerable organisational change is often required.

Because CAPM systems cover a number of different functional areas, they require high levels of cooperation between these functions in order to create an integrated information network. This often exposes the underlying differences between functional areas, whether as a consequence of previous political conflicts, differing priorities, competition for resources or simply different ways of seeing the world. Thus it poses a classic challenge for organisational development. Unless the organisation can find ways of achieving closer integration between functions, it is unlikely that an integrated information system will be able to operate to its full potential.

In the case of CCL the problem was compounded, because the decision to invest in a CAPM system, and the selection of the particular system to be implemented, were both carried out for them by the parent company. As a result, CCL had no feelings of ownership towards the system, and thus had an excellent scapegoat to blame when things went wrong!

EXISTING TECHNOLOGICAL SYSTEMS IN CCL

Although the CAPM system was purchased by CI in the late 1970s, it wasn't until 1982 that CCL were encouraged to consider its full implementation. This tardiness was deemed permissible, as CCL was the youngest and smallest company in the CI group. Thus CCL had been allowed to develop at its own pace, with its managers arguing that their company was not big enough to warrant sophisticated computerised systems, and was better off maintaining its complex manual systems.

As a result, CCL had fairly limited experience of advanced technology implementation. The company had a computer-aided design (CAD) facility, and a sales order processing (SOP) and general business system (GBS) in place, but beyond that most systems were still manually run. There was a certain irony in this situation, as the managers readily acknowledged:

> It's rather embarassing. We're selling a very high-tech product, and it's pretty apparent to anyone who comes down here that we're not automated. It's obvious that we're totally reliant on manual systems, and I suppose that's not conducive to the industry we're in.

The SOP, GBS and CAD implementations were viewed as extremely successful, enabling the company to increase the amount of data processed, thereby allowing it to grow. However, none of the systems were recognised as significantly changing the organisation and the way in which it worked – only the speed at which tasks were accomplished.

CCL'S IMPLEMENTATION OF THE CAPM SYSTEM

As might be expected, although CCL is given a high degree of independence from its parent company, it is bound by a number of the group policies and philosophies. These have shaped the CAPM implementation strategy adopted by the company.

A key CI philosophy is that of autonomy. Within CCL each department is responsible for its own actions. The results of this philosophy are clearly visible in the method of implementation adopted by CCL. A steering committee comprising the heads of each function was set up to oversee the implementation. Through a process of negotiation, modules were allotted to individual departments, to be implemented without interference from any other department. Thus the system was systematically disintegrated, and legitimised by the accepted CCL philosophy of autonomy and non-interference.

A second company philosophy had a direct impact on the implementation of the CAPM system. This was the idea that departments such as personnel, training and data processing (DP) should be seen as overheads, and therefore should not exist. Instead, departmental managers are given a budget and are encouraged to take responsibility for all aspects of these functions. The production manager said:

> I think we're deliberately trying to have people on-line and involved in the business with a good knowledge of the way the business operates, rather than having DP professionals who might just be looking at the thing from an academic systems viewpoint, without practical experience.

Finally, the company has an 'organic' philosophy to its business, believing that change sets its own pace. This approach has influenced the implementation of the CAPM package. The steering committee has met on a monthly basis simply to monitor the implementation process. Said the production director:

> I think that it's fair to say that there has not been a specific policy statement. The company as a whole has *not* said, "These are our milestones, we must have this operating by a particular date." The committee has worked out (as time's gone by) a programme of activities on a month-to-month basis . . .

CCL'S PROBLEM WITH IMPLEMENTATION

By 1988, six years after the implementation programme for the CAPM system at CCL began, few actual changes have taken place. The reasons for this slowed implementation are a mixture of group-wide problems and company-specific issues. As the system was implemented throughout the group, significant software bugs were discovered, and horror stories of crashed systems and excessive inventories emerged. These have made CCL extremely cautious about the system and its implementation.

As a direct consequence of these stories, and fearing that the profits may suffer, CCL's top management have neither endorsed the system nor made any extra resources available for its implementation. Rather, the managing director has been widely quoted as saying, "Implement the system, but if it fails it's your responsibility, and don't come crying to me about it."

Within CCL itself, yet another factor is severely hampering the system's implementation: the company itself has split into two fiercely adverse factions. These comprise those in favour of implementing the system, championed by the production department, and those strongly against its implementation, led by the purchasing department.

This split has been further exacerbated by the tasks which need to be accomplished in preparation for the implementation. Firstly, a cleansing and updating of the parts master file must be undertaken. Such an operation would ensure that all companies throughout the group have consistent numbering of parts. Purchasing and engineering are the only departments holding the full current parts number lists, so one of these departments had to undertake the parts numbering task. At this stage of the implementation, engineering did not recognise the importance of the system to their role, and although purchasing were highly sceptical of the use of the system, they did attend the steering committee meetings. Purchasing, the department actively opposed to the system, were therefore asked to undertake the cleansing and updating exercise.

CCL's step-by-step, organic approach to implementation, together with its policy of non-interference, ensured that purchasing were in a strong position to stall the system's implementation, leaving the pro-CAPM lobby in a virtually powerless position, with other departments hesitant in their approach to the system.

DEPARTMENTAL PERSPECTIVES

Each department involved in the implementation has a different perspective on the scheme:

The purchasing department

The purchasing manager joined CCL in its start-up phase, and was a key figure in shaping the current practices of the company. Having left his previous job because it had become increasingly automated and demoralising, the manager was able to develop CCL's manual systems from scratch. He therefore had considerable commitment to the company's non-automated style of operation, and this colours his views towards the CAPM implementation:

> It was refreshing to get back and to create a manual system to suit the particular problems that CCL had. All I would do is to computerise those, because they've been put in for a reason.

In sharp contrast to his previous job with a computer company, where systems were literally developed to his own specifications, the CAPM system is bespoke to group company needs rather than to individual requirements. This has made the purchasing manager extremely apprehensive about the CAPM system and its implementation. At present the manual purchasing systems which he devised are functioning adequately and have not collapsed, whereas a computer system always has the potential to fall over, and as a result to demotivate his staff, causing labour turnover.

> If you've got a good team, you want to keep them. I was demoralised by computing. I was surrounded by them; I worked with them; we made them; I dreamed about them; my wife was a senior programmer; all our friends in those days were in the computer industry, and they [the computers] were always going wrong, or it seemed as though they were.

As far as this manager is concerned, the introduction of the system will cause him many problems in the short term, with little reward later on. Most immediately, technical problems are to be confronted. The system as yet does not work to his requirements. Organisational problems are also in evidence, while resources and training are being seen as areas which need more company commitment. These issues are further complicated by the overall organisational climate, which is influenced by the managing director's attitude towards the implementation. The 'bottom line' of the company is to make profits, so the implementation is to be undertaken at the same time as running the department:

> I don't think that they [the other members of the company] are aware of what needs to be done in preparation, and you've still got to operate and keep the company alive. So you can't just say, "Right, we'll switch off for three months." You've got to fit this in ... Otherwise the company would just dry up and not shift anything out, and you'd get a beautiful implementation but go skint in the process.

The purchasing manager sees the system simply as automating what has gone on before. Instead of manual slips for goods in and out, these will now be computerised. It is anticipated that the computerisation of this department may save time in terms of getting hold of information. But the trade-off is seen as the job becoming less exciting (less firefighting) and more routine.

> It would be boring if the computer was right all the time – living with it 50 or 60 hours a week and it being right. OK, you'd take the accolades, but that soon gets to you. It's nice to be able to go home thinking, "Great! I solved that problem today!" It's great, you feel good.

The production department

The production department, by contrast, are strongly in favour of some computerisation of systems, though there appears to be an internal debate over whether the company should go as far as implementing MRP. However, the department have little actual input into the present implementation programme. It has attempted to fast-forward the implementation of the system by circulating documentation on time-scales and implementation, by giving talks on just-in-time (JIT) and materials requirements planning (MRP), and by taking on roles such as secretary to the implementation steering committee.

Both the production director and the production manager have been recruited to CCL within the past four years. As a result they see themselves as slightly outside the traditional CCL position. The implementation strategy favoured by production does not follow the 'organic' cultural style adopted elsewhere in the company, but instead focuses on a structured approach to implementation, with milestones. Both have worked with MRP systems in their previous positions, and have actual knowledge of working systems. This again causes them to differ significantly in their views from their colleagues. Says the production director:

> A project of this complexity needs a full-time project manager who does nothing else but look after the implementation, chart the milestones and everything else. It's a role I have tried to establish, but it hasn't come off that way because of the reluctance from other people involved to accept authority and to accept the constraints of a formal plan.

Perhaps because of their past experience and knowledge of the implications of such a system, they are able to look beyond their own departmental boundaries. They can see the strategic role that could be played by a CAPM system. The production director continues:

> I think that at the end of the day the opposition there is in this company in going to MRP will have to be overcome, because in the end that's what we're looking for – the information that MRP gives you, for example, showing the difference between orders and parts coming in and stock. This is where we're aiming, all of these [other modules] are stepping stones to getting to that point.

Although the production department have past experience and know-ledge in the field, which leads them to view a CAPM system in a positive light, they recognise that other departments in the company have a more hesitant attitude towards the system. This, they suggest, is due to two major factors. Firstly, the system has received bad press, and secondly, there is a fear of the unknown. The production director comments:

I think what is significant is that we have operated in this environment in other companies, so we know the pros and cons of going down this route. Whereas resistance is tending to come from those who have no previous experience, those people are tending to rely on others outside the company feeding in the bad news. It's human nature to pick up every piece of bad news going, and to use that as the reason as to why we shouldn't be progressing too quickly on this implementation.

The production department can see the benefits of implementing the CAPM system, but recognise that these are hindered by the implementation strategy that is being followed by the organisation. At present, new product development is identified as the number-one priority, with the implementation of the system as only number three on the priority list.

Past attempts by the department to speed up the implementation of the system have failed, and cowed by this they now feel that the only way CCL will accept the system is if it simply duplicates the present operating systems:

I think there's an argument that says to get the maximum benefit out of a system we have to change our ways of working. But in the process of converting people over to the system, we're almost attempting to mirror the way that they're working manually.

The engineering department

This department is a recent recruit in support of the CAPM system. To date, the system has not been seen as relevant to engineering, but with the proposed implementation of the bill of material (BOM) module, the system has now taken on some meaning for the department:

We've been having these implementation meetings, but I haven't been taking them very seriously until it reached a stage where I knew that we'd have to get involved and could actually contribute. I get all the minutes and can read them, but until you get in front of a computer it doesn't actually mean a lot.

This lack of interest in the system has cost the company considerably in lost time and resources. Lack of interest on the part of the engineering department led to the parts master file being taken on by the purchasing department. Recently it was decided that this information should reside with the engineering department. But the parts master file has been coded in buying rather than in engineering terms, and has to be rewritten.

The engineering department is the only department that is making any organisational changes. It is to create the two new posts of database manager and assistant. The recent conversion to CAPM has allowed the department to develop an enthusiasm for the system which is not seen elsewhere in the company:

> So far we have had zero impact from SOP [sales order processing] or the finance functions. But when we get onto the CAPM system, then it's got to be driven by engineering drawings. They have got to take responsibility for the technical side of the database, going in with the structure of the BOMs, parts lists, etc. We've got to go up a very steep learning curve now; people who have had no involvement with the minicomputer are suddenly having to turn into database controllers and terminal operators, and we've got to get everybody using the system.

The manager continually highlights the benefits of the system, though the steps towards implementation such as training throughout the company seem less well defined. The system is seen as contributing to a formalised process, especially in terms of new product development:

> People think that the computer will slow down the process of product development. However, the benefits from an informal system are largely illusory. Because people don't write a parts list down, they forget to put all the items down. Hence the costings are out, and it's a bit late when it's gone to production.

Training is not considered a problem in this department. Three paths to training have been identified, the first being to sit in with another company already operating the system (sitting with Nellie); the second is to get support from the in-house systems support, and the third is to learn by doing. The latter point is underlined by the previous experience which the department had with the implementation of the CAD system:

> We were very concerned that we were going to have a training problem. This was not true, because with the right package and motivated staff the learning curve is very steep.

For the engineering department, the system is seen as a potentially useful tool in solving a number of informational problems, allowing for the integration of the database and thus saving time and money. Although in the past there has not been a significant interest in the system, now that the benefits have been highlighted and the system actually appears to be affecting the running of the function, the engineering department are interested. Training of staff is recognised as essential but not so problematic. There is a 'where there's a will there's a way' approach.

The accountancy and finance department

The accountancy department have already implemented the general business system (GBS) module. This has proved to be a success, saving time and therefore cost to the company. Further CAPM implementation is viewed in the same light. Finance is reserving judgement on the system until it has been convinced that the other departments can see merit in its installation. This position has an underlying power as the finance director acts as unofficial head to the CAPM steering committee meetings. He also feeds back company feelings about the system to CCL's managing director.

Recently finance have recognised that by computerising the standard costs operation they could save considerable time. At present, the manual operation takes seven man weeks. But using the system, the information would be available at the press of a button. This has caused them to move ground significantly in their attitude towards the CAPM system. However, in terms of further developments of the system, such as implementing the MRP module, they are still reserved in their judgement.

Having examined the past implementation of SOP and GBS, the finance department recognise that successful implementation appeared to rest upon having dedicated, experienced staff to smooth the process. In addition, user commitment to the system is seen as an important variable. However, the system is recognised as being significantly different from other installations, as it is significantly more complex. Particular emphasis is placed on the importance of good forecasting leading to MRP. They suggest that in CCL's case the variable business and complex product might mean that MRP is not the answer.

The accountancy function can see to a certain extent the value of such a system. Again, its value is talked about in terms of saving time and tightening up the system as it stands. There is no perception that the organisation will change in any strategic way from its present situation.

In addition, some comments suggest that there is a fear of moving too far towards computing because it involves a position of increasing vulnerability as the system becomes reliant, firstly on computer technology, which might fail at any time, and secondly on highly skilled personnel, who may leave at any time. Given the highly specialised training that is needed on account of the bespoke nature of the system, this is seen as a significant issue.

CONCLUSIONS

Gradually, the other functions within CCL are beginning to recognise some of the time-saving benefits of the proposed CAPM system. However, the company does not anticipate change in its implementation policy, and will not be increasing the resource allocation to the system. Such an approach, when combined with the external electronics market culture of constantly improving the product for market (rather than the processes by which the product is managed) means that within CCL the CAPM system has a very low departmental priority rating.

In addition, the CAPM system can be considered a threat to CCL's existing organisational pecking order. At present those managers with the longest tenure hold the positions of influence in the company. Integrated technology could potentially make their positions more visible, and remove some of their organisational mystique, bringing into question the accepted organisational roles and boundaries.

Such environmental and political factors, combined with the perceived technical limitations of the system (its age and slowness), will ensure that the system is certified dead long before anything like full integration is achieved.

CASE STUDY TASKS

CI are committed to the implementation of the CAPM system throughout their group of companies. Not to implement the system would be seen as a direct criticism of the most senior member of the CI board.

Imagine you are a senior project manager sent from CI's head office. Your brief is to identify the reasons behind the slowed implementation and to attempt to 'rescue' the implementation project for the CAPM system. Your objective is to find ways of introducing the technology in such a way that the different functions involved feel a sense of 'ownership' and involvement in the project, and so that the resulting system is a strategic integrated information system and not simply an automated version of current manual systems.

Specific questions which may help your planning include:

1 What in your view are the major problems confronting CCL in the implementation process, and how have they arisen?

2 Is there a clear methodology for implementing such strategic change? And if not, can you suggest a possible framework?

3 What changes are likely to be needed in the organisation to help it to make effective use of such integrated applications of information technology?

4 What is the role of training in helping to adapt to such new technology?

5 What would you do about the communication and other problems between the different functional areas involved in the project?

6 If you could start the whole project again from the beginning, what would you do to ensure effective and successful implementation?

ESSENTIAL READING

Buchanan D, Boddy D, *Organisations in a Computer Age: Technological Imperative and Strategic Choice*, Gower, 1983

Corke D K, *A Guide to CAPM*, Institute of Production Engineers, 1985

Wight O, *The Executive's Guide to Successful MRPII*, Oliver Wight Publications, 1982

FURTHER READING

Ettlie J E, *Taking Charge of Manufacturing*, Jossey Bass, 1988

Handy C, *Understanding Organisations*, Penguin, 1987

Morgan G, *Images of Organisation*, Sage Publications, 1986

Wallington D, CAPM in practice, *Proceedings of the EPEE*, 1985

10 System specification and usability: Booths Ltd

Mark Lansdale and Ian Newman

ORGANISATIONAL CONTEXT AND BACKGROUND

Booths is a family firm which specialises in the wholesaling of confectionery and tobacco goods from eleven depots around the country, and managed from the head office in the home counties. It sells to small retail outlets such as newsagents as well as to large chain stores and supermarkets, mainly on a cash-and-carry basis at the depots.

The company relies upon high-volume sales at a relatively low profit margin. At the same time, head office aims to keep the capital invested in stock at the depots to a minimum. The objective is to order that quantity of each line which would ensure that the last item from one delivery of a line is sold on the evening of the day on which the next delivery takes place. Unfortunately, there is some difficulty with this strategy in practice (due to variations in demand and unpredictable deliveries), so a margin of safety is added to try to ensure that depots do not actually run out of stock, particularly for high-selling lines.

The ordering of stock for the depots is coordinated at head office, despite the fact that the individual depot managers are responsible for the profitability of their depot (indeed, each one's salary bonus is determined by his or her depot's profitability). Depot managers feed in their ordering requirements to head office who deal with the manufacturers on their behalf, negotiate country-wide deals and have the goods delivered directly to the depot. The business is complicated in that the goods do not have a shelf life, and the seasonal demand for goods such as Easter eggs requires particularly detailed knowledge of stock held and projections for future sales.

The managing director of Booths decided to install a centralised, integrated information system, which would handle all stock control, ordering and financial management. This would replace the ageing stand-alone microcomputer systems which were installed at each depot. These had become very unreliable because of hardware faults. Furthermore, the managers at head office felt that they were not being provided with suitable management information from the depots, even

145

when the depot systems were working. For example, the weekly returns of stock levels and the turnover statistics were thought to be insufficiently frequent, accurate or fine-grained to enable the management at head office to monitor the performance and profitability of the depots.

The managing director took advice from the company secretary and from external computer equipment suppliers (later to be employed in designing and installing the system in question), and decided to reduce the autonomy of the depot managers and carry out all data entry (except for that coming directly from the tills) at the head office. The principle was that data entry by specialist staff would reduce errors and also minimise the total number of staff hours devoted to data entry.

However, data entry at head office meant that some unusual procedures had to be instituted to deal with the entry of delivery information. A copy of the order being sent to the supplier was to be posted to the depot; the delivery would then be checked against the order and any changes written on the copy order, which would then be faxed back to head office for entry into the system (fax machines would be obtained specially for this purpose).

The implementation

A system manager was appointed at head office to oversee the specification, procurement and installation of this new system. He negotiated with a firm with whom he had previous contacts, and the system was installed and commissioned relatively quickly. It would be nice to say more about this process in terms of how a requirements specification was produced, how the change was to be managed, and so on. The bare fact is that no documentary evidence exists in Booths to indicate how it was done, or whether it was done on anything other than an ad hoc basis. (Neither the system manager nor the suppliers were forthcoming on this matter.)

The essence of the implementation was that a minicomputer in the head office was connected by landlines to peripheral microcomputers in each of the depots, which in turn supported workstations for the depot managers and ran the checkout tills. Information gathered from the tills and other workstations in a depot would update databases in that depot and at the head office. Similarly, information entered at the head office would update the database(s) at the appropriate depot(s) as well as the one at head office itself. All of the updating would take place in 'real time' to ensure that both the depot managers and the head-office management knew exactly what was happening to the business all the time. Additionally, the system was designed to support all aspects of head-office administration, including payrolls, company ledger and word processing. It was intended as an integrated, comprehensive business package.

The implementation was based on existing software developed for the building trade to provide ordering, stock management, invoicing, company ledgers and sales analysis for a centralised business. This route was taken because the software existed and had proved itself, albeit in a different environment. It was believed that this would enable implementation to be completed quickly, thus minimising the upheaval associated with the change, and quickly overcoming the problems caused to the depots by the unreliability of the existing equipment.

Implementation did indeed happen quickly, although some special software had to be written to provide for distributed operation and maintain the duplicate databases. The reliability problem was also overcome by the installation of two microcomputers at each depot linked to a separate till controller. This arrangement meant that a depot could operate satisfactorily if communications with head office were lost, even if one microcomputer failed, and that the tills could still be operated if both microcomputers failed.

The problems begin

Six months after the system had been installed, despite the improvement in reliability, the management were becoming anxious, and for a number of reasons.

Firstly, the system was notorious throughout the company as being difficult to use. Who, for example, wants to be told that there are 230.00 boxes of Milk Tray in stock – or even worse, 2.30? What is more, errors could cause considerable disruption (see *A checkout operator* below).

Secondly, the stock levels recorded by the system were completely untrustworthy, and the physical stock levels of some lines were rising significantly. Indeed, some of the depots were literally running out of space, and the company could ill afford the capital tied down in this way. In one depot, for example, goods had been stocked to such high levels that they were a hazard. The manager there remarked wryly that it was bad enough having his office reduced to standing room only by several gross of gobstoppers, without running the daily risk of death under an avalanche of chocolate rabbits!

At first, when the managing director approached the system manager to see what could be done, this had produced the response that everything was going very well. It was also pointed out that the suppliers were bringing prospective customers to show them the operation at Booths "because it was such a success". A little later the reply was that everything would be satisfactory, provided that more staff were taken on to help with the management of the system. Finally, the system manager retreated into a siege mentality. He became increasingly defensive and secretive about how the system did, or did not, work, but still maintained that it was basically a good system.

Six months later, at the point where this case study begins, the situation had become even worse. Relationships with the system manager had collapsed completely, and such was the lack of trust that the managing director had terminated his contract overnight, with suitable compensation, only allowing him back on the premises to collect his personal belongings. For such was the ill feeling surrounding the system that the managing director feared the system manager might use his term of notice to sabotage the system, as indeed he believed (rightly or wrongly) he had been doing for some time. Most other workers had by now declared outright hostility to the system, and to the company for installing it; and the stock levels had gone even higher.

At this point the managing director called in consultants with a view to getting advice on what could be done. Suggestions mooted included completely scrapping the system and sueing the suppliers of either the software, the hardware, or both.

THE PROBLEM AS PRESENTED

The consultants' brief was simply this: to appraise the existing system and make recommendations to the company as to how to overcome the evident problems.

They were invited to interview a number of people at different sites, including the head office. The sections which follow give the range of opinions expressed by the interviewees:

A senior manager at head office

The stock-control system is out of control, and will eventually break the company. It cannot continue. Furthermore, the maintenance contract on this system is bleeding us dry. I'm all for sending the whole lot back. No one seems to understand what the system is doing anyway: the manuals are incomprehensible.

My assistants in the central ordering office are all fed up, and some are leaving. They spend half their time correcting mistakes on the system, and the other half watching a dead screen waiting for it to come back to them. It's ridiculous: if I activate the basic ledger program (if I can, that is), then everything else stops – and even then it takes all day and all night to run. I could do it quicker by hand. If I could get my hands on . . .

A depot manager

From my point of view, it's not as bad as some people seem to say, but I do spend a great deal of time soothing customers at the checkouts. Head office are always on about stock control too, but what can I do? They do the ordering, the stock levels on the computer are not reliable, and if I say anything they don't believe me either.

Often the information about deliveries we've received doesn't get entered on the head-office computer until the next day, and it can be hours after that before the stock record appears on our system, even if the communications are working. By that time we have often sold some of that stock. Sometimes stock levels are right, but if the communications fail, what it says is anything up to two days out-of-date, and sometimes it's just totally wrong (usually after the main system has been down). I've checked, and I'm sure I'm right.

It puts me in a difficult position if a client asks for five gross of Tiger Bars, because I don't know whether I've got them or not. And with the depot in the state that it's in, it's not a simple matter to go and count them. The backdoor man who receives the deliveries is always complaining too, about the fact that the chits he gets from the system don't correspond with what gets delivered – while head office keep telling me to give him a talking-to because he messes up the deliveries and accepts the wrong goods.

A checkout operator

I only put up with it because Mr Jones [the depot manager] tells me it will be put right soon. If there's a mistake in tallying up a customer's purchase, for example, there's no way of correcting it apart from starting again. Once we had to get one customer to empty his van of eight trolley loads, and I'm sure he would have thumped me if I'd been a bloke. He's never come back.

A head-office clerk

It's terrible when its slow. You wait around for minutes, just for it to tell you that it recognises the order number. If you make a mistake, it takes forever to put it right. And it's so easy to make a mistake: I'm always confusing one screen with another, and it makes you do so many things you think it could do for itself, like repeating the order number. Also, the numbers always have to be checked. Tiger Bars come in cartons containing ten boxes, but we account by the box, not the carton, so you have to multiply the numbers by ten. On the other hand, Suckits are in cartons of four boxes . . .

CASE STUDY TASKS

Imagine you are a consultant who has been brought in to sort out Booths' problems. How would you proceed? One aspect is to consider what further information you would need, and how you would go about getting it. You must also generate some reasonable hypothesis as to how this state of affairs has arisen, and what type of solution might be appropriate.

The following questions are designed to focus your mind upon particular aspects of the case:

1 Both separately and as a whole, what conclusions might you draw from the comments made about the following?

   a the response times of the system;

   b the reported behaviour of the system manager;

   c the delays in the real-time updating of information;

   d the documentation as described by the senior manager;

   e the handling of delivery notes (the depot manager);

   f the quantities on the order forms (the head-office clerk).

2 What techniques might you apply to learn more about the problems referred to in the previous question? What do you think you might need to know?

3 Can you speculate as to the reasons behind the high stock levels?

4 Consider, both separately and as a whole, the comments made about:

   a the errors and the problems in correcting them;

   b the format of information on the screens;

   c the response times.

   What do they tell you about the relationships between the system, the users, and the designers and implementors of the system?

5 How might you get more information about matters referred to in the previous question, and also about user attitudes generally? What information would you want?

6 To what extent do you think each of the following measures might contribute towards a solution to the problem? Give reasons for your answers.

   a a total replacement of the system;

   b training the users how to use the system;

   c making modifications to the existing system.

7 How would you deal with the disaffection in the workforce?

8 What lessons should be learned from this case study about the process of managing change?

ESSENTIAL READING

Bjørn-Anderson N, Eason K D, Robey D, *Managing Computer Impact: An International Study of Management and Organisations*, Ablex, 1986

Clegg C et al, *People and Computers: How to Evaluate your Company's New Technology*, Ellis Horwood, 1988

ADDITIONAL READING

Hirschheim R A, *Office Automation: A Social and Organisational Perspective*, Wiley, 1985

Shneiderman B, *Designing the User Interface: Strategies for Effective Human–Computer Interaction*, Addison-Wesley, 1987

Section II

Service and Information Sectors

11 General Insurance

David Boddy, David Buchanan and Margaret Patrickson

ORGANISATIONAL SETTING

General Insurance was a Canadian insurance company created in 1972. It had grown rapidly both in the volume and in the types of business handled. A policy of giving branch managers greater autonomy was instituted during the early 1980s, supported by investment in computer systems. This case study draws on the experience of those changes, and some of the dilemmas that had to be managed.

BACKGROUND TO THE CASE

The company's recent growth had been rapid and annual premium income had risen strongly. In 1987 it was employing about 560 people, about 70% of whom were under 32 years of age. By then it had issued about 250,000 policies, mainly in the domestic and motor vehicle area. During this period the company strove to build its corporate image, and management worked hard to make the company a household name.

The scope and appearance of the branch network was also planned to develop the corporate image and improve competitive advantage. Branches were located where possible in or close to major shopping centres, and were well decorated and furnished.

There were five assistant general managers, and a deputy general manager who reported to the general manager. Activities in the branches, of which there were 18 in 1987, were coordinated at head office by the branch sales division, and were the responsibility of the assistant general manager (AGM) for general insurance. This division also included staff working on product development and supporting services. Figure 11.1 shows the general structure of the company.

Throughout the 1980s the role of branches had been gradually redefined and expanded so that they could offer customers a total insurance service, instead of operating simply as sales outlets under strict head-office guidelines without the authority to vary the terms of any insurance contract. At the same time, some branches had begun to

155

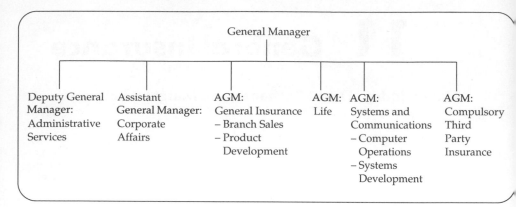

Figure 11.1   The Structure of General Insurance

handle the large commercial customers, whose business was more competitive and potentially more profitable. Greater branch autonomy became necessary, and was encouraged by senior head-office management, until by the mid-1980s the branches had developed into profit centres. The employee handbook stated:

> Each branch is the front-line contact with our existing and prospective policy holders. Branches operate autonomously so that the particular needs of each area can be identified. Branch managers play an important role in budget planning, so that the targets set are achievable and performance can be measured against the final result.

By 1987 branch managers were writing their own business plans, and setting their own revenue and expense budgets. The new sales orientation also meant that they had to develop new skills, so that they could become active salesmen with a visible presence in the local community. They had to relinquish direct staff supervision, and become field workers servicing in particular the needs of large commercial clients.

The move towards a results-oriented role for branch managers was not triggered by computing developments. But the new direction was supported by computer-generated information that helped branch managers to understand the operation of their business more fully and thus to run their branches autonomously.

In 1987 the company had a computer suite at head office, which employed 16 people and used equipment worth about $13 million. This section was the responsibility of the assistant general manager for systems and communications, who reported directly to the general manager. The company was one of the first organisations in Canada to recognise the strategic importance of computing systems in this way.

The company had also started to develop a networked system, and by 1987 there were approximately 400 terminals in use. These systems were built around a policy management system (PMS) package, which covered almost every aspect of operations, from new business to payments, through standard statistics, claims, renewals, and so on. It was used both to store details of individual customers and to provide regular management information.

With PMS a full client record could be retrieved by keying the policy number or customer number. This reduced the time spent on correspondance, and saved a lot of wasted time and frustration searching for information. Some branches also had their own personal computers, which were made available provided the branch could make a good case for them and had staff with the skills to use them. By 1987 a pilot electronic mail system had been introduced. Computer literacy was high in the company.

The monthly reporting system revealed in detail where expenses were being incurred, and where revenues and profits were coming from. It showed market share, and where it was being gained and lost. In the latter half of 1987, a new report was produced, comparing branch performances on the basis of a number of key criteria. This was supported by a series of individual reports examining the performance, productivity and profitability of each branch in detail, including other statistics on, for example, staffing and absenteeism.

This increase in the amount of available useful information allowed branch managers to set their own targets and budgets, and to justify them more realistically, making a case based on experience and judgement, but also supported by statistical analysis of the business performance and trends. The computerised analysis of the business also helped head-office support staff and branch management to identify profitable new products, mainly in the commercial field. Branch managers were thus expected to take a broader view of business profitability, based on an increased understanding of the way in which the business functioned, and not merely to concentrate on gross premiums as they had done in the past.

There was, however, only limited on-line access to management information. Monthly reports were sent to branches in various computer printouts. Some useful information could not be extracted easily from the database. Branch managers might have wanted, for example, to run a direct mail campaign to a select target segment. But they could not get the required information on clients directly from the database. To do this they would have had to use easytrieve – a difficult procedure that was controlled by another division and was therefore not used at all. Most staff felt that the system had to be easier to use.

Head-office staff felt that although senior managers seemed to endorse the new sales- and results-oriented approach, the full implications of these changes in corporate culture had not been understood and accepted. Some staff felt that the policy of increasing branch autonomy was not supported by all of the assistant general managers, and that at least one assistant general manager resisted this change. Branch managers too sensed this ambivalence on the part of senior management.

The ambivalence was reinforced by other controls on branch management. The sales orientation encouraged the branch manager to pay less attention to administrative detail in running the branch. But in terms of branch auditing, this was still regarded as an important facet of the job.

This created a conflict of interests for branch managers. Where they had adopted the new approach enthusiastically, with less attention to traditional administration, they had on occasion received unfavourable monthly audits. The audits encouraged an emphasis on branch administration, perhaps at the expense of the more proactive, visible component of their work. The internal auditor reported to the general manager, pulling a lot of the required information from the computer system, and examining whether branch management procedures as laid down in the company's manuals had been followed.

One member of the head-office staff expressed a view that was generally felt: "We need to give branch managers a clearer specification of senior management expectations. We haven't necessarily told them that."

The head-office branch sales division provided a support function as well as having a management responsibility for branch operations. The computerised management information enabled them to scrutinise branch profitability more closely. This facility was used to help branch managers look at trends and examine future developments, and also to help them develop their budgets, run 'what if?' analyses (on a personal computer), investigate loss ratios and identify any action required to maintain or develop business. The branch sales division had a personal computer, which was used to set out model budgets, with graphs showing business summaries and trends.

Head-office staff unanimously appreciated that branch managers had come under increased pressure as a result of the shift in emphasis to sales and results. This was evident from the views expressed by various members of head-office staff:

> I think it has made the branch manager's job more difficult. They used to sell insurance and keep their people in line. There was much less emphasis on long-term planning. But the computer system enables them to do that. They possibly had more personal involvement in the business than they have now. They are more

deskbound, with more piles of paper, under more pressure, and the business is more competitive . . .

Overall impact? The branch managers are under pressure from the requirement to do their own business planning and budget setting. These activities demand time and commitment. But the effort spent in preparing these documents is often not acknowledged. Do they get enough information on new products and market trends? They may feel let down through lack of market and product information from head office. I don't feel they get the feedback they should. I think they are maybe left too much on their own, with not enough support . . .

Branch managers are now under more pressure. But the process of change has been initially stressful. From the end of this year, the technology will all be in place; skills should be developed and proficiency established. Pressure has come from the learning process, and should be temporary, not a permanent feature of the job . . .

Branch managers' attitudes to the 'new technology' ranged from neutral to negative:

The computer systems haven't really changed the branch manager's job. We still get hard-copy reports which we have to collate and compile manually. It hasn't really helped us at all . . .

Our systems have had no impact on the way management decisions are made. The computerised information system doesn't affect the running of the branch . . .

I think our computer systems are disgraceful, and I have given up using them. We have an excellent opportunity to obtain information, but the system does not work in an understandable language. The output needs to be interpreted using a codebook. You can't just read it. I don't have my own terminal, and I have never had one. I have seen better systems that tell you what you want to know in a language that you can understand. I do my monthly reports by hand . . .

One branch manager stressed the benefits of improved access to information:

The reporting system is very good. Our regular monthly reports are good. There are sometimes delays, but the reports are good when they are on time. It can save time. I write it down, someone else keys it in. It's a useful tool. And if some other report is required, I can get the information and punch it into the system. We get information on gross premiums, claims, staffing – all monthly.

The volume of paperwork circulating in the company was felt not to be as extensive as it used to be. But in the words of one of the head-office staff, there had been "an increase in the number of computer printouts hitting the desks of branch managers."

This had led to the possibility of management information overload, consuming excessive amounts of the branch manager's time. Some branch managers also felt that the number of requests for information which they received from head office sections had become excessive.

The company's branch network was geographically dispersed. The exchange of information between branches, and between branches and head office, was critical to the operation of the business. The networked computing system gave each branch a new set of communications tools in the form of limited on-line information retrieval and electronic mail. The latter might be considered an important new communication channel in this context, considering the time involved in sequentially telephoning 18 branches in order to give or request the same information in each case. Email thus offered a significant improvement in the use of staff time.

At the time of this study, however, the email system was suffering teething troubles. As one member of the head-office staff explained:

> Branch managers started to gain confidence in the system, but then the new version was introduced and crashed almost immediately. We need to re-establish that confidence which may have been lost.

Although the problems were not proving too difficult to solve, some staff had lost confidence in the system. It had been 'down' for six weeks, following the introduction of an updated and improved version which had not functioned as intended.

Despite what might appear in this context to be the obvious advantages of an electronic mail system, the conventional communications technologies of telephones, memos, paper files, letters and couriers were still popular and indispensable. Many staff still preferred to use the telephone for contacting specific individuals and known colleagues, reserving email for simultaneous transmission to larger numbers of people. A head-office manager confirmed this view:

> Email is bad news. It's complex. It takes time to log in, and it takes time to move between enquiry and email modes. It's not operating all the time, so people have no confidence in it. We used to use it a lot, but we have to phone and ask people if they have in fact received their email! Some branch mangers may only check their email once a week, and tend to take faster action on hard copy. We need to develop the discipline of checking the email more frequently, and many branch managers just will not do this.

Two branch managers expressed a widely shared opinion of the system:

> Email is hopeless. I don't use it, don't look at it. It doesn't talk to you. I shouldn't have to go and check. Messages should be on my desk or on my printer. It would also help if I could see a sign on my screen telling me there was a message waiting to be read. And with outgoing email there's no indication that the message has been received . . .

> I have had no instructions in the use of the new email system, and I have no time to sit down and find out either. It has only been available for a week, and I have only been able to log on once . . .

The branch managers wanted to see facsimile (fax) transmission more widely used. A lot of the business was based on the filling in of forms, which when completed could be sent immediately through fax. Some branches also dealt in properties; when opening new outlets they worked with architects, who wanted to see leases and other documents. For these applications, fax was much more convenient and faster than conventional mail or email:

> We'd be better off with fax. I don't have one here, but I should have. Communication could be more economical on fax. When head office send a memo to all branches, it's cheaper by fax, especially compared with sending out a document to 18 branches manually. Depends if you want hard copy. And some managers are reluctant to use a keyboard . . .

> The claims people use email, but again fax would be better. They have to complete a claims form, then key the information into the system to send it to head office. Fax would help here. Apart from claims, we're not using email for anything . . .

The limited use of the email system, and the mismatch between branch activities and email capabilities, may be explained in part by the apparent lack of contact between head-office-based systems staff and branch employees. One branch manager said:

> What contact do we have with our systems people? We're lucky if we ever do have contact. It's been at least a year since I saw one of them. We see the hardware people more often, when our equipment breaks down. But we have to go through our branch sales division to get to systems for ad hoc reports, so I don't use that facility. Will the new improved version of PMS help resolve some of these problems? I don't know a lot about it. Communications about it have been low-key, and I don't know what it will do for us.

The systems had altered the relationships between branch managers and branch staff, and also between branch managers and head-office management. Branch staff, who handled clients, had to be able to operate the systems to access and use information. They had developed new skills to enable them to do this effectively, and as a result they had achieved a high degree of autonomy from branch managerial super-vision. One branch manager explained:

> I have to ensure that they can handle this sort of thing. They are the ones in constant communication with the customer. The staff in fact learn the codes better than I do, because they are using them constantly.

Another branch manager confirmed this effect on staff competence and autonomy:

> These developments have restricted the need for communications between me and my staff. Only if there is a problem. They know their job, and they do it. It has made them more autonomous. The computer can answer many of their queries, or they can contact head office direct. We expect a lot more from them.

At least one branch manager felt that the company's information and communications systems had improved interpersonal relationships at different levels in the organisation. The improved, shared information had not only improved communication, but had also brought about benefits in the area of management decision-making, as he went on to explain:

> Relationships with other company staff have become more harmonious and more meaningful, as the information is accurate and easier to get. Relationships with other branch managers have become more meaningful. We face similar problems that show up in our reporting system. We can spot absenteeism, for example, and compare one branch with others and with the company as a whole. We can monitor costs and try to alter them. We get better reports on branch performance.

> In June 1987 we started to get an individual branch productivity report. We can get a closer view of our clientele, our office staffing structure, who we are working with, and absenteeism, and we can compare this with the company average. So our conversations are more amiable, less stressful. Our budgets are based on precise knowledge, factual information, whereas in the past we worked on gut feel, hunch.

> This brings the branch manager and the more senior management closer together, because we have a shared understanding of the issues, and the same accurate information. It's easier to relate to each other. We get systematic branch productivity and perform-ance comparisons. Different branches work in different environ-

ments, so comparisons are not simple. Now we take realistic account of the socioeconomic differences which influence the business mix and performance of different branches. We get better branch profiles.

CASE STUDY TASKS

Your objective is to provide convincing observations about the present situation, and to raise questions which would enable the company to see a way forward.

1 Summarise the view of the situation as expressed by:

a the branch managers;

b the head-office managers.

2 What would you do to increase the commitment of branch managers to the computer systems and to the policy of branch autonomy?

3 Has the company adequately revised its structures and systems in a way that supports the policy on branch autonomy? While considering this question, decide what you should do about:

a the reporting structures;

b branch audits and staff appraisal;

c performance-related pay;

d the training of branch managers.

4 The computer system has made possible the move towards branch autonomy, though it did not actually cause it. In practice, has it helped? What would you do about the following problems?

a the amount of information that branches have to send to head office;

b the lack of relevant information available from the system;

c the limited use which branch managers make of the information they receive from the system;

d the lack of fax facilities;

e the poor use of email.

5 What evidence is there about the quality of the working relationships between systems staff and branch managers?

a What are the effects of difficulties in this area?

b How could they have arisen?

    c How would you improve relations?

6 How committed do you feel that senior management are to the policy of branch autonomy? List the reasons for your conclusion, and then set out the options which face the company in managing its branch network.

ESSENTIAL READING

Boddy D, Buchanan D A, *Managing New Technology*, Blackwell, 1986, chapters 1, 6, 7, 8

Handy C, *Understanding Organisations*, Pelican, 1985, chapter 7

Rockart J F, Chief executives define their own data needs, *Harvard Business Review*, May/June 1979, pp81–93

ADDITIONAL READING

Boddy D, Buchanan D A, *Technical Change Audit*, Manpower Services Commission, 1987

Buchanan D A, McCalman J, Confidence, visibility and performance: The effects of shared information in computer-aided hotel management, in Boddy D, McCalman J, Buchanan D A, eds, *The New Management Challenge: Information Systems for Improved Performance*, Croom Helm, 1988, pp17–29

Dagwell R, Weber R, System designers' user models: Comparative study and methodological critique, *Communications of the ACM*, 1983, vol 26, no 11, pp987–997

Handy C, *Understanding Organisations*, Pelican, 1985, chapter 5

Leavitt H J, Dill W R, Eyring H B, *The Organisational World*, Harcourt Brace Jovanovich, 1973

Peters T J, Waterman R H, *In Search of Excellence*, Harper and Row, 1982

12 Competition and control: The strategic use of IT in a life insurance company

David Knights and Fergus Murray

INTRODUCTION

Mutuality is a comparatively successful life insurance company that specialises in pensions. However, a recent retirement has led to the appointment of a new, young chief executive, who has sought to modernise the company in the belief that it has previously been successful more by luck than by design. He is convinced that intensified competition in the financial services market (resulting from market deregulation and new legislation imposing higher standards on the industry) could quickly erode the apparently cosy climate of the last few decades, during which Mutuality has enjoyed unprecedented growth. So he has set about transforming organisational practices.

As the first stage in this process, there has been a complete turnover of the senior executive team, involving the strategic replacement of the heads of finance, marketing, information technology, customer administration, investment and personnel.

This case focuses on the IT division, although it draws on a broader understanding that has been developed during a more intensive study of the whole organisation.

BACKGROUND TO THE CASE

Financial services is a sector where information technology has played an increasingly important role since the early 1960s, when banks and insurance companies computerised their administrative systems. Within insurance, information technology has evolved through a series of progressive stages and applications, the most advanced of which utilise distributed processing, whereby local offices can process and modify data on minicomputers that are linked to the mainframe.

Mutuality has not yet reached this stage of development, but is desperately seeking to modify and improve its somewhat dilapidated systems to meet the requirements of intensified competition and the new regulatory demands with which the industry is presently confronted. This case examines a brief episode in this struggle: the attempt to develop IT systems which could provide the products and service supports for an increasingly competitive pensions market, following the partial privatisation by the state of the pensions sector.

ORGANISATIONAL SETTING

As the name suggests, Mutuality is a mutual life insurance company. It is only medium in size, with managed assets of £2,600 million compared with £18,600 million for the Prudential, which is the largest UK life insurance company. But Mutuality has been growing at a slightly faster pace than some of its competitors. Over recent years, for example, it has moved from the 24th to the 17th position in the league table of the top life companies. Approximately 21% of life insurance companies are so-called mutuals, in which policyholders are nominal shareholders and can thereby expect to secure a pro-rata share of the allocation of profits in the form of with-profits policy bonus distributions.

Mutuality secures business only though the independent market, and not through company agents. It therefore has to remain competitive on its investment returns, as this is one of the major criteria (indeed legally binding since the introduction of the best advice principle (see note at end of chapter) within the Financial Services Act 1986) upon which life offices are selected by the intermediaries. The firm employs over 1000 personnel at its head office, and another 300 staff in its 33 branches, who service the intermediary market (ie brokers, accountants, building societies and banks), through which the company distributes its products.

The life insurance and pensions sector has enjoyed remarkable growth in the postwar period, thanks to a rise in real incomes, a restructuring and differentiation of insurance products in accordance with the values of private economic accumulation, and the development of more sophisticated marketing and sales techniques. An illustration of this rapid growth is evidenced by the fact that between 1980 and 1985 life business grew by 50% on a £20 billion/year base.

This expansion has been reinforced by a number of other factors. To take but one example, the demand for domestic independence on the part of nuclear families, and the associated decline of the extended family, has rendered the elderly more financially vulnerable. Moreover, threats to the public provision of pensions and other welfare benefits have further intensified the financial vulnerability of the aged, thus necessitating a greater reliance on private insurance as a means of providing security in old age.

Until quite recently a legal monopoly on the production of life policies, a degree of protection from international competition, and the fiscal advantages enjoyed by life and pensions products, combined to create a climate of benign competition between firms in the sector. This did not prevent the rise of a number of large corporate composite (life and non-life) insurers through merger activity (eg Guardian Royal Exchange, Prudential, Royal, Sun Alliance), but it was a climate that facilitated the survival and growth of the industry's small and medium-sized life players.

Historically, life insurance companies have been slow to change their business strategies and practices. This is partly because the industry has been dominated by the actuarial profession, whose focus tends to be on a prudent calculation of risks, premium rates and bonus allocations to contracts. Until comparatively recently, therefore, little attention was given to modern proactive or aggressive modes of management in spheres such as marketing, sales, accounting, investment or new technology.

Despite this, the industry has benefitted from the adoption of computing systems, and more recently from the development of information technology. In the early days, however, computing was utilised primarily as a means of processing complex administrative data such as payroll and customers' policies, the latter of which constituted the principal activity of the head offices of life insurance companies.

The computerisation of administrative processes was advanced with no apparent or explicit purpose of increasing the productivity and control of labour. Indeed, it has been claimed that insurance companies specifically avoided using the new technology in these ways, in order to ensure staff cooperation in the large-scale changes that were needed for the adoption of computerised systems. Regardless of intention, however, developments (especially in the use of information technology) have usually had the effect of intensifying production and thereby reducing unit labour costs.

Whereas the early adoption of computerised processing tended to be purely administrative, more recently companies have begun to see IT as a potential weapon for seeking competitive advantage in the marketplace. So, for example, IT is increasingly being used as a means of developing products that are more flexible and attractive to consumers, and of providing an improved service and system of sales distribution to intermediaries. The life sector is therefore a major IT user, and it is increasingly the case that the most significant costs of new developments resulting from legislation and/or competition are those relating to data processing and systems.

Mutuality, however, is not an IT innovator, but has tended merely to follow general trends in the industry. Thus there has been a gradual shift from batch to on-line processing, and towards the installation of minicomputers in branches. The company develops its own systems, and has an information services divisional development staff of around 100. Many staff have joined the company in the last five years. The majority of Mutuality core data systems were developed in the 1970s, although some of these have since been updated. Many of the modifications have involved piecemeal and uncoordinated amendments to the systems, with the result that changes are adhoc and poorly documented, while procedures are only informally understood, thus leaving the process of modernisation incomplete.

CONTINUITY AND CHANGE AT MUTUALITY

As has already been intimated, the chief executive's philosophy, style and strategy differed considerably from that of his predecessor, who had acted more as an establishment figure within the industry's trade, professional and quasi-governmental associations. A firm believer in tight and tough top-down management, the new CE rapidly sought to establish a corporate strategy that entailed the development of closely monitored business plans, with a six month rollover period and detailed action plans designed to ensure their day-to-day operation in departments. As a result of these strategic changes, all areas of operations began to be monitored quantitively through a rigorous system of reporting in monthly executive meetings. Much of the change was geared to reorganising key divisions in support of a marketing-led strategy of retaining or advancing the company's market share.

However, no major innovation was envisaged other than the development of products at the forefront of the industry's capacity. Indeed, after considerable strategic discourse, senior management outlined their corporate strategy as one of "continuing to do what they were good at, only doing it better." Clearly, beneath the CE's confident dynamism lies a conservatism that fears breaking the 'magic circle' of success established by his predecessors. So, while continually admonishing managers for slipping into the 'old ways', the CE displays an ambiguity as to the extent of change required. For example, his response to the various regulatory and deregulatory effects of legislation in the financial services is to espouse the view that the company will only change when that change seems almost inevitable.

THE PENSIONS SHAKE-UP

One of the inevitable changes that has created major IT problems for the company is the partial privatisation of pensions created by the Social Securities Act 1986. In 1984 Norman Fowler's green paper on pensions reform was published, indicating a gradual running-down of the state earnings-related pension scheme (SERPS) originally established by a Labour government in the 1960s. In its place the government was to allow a transfer of state contributions to a private pension scheme, with the consequence that, as the CE at Mutuality expressed it, "a bloody big pensions bonanza" could be expected. Unfortunately the green paper was surrounded by a good deal of political uncertainty, because an imminent general election meant that the legislation was contingent on the return of a Conservative government for a third term. Nonetheless, because of the significance of the proposed changes, Mutuality's senior management had to develop some contingency plans ahead of the actual legislation.

The major problem for the company was that the systems area, where most of the initial cost of responding to the product changes would fall, did not possess the flexibility that the uncertainty surrounding the proposed legislation demanded. For this reason, decisions had to be continually deferred awaiting more detailed information from the legislators. The consequence of this was that the new developments had to be superimposed on an already outdated and 'scrappy' systems architecture, thus adding to the piecemeal and adhoc nature of the company's information technology operations.

In effect, senior management had to make three key decisions:

- Firstly, should they prioritise the pensions business over and above the forthcoming development of a new universal life product (see below), which in contrast to existing life assurance policies would have a comprehensive range of options and a flexibility of premium, risk and investment levels built into a single contract?

- Secondly, which pensions products should they actually develop?

- Thirdly, which pensions administrative computer systems needed to be updated as part of the IT strategy that had been started in 1980?

Prior to the proposed legislation, the company had developed a new executive pensions product in order to diversify and extend its penetration of this fast-expanding market. This having been achieved, the next priority had been to engage in some product diversification by developing a universal life policy, the prototype of which had proved successful for US insurance companies. The third priority had then been to update the company's best-selling personal pensions product. The pensions legislation, however, combined with systems resource constraints, was putting pressure on the company to reverse the order of this priority, although the political machinations involved were far from straightforward.

Following a firm lead from the CE, it was eventually decided to prioritise pensions and defer the universal life product. Senior management therefore set about defining the appropriate mix of products and systems. A prime consideration here was the CE's concern to maximise new business and develop a full range of pensions products to convince the financial intermediary market that Mutuality could provide a comprehensive pensions service.

IT PROBLEMS

As with most product developments, the systems requirements for the new pensions business involved firstly contract terms, secondly a quotations system, and thirdly administrative systems. One way of reducing the IT extensiveness of such new developments was to add on contract terms, quotations and options to current products, as this would only require adhoc modifications to existing systems. The problem was that this would place even more strain on the creaking systems at Mutuality.

Product and systems development requirements were initially quite modest, and a six-month postponement of the product launch (due to administrative problems at the Department of Social Security) gave Mutuality a welcome breathing space. But as the launch drew closer, further rule changes brought a rapid shift in market expectations. Further development commitments had to be accepted in response to pressure from the sales and marketing division for additional new products and on-line administrative systems to meet changing perceptions of what would be most popular in the marketplace. At an even later stage, yet another variation on the main personal pensions product was added to the schedule.

This led to chaos as the IT resource was stretched ever thinner. Project management broke down at middle and junior management levels. Development work was increasingly frantic, and non-essential parts of systems were deferred until after product launch. In order to meet what were seen as the most important requirements of the new market for pensions, on-line conversion of some product processing systems was cancelled or put back two and three years.

Nevertheless, in June 1988 Mutuality launched a family of new pension products. These were backed up by rather shaky systems, the cost of which was a much lower rate of productivity improvement than had been predicted. For example, processing times for one of the new group pensions products were approximately 200% higher than expected.

The project to develop these products and systems had been the biggest IT programme ever undertaken by Mutuality. Following hard on the heels of another major product development (the executive pensions contract), the project seriously disrupted an earlier IT strategy that had been initiated to update the core administrative systems.

A number of systems development staff were particularly frustrated to see such a large project building on (and adding to) out-of-date systems that had already proved expensive to maintain. They would have preferred to use the pensions project as an opportunity to push through a complete overhaul of core systems, upon which this and future developments might build with a clear expectation of efficiency and reliability. Instead, new systems were being continually compromised by the necessity to interface with the old systems. Various estimates put the additional expense created by this requirement at 40% of total development costs, while the failure to build much-needed administrative on-line systems for other products (eg the executive pension scheme) would cost at least £250,000 per annum in extra clerical costs. Furthermore, those administrative systems that *were* developed suffered major design faults, which in turn led to unit policy processing times of 27 hours rather than 14 hours in their first three months of operation.

Despite the failures and compromises, the exercise was defined as a great success since, as the IT senior executive put it, "The products were there on day one." At a series of presentations to all head-office staff, sales hype projected the new products as the ultimate that could have been achieved. Any difficulties encountered were blamed on changes external to (and out of the control of) the company. The strategic IT course followed by the company was portrayed as the almost inevitable outcome of the scale and pace of changes created by government legislation on pensions.

There were, however, alternatives to the strategic choices that had been taken by the CE and his allies in sales and marketing, IT and finance.

ANOTHER VIEW

The customer services executive (ex-IT senior executive) and the assistant IT executive attempted to open up the debate around these choices. In particular, the assistant IT executive believed that a different course of action would have been both desirable and possible. Namely, he had wanted to continue the IT strategy of systems renewal that had been started in 1980, while simultaneously building the new product and administrative systems.

This would have required a considerably larger outlay in terms of systems development, and probably also the use of external software developers for all or part of the project. But despite the greater outlay involved, the assistant IT executive believed his plan would have had the merit of securing the long-term future of Mutuality's systems. It would have resulted in the creation of a sophisticated suite of systems that would have been quick and cheap to amend, giving the company the ability to respond rapidly and flexibly to future market and regulatory changes. In an interview after the launch of the products he said:

> We have taken a rather expedient route by using existing systems where it was thought they would be quicker and more sure to deliver. This will give us continuing maintenance problems, and some of the systems will have to be scrapped in a few years.

Thus the assistant IT executive believed that the low-risk strategy of adding on to existing systems had been adopted because the new IT senior executive had not realised the extent and severity of the problems associated with existing systems.

Other evidence suggests, however, that the senior executive was also hedging his bets in order to avoid risks and exposure to criticism. He perhaps had good reason for doing this, since in the company where he had previously worked, a comprehensive renewal of systems had been advanced with disastrous organisational and financial consequences. He had been appointed there by the assistant general manager (later to become chief executive of Mutuality), who had been responsible for some of the mistakes, and his brief had been to sort out the crisis, which he had done by cancelling all except one of the project developments. As this had relieved the company of a £3 million software contract bill, the strategy had been defined as a huge success, but the experience must clearly have left him and the CE cautious about large-scale IT systems restructuring in their new company, Mutuality.

A different evaluation again was suggested by the consultant project manager who had been brought in to rescue the pensions project. He identified the origins of systems problems in the short-term, market-led approach adopted by the company. He summed up the dilemma as follows:

> The problem is that continuing with the old systems is very expensive, but so is replacing them. Whichever way you jump, the situation is getting worse and the more it will cost you. It's a question of opportunity costs. If one option [developing the products] generates profit and the other [system renewal] costs you money, you choose the profits as the soft option. It's an imponderable problem to which there is no right solution.

CASE STUDY TASKS

In this case study you are asked to place yourself in the position of the assistant IT executive at the point when major decisions concerning strategy are about to be taken in relation to the pensions project. You recognise that developing new products on top of old systems will incur high costs and store up problems for the future. Therefore you decide to try and counter, or at least modify, the strategy generated by the CE's short-term, marketing-driven approach. Your task is to consider how to develop an alternative IT strategy. In so doing, you might like to consider the following questions:

1 How would you initially formulate an alternative strategy?

2 How would you attempt to mobilise the strategy?

3 How might you seek legitimacy for the strategy with reference to internal and external events?

4 Who would you need to win over to the strategy for it to have any chance of success?

5 Given the importance of keeping on the right side of the CE and his colleagues, consider the implications of vociferously mobilising an alternative IT strategy that may provoke considerable conflict between yourself and the management team.

6 Lastly, consider whether a strategy is likely to be adopted and acted upon just because it appears to be objectively rational. Perhaps the power mobilised in support of a strategy, and the legitimisation provided for it, are more important for its successful adoption than its substantive content. What do you think?

In carrying out these tasks it is important for you to indicate problems, together with alternative solutions to the problems that you deal with directly. You should also refer to other literatures that are of relevance, and more particularly you should place your approach within a field of theoretical debate.

Note

The 'best advice' principle was introduced to prevent insurance brokers recommending to clients those companies which paid them the highest commission. 'Best advice' simply meant that they had to advise clients as to the best policy and company appropriate to their specific needs.

ESSENTIAL READING

Barras R, Swann J, *The Adoption and Impact of Information Technology in the UK Insurance Industry*, Technical Change Centre, 1983

Knights D, Sturdy A, Shifting work: New technology in the insurance office, in Varcoe I, McNeil M, Yearsley S, eds, *Deciphering Science and Technology*, Macmillan, 1989

Knights D, Willmott H C, The executive fix, in McGoldrick J, ed, *Business Case File in Behavioural Science*, Van Nostrand Reinhold, 1987

ADDITIONAL READING

BIFU, *Jobs for the Girls: The Impact of Automation on Women's Jobs in the Finance Industry*, BIFU, 1985

Child J, Smith C, The context and process of organisational transformation: Cadbury Limited in its sector, *Journal of Management Studies*, 1987, vol 24, no 6

Knights D, Roberts J, The power of organisation or the organisation of power, *Organisation Studies*, 1982, vol 3, no 1, pp47–63

Knights D, Sturdy A, Women's work in insurance, in Davidson M J, Cooper C L, eds, *Women and Information Technology*, John Wiley, 1987

13 Implementing systems standards in a merchant bank: An IPSE at Mbank

Frank Land, Peter Le Quesne and Indrajit Wijegunaratne

PROLOGUE

At least half the world's development staff are busy maintaining systems, and at least half this effort is non-productive. One-quarter of the remainder are building systems that will never be used. Most development staff are working at about half the efficiency called for in the plan.

Recent statistics provide vivid examples of this problem:

- A study of US Army IT projects costing about $7 million in total revealed the following usage figures:

  - 47% of code was delivered but never used;

  - 29% of code was paid for but never delivered;

  - 19% of code was abandoned or reworked;

  - 3% of code was only used after change;

  - 2% of code was used as delivered.

- Another study showed that only about 1% of large systems (ie those over 50,000 lines of code) are finished on time and within budget, and actually meet users' needs. The average large system is a year late and costs twice the original estimate.

Many of the problems highlighted in these studies stem from inadequate methods and tools for systems design and construction. In the past few years new computer-based products have been developed to attack the problem. One of these is the *integrated project support environment*, or IPSE.

An IPSE is essentially a software product. Certain IPSEs come with their own hardware, while others are designed to work in a specified computer environment. An IPSE supports the activities of systems development by providing automated tools, which assist in the following ways:

175

- They provide techniques for the analysis, design and construction of the system, for example:

  • tools for analysts to create and store documentation;

  • tools for builders to refer to and use in constructing the system.

- They assist in the management of the project, for example:

  • by computing estimates and tracking actual use of resources;

  • by helping with scheduling through the development of PERT network planning charts.

In principle an IPSE would be expected to have facilities relating to each phase of the development cycle (analyse, design, build, test, install, operate and maintain). In practice, however, IPSEs differ in the range and quality of support they offer.

The techniques for systems development (that IPSEs support) impose particular ways of working on the teams using them, as they have to conform to prescribed ways, both of representing data and processes, and of proceeding with their work. This combination of techniques and procedures is usually given the term *systems development methodology*, or *systems development standards*. The trend is further complemented and reinforced by so-called *project management techniques*: formalised task assignments that track the progress of work by the completion of timesheets. The application of IPSEs thus supports this general trend.

A critical factor in the successful development of information systems is not the design of the system or the suitability of the technology, but the management of the change process . . .

More information systems failures are due to poor implementation strategies than to any other factors . . .

THE CASE: INTRODUCTION

The present case is based on a research project funded by the UK Alvey Directorate. The research was seeking to uncover factors which influence the level of success (or failure) that an organisation achieves in bringing a new technology or new work methods into the workplace. Underlying the research was the conviction that organisational, managerial and social factors, as much as technology related factors, bear upon the outcome of the implementation process.

The technology to be introduced into the workplace was an IPSE. The workplace was the information systems department of Mbank, an established merchant bank in the City. The time was in the mid-1980s, when the bank was preparing itself for the major changes in the financial sector that were brought about by deregulation, culminating in the so-called Big Bang of 1986.

The IPSE purchased by Mbank

The particular IPSE chosen by Mbank is strongest during the early phases of the project lifecycle, and especially in building up models of the systems under development. The IPSE uses representational methods and procedures associated with the set of techniques commonly known as structured analysis techniques. It includes a central database storage facility under the control of a system administrator. This database can hold dataflow diagrams, data dictionary entries and process descriptions derived from the work of analysts employed as part of the project team.

However the version of the IPSE used at Mbank did not provide equivalent support for the subsequent stages of the project: technical design, programming and testing. Its project management facilities were not particularly strong, and the version at Mbank provided only very simple timesheet production facilities.

The organisational setting

The information systems department of Mbank is located in the City as well. Figure 13.1 and Table 13.1 show the organisational structure of the department, together with an outline description of their main systems.

The two major systems – the investment system and the banking system were developed in the early 1970s. The maintenance of both these systems has been contracted out. There were no major initiatives thereafter until the 1980s. A few major projects have been initiated in the 1980s, but their progress has typically not been smooth.

The department grew rapidly in the 1980s. Starting from about 50 in 1983, the staff levels peaked to about 190 in 1986, with several developments going on. But in 1987 staff strength on these systems was radically cut back, so that by the time of this study (early to mid-1987) the department's staff strength was back to about 70.

There is a mix of contract and permanent staff in the department. The senior management are all long-serving Mbank employees, having risen through the ranks of the organisation over the years, from technical roles such as programming. The style of management is relatively informal, the emphasis being on the verbal as opposed to the written. Directives are typically treated in a liberal fashion, and their compliance more often than not is a matter for negotiation. The department has a tradition of autonomy and individualism at project level. This has tended to foster a milieu in which each project group has developed its own way of working.

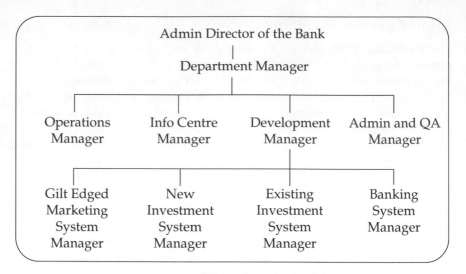

Figure 13.1   Department Organisation Chart

Functional area	System	Comments
Investment Management & Securities	'Old' Investment System 'New' Investment System	Developed early 70s New project under dev
Corporate Finance, Personnel etc	Micro Based Applications	Info Centre
Banking and Investment	Banking System	Developed early 70s
	Gilt Edged Market Making System	Package bought for Big Bang. To be replaced end 1987
	Front Office Dealing System	Terminated after requirements analysis stage
Treasury and Trading Development outside Dept's ambit. DP to take control of operation	VECTOR System	
	Jobbing System	Developed to complement Gilts System

Table 13.1   Main Systems and Functional Areas They Serve

THE PROGRESS OF IPSE IMPLEMENTATION

Standards history and pressures to act

The above indicates that there had not been a tradition of standardised work in the department. The staff within each group tended to express support, perhaps on the basis of prior familiarity, for certain commercially available systems-development methodologies at the expense of others. There was in general no regular or consistent adherence to any one of them.

There was, however, a desire among senior management to move in the direction of standards. This was motivated by the realisation that the department was growing rapidly, and that as a consequence more formal methods were needed. There were also external pressures for greater accountability and efficiency, arising out of a general move towards greater cost consciousness on the bank's part.

Perhaps in tune with the culture that prevailed, the senior managers in the department held different views on the candidate areas where the need for greater standardisation was most urgent, usually depending on their own areas of responsibility. The general view among management was that standards ought to be amenable to modification to suit the needs of each major project. Standards implementation was perceived as an educative process. A senior manager's comment neatly sums up this view:

Standards is a matter of intelligent people reading the manual and applying it intelligently, but I wouldn't expect a coach and horses driven through it.

Vincent Brown, a senior analyst, was assigned to look at the question of standards, and by late 1985 a standards committee was in existence. The committee spent some time debating the issue. There were discussions about the merits of developing one's own standards versus getting a packaged product, as well as about the various standards approaches. Two particular needs emerged from the discussions – a need for standards for project management, and for a methodology for systems development.

In January 1986 approval was granted to proceed with a major project to create a system that could replace the ageing investment system. This gave added impetus to the perceived need for standards.

By this time the standards committee was meeting for an hour and a half each week. As the committee addressed the problem of what system to adopt, the emerging consensus was that most proprietary standards were generally equivalent. An increasingly general range of areas was envisaged, and was even widened, for example, to include maintenance activity. Known project management products based on micros were seen as unsuitable for a multi-project situation. Increasingly an IPSE-like product was viewed as the only choice capable of supporting the different requirements that emerged from the committee's deliberations.

The acquisition process

The IPSE was first brought to the attention of the department during a feasibility study of the new investment system. In 1985 Vincent Brown had been assigned to undertake the initial investigation of the IPSE. After attending a presentation by the IPSE vendor, he reacted noncommittally, recommending that if nothing else were found, the IPSE be looked at again in one year.

Notwithstanding this recommendation, the Mbank management continued to signal a serious interest in IPSE. They wrote, for example, to the vendor, pointing out that the IPSE would need to provide them with a costing and budgeting functionality. The vendor responded in very general terms, but the IPSE's ability to address these requirements was not investigated further.

In January 1986 a proposal was made that the IPSE system should be installed as a basis for systems standards and project control procedures, and a request was made for further investigation into the standards that could be provided by the IPSE supplier. The IPSE vendor's development standards were felt to have an advantage, as they were supported by the IPSE. The other contender at this stage was the standards system available from the department's primary training supplier, which had the advantage of being consistent with the training that some staff had already received.

Vincent Brown sent a set of broad proposals for possible Mbank standards to the IPSE vendor, and subsequently the latter suggested conducting a standards outline exercise (on a consultancy basis) prior to the proposed installation of the IPSE. A site visit was arranged by the IPSE vendor, and the manager at the site offered a positive picture. It was clearly noted at the time that the project control facilities of the IPSE were not being used. A bundled price was offered, covering the IPSE system (hardware and software), consultancy for the standards outline and system installation. An order was placed in March 1986.

There were several strands to the evaluation process, but on the whole it was informal. The IPSE concept was attractive to all concerned, and the respective managers all expected the IPSE to provide support in the area of greatest concern to them. The department manager hoped that the IPSE could support department-wide resource monitoring and allocation. The administration manager, who had an accounting background, indicated that the IPSE might give assistance for budgeting. Certain project managers were keen on the project management functions of the IPSE. At project leader level and below the greatest expectation was in the area of techniques for systems development.

The department manager remarked that he would authorise the acquisition of the IPSE on the basis that it was an experiment. This view, however, was not well known in the organisation. Cost, according to the department, was another issue: too much expenditure before it was known whether the system would suit the department was considered unwise.

Installation

The contract was for an IPSE system, a standards outline and 50–60 man days to tailor and install the outline. Of these, the outline plus the consultancy carried a higher price. The purchase overall, while reasonably expensive, did not represent a large investment in the context of the department's typical expenditure at the time.

The standards outline was essentially a framework around which the detailed standards could be subsequently developed. The need for the outline exercise, according to the supplier, sprang from their recommendation that automation is not worthwhile without a clear idea of what one's standards are.

Work on tailoring the outline began in March. A consultant from the supplier was assigned to Mbank. The intention was to customise the standards outline so that the detailed standards could subsequently be developed by the department within the framework provided.

The systems development manager at the department was the official liaison person. The consultant was to meet a cross-section of relevant staff from the department, and to secure an agreement on the nature of the stages and the checkpoints within the development process. The exercise was to include presentations to the department once the outline was done, and would take approximately two to three months to complete.

Up until the order for the IPSE was placed, the central Mbank person involved in the process was Vincent Brown. He was relatively senior, and had a relatively high profile in the department. Before its arrival, however, because of other pressing demands on the department, he was assigned to manage the microsystems development area, and his subsequent involvement with the IPSE was greatly reduced.

Thus only two weeks before the IPSE was due to arrive, the responsibility for standards and for the IPSE was reassigned to John Grant. He had only four months' prior experience in the department, and did not have much background in standards or in quality assurance (QA). He had joined Mbank with the intention of working in analysis and in project leadership.

A few months after the IPSE's arrival, the overall responsibility for IPSE and QA shifted from the development area to the administration area. The administration manager was an accountant, and his primary brief was in accounting matters – budgeting and management accounting – relating to the department's affairs.

USAGE

The IPSE was not a piece of software that ran on the department's existing hardware; it had its own hardware. The original system came with four terminals attached, and four more terminals were attached soon afterwards. Of these, three were allocated to the application areas – one each in the new investment, old investment and banking system areas. Four were placed in the QA group's area, where the two printers were also installed.

The deregulation of the financial sector, and the computerisation of many of the Stock Exchange's functions (the so-called Big Bang), meant that financial sector institutions (especially merchant banks) had to be adequately prepared by the scheduled date; this involved modifying existing computer-based systems and developing new ones. Around this time, the Big Bang activities were imposing very heavy demands on computer and staff resources at the department. There were many issues that needed attention: looming deadlines, pressures from users, delays in current projects and cost concerns.

John Grant's appointment was not announced generally to the department. Neither was the installation of IPSE terminals accompanied by much fanfare. In the absence of a formal plan to implement the IPSE within the department, the use of the IPSE terminals for systems development work was largely determined by individual initiative.

The standards outline exercise did not prove fruitful either – at least not in the way that the vendor perhaps expected. The outline was delivered in the form of a document soon after the IPSE was installed, but the presentations that had been envisaged earlier did not materialise. One opinion expressed at Mbank was that the outline was not tailored enough to their needs. The vendor's view was that the outline exercise may have suffered through insufficient involvement on the part of department staff. In the event, there was no effort to progress the outline further to produce detailed standards.

A new treasury and trading system was being developed at the same time by a team from the IPSE vendor company (a separate assignment). This team made systematic use of the IPSE. They had been producing documentation manually, though in a format which could be stored and manipulated on the IPSE. This work on occasion would deprive other users of machine resources, and this was a source of irritation to the

Mbank users at the time. This other project was subsequently cancelled.

Within the new investment project, a decision had been taken, given the absence of departmental standards, to develop a set of standards internally to the project and to use them specifically for the project. This decision had been made before the outline from the IPSE vendor had been completed. The outline was therefore not considered by the new investment project team. The IPSE was used by some members of the team, notably for diagramming. But the IPSE's diagramming capability was thought to be less good than that of specialist tools marketed for this purpose, so its usage gradually fell away.

On the project management side, the general feeling was that the IPSE was a project control device, primarily for activities such as timesheet completion and status reporting. Management accounting would be aided by capturing information on what people were doing and feeding it to the budgetary control process.

When the IPSE arrived, staff found that the phase/subphase/task approach to project management could not be applied to the way in which they organised maintenance and enhancement work. There were several discussions on developing a mutually acceptable project structure, but nothing concrete emerged.

Systematic entry of timesheet data was organised in one area (the old investment system area) by a contract employee who had project management responsibilities. But during the first few months the exact nature of the product's project control facilities became apparent, and people began to find that these did not live up to their original expectations. There were two issues of contention:

- the limited nature of the IPSE's project control functionality;
- given these limitations, the difficulty of access and transport to another machine.

The administration manager had some discussions with the IPSE vendor, especially on the need for a utility for management accounting. The vendor proposed extra facilities at additional cost. This proposal was not taken up (incidently, a micro-based system was specified and developed internally for this purpose). IPSE use for timesheets continued for some time in varying degrees, depending on the preferences of the individual project managers, but it gradually tailed off.

The IPSE did make some inroads in the area of word processing. Although access to terminals was limited, some individuals began to use the IPSE for their word-processing needs. They appear to have found it more convenient, for example, to develop user manuals themselves on the IPSE instead of submitting handwritten jobs to the department's word-processing group.

Some eight months after the IPSE was installed, the department's word-processing staff, which had originally numbered about six or seven, was reduced to four. The IPSE was not the deciding factor in staff reduction, which was partly due to a general reduction in workload, but the IPSE was clearly influential.

THE CURRENT SITUATION

The IPSE's future at Mbank is highly uncertain. During the period of this study, the use of the IPSE was restricted essentially to a small proportion of the department's word-processing and timesheet activities. The IPSE was not being used for any systems analysis/design activities, and further uses for the machine in the future were not envisaged.

John Grant left Mbank towards the end of this study and took up a position in mainstream systems development project management. He complained that he had not had sufficient authority or management support at the department for implementing the IPSE and standards. His superior at Mbank was, however, of the opinion that John Grant had indeed had sufficient authority, but that his rather abrasive manner had hindered the process of 'selling' the IPSE and standards.

The new investment system project, which in part fuelled the quest for standards, has since been radically changed in its constitution. There is no longer a project manager, and responsibility for the development of the project has been transferred to the relevant user department. As soon as development is complete, the DP department is to take over its operation.

The relationship between the IPSE supplier and Mbank is also somewhat uncertain. Meetings were held with the vendor, at which the problems encountered by Mbank were raised. The department requested changes to the product to tailor it to their needs, but at no extra charge. The supplier, however, regarded major changes as unfeasible, while other changes would be subject to charge.

Mbank also asked for further support for users, again without extra charge. But the supplier explained that the amount of support covered in the purchase price had already been delivered. Department staff, however, continue to feel that insufficient support was provided with the product. Contact between Mbank and supplier has since diminished.

CASE STUDY TASKS

You are to undertake a review of the purchase of the IPSE at Mbank, and of its subsequent implementation and use. Answer the questions below, either individually or working in small groups. You should first approach the case in practical terms, answering the questions with reference to the data presented. But you should also go on to consider appropriate theoretical approaches and analyses.

Questions

1 What do you think are the major reasons for the fate of the IPSE at Mbank?

2 What would you do now to try to rectify the situation?

3 If you were in charge of selecting a suitable IPSE and implementing it within your organisation, how would you go about the exercise?

ESSENTIAL READING

Land F, Le Quesne P, Wijegunaratne I, Effective systems: Overcoming the obstacles, *Journal of Information Technology*, 1989, vol 4, no 2

Le Quesne P, Individual and organisational factors and the design of IPSEs, *The Computer Journal*, 1988, vol 31, no 5

ADDITIONAL READING

Boland R, Hirscheim R, *Critical Issues in Information Systems*, John Wiley, 1987

Piercy N, ed, *The Management Information Systems: The Technology Challenge*, Croom Helm, 1987

Sommerville I, ed, *Software Engineering Environments* (IEE Computing Series 7), Peter Peregrinus, 1986

Swanson E B, *Information Systems Implementation: Bridging the Gap Between Design and Utilisation*, Irwin, 1988

14 Banal (and fatal?) barriers to adoption: National Community Bank

Dian Kjaergaard

ORGANISATIONAL SETTING

The National Community Bank (NCB) is one of the largest banks in Denmark, whatever criteria one uses – the balance sheet, the number of branch offices and other operating units (several hundreds), or the number of employees (several thousands). During the period described here, NCB was aiming for a substantial increase in the number of business customers. Part of the bank's strategy was to speed up applications for loans and other forms of credit, and improve the quality of its evaluation. This entailed improving services from the credit offices, of which there was one for every fifty branch offices. It also meant improving the skills and increasing the authority of the elite branch-office bankers who specialise in business customers; this would allow credit office involvement in individual cases to be gradually reduced. So one important goal of the project was to decentralise decision-making authority.

In this connection, two main activities were picked out for improved computer support:

- evaluation of creditworthiness (based primarily on the analysis of financial statements);
- customer-account profitability analysis (CAPA).

The research underlying this case study was concerned with the latter, and with a program called PC-CAPA. PC-CAPA replaced a mainframe-based system which had been used in credit offices for about 10 years. The program made it possible for credit offices to carry out faster, more flexible analyses. In addition, PC-CAPA was distributed to branch offices so they could begin making their own analyses. This case study examines the problem of adoption at the branch offices.

THE TECHNOLOGY AND ITS PROPOSED FUNCTIONS

PC-CAPA was designed and implemented as a small stand-alone (PC-based) program; the compiled code filled less than half a megabyte.

The program's only function was to calculate expected or realised profitability on customer accounts. This would enable 'what if?' calculations on the profitability of different kinds of deals (prices and terms) with a customer.

The thinking behind the program was that adjustments to various products within the customer's portfolio should be seen in relationship to the entire account; users should employ their own judgement to evaluate the customer's profitability in the light of the entire relationship. Other criteria defining good customers included creditworthiness and security, growth potential, political value to the bank, and so on. These criteria were deliberately left vague (a marked contrast to the trend in many other banks that now use expert advisory systems in connection with customer evaluation).

PC-CAPA is a decision support system (DSS) for 'institutionalised' decision support. It is designed partially to automate certain aspects of complex, 'repeated' decision-making without attempting to replace decision-makers. Deals with customers are repeated in the sense that the same basic kind of decision is made many times a year by many different people in an organisation. Decision support of this kind aims to:

- relieve decision-makers of time-consuming details;

- introduce a more uniform quality of decision-making.

The use of this kind of DSS is often mandatory.

No computing application is simple in the same way as paper-and-pencil technology is. To be used well, every computing requires a large number of complex 'co-requisites' to be in place. In the case of PC-CAPA, the need to carry out a profitability analysis and the ability to use it in setting terms for a customer are not enough. It is also important to have a number of apparently banal things in order.

A few practical examples will illustrate the point. Users would need:

- access to a shared PC in good working order;

- the latest version of the program (how would they know?), ready to run;

- a properly connected printer, loaded with paper and correctly set;

- knowledge of how to format the disks on which calculations are stored, and how to back them up.

These examples may sound trivial, and to regular users they would quickly become so. They are, however, important for infrequent users (eg in the branch offices), especially those with little computing experience. For them, access to an up-to-date user manual is also crucial. But since systems like this are often modified, it is important that someone (who?) has updated the documentation. And help from a local expert is essential; is there someone with the skill and time to help? Busy branches are also subject to interruptions from customers waiting for service, and this makes their task more difficult.

NCB's computer staff envisaged that applications like PC-CAPA would eventually be integrated into a three-tier computerised infrastructure. However, at the time of the study PC-CAPA could not extract data from existing databases; everything had to be keyed in by the direct user. As a result, some of the co-requisites for using PC-CAPA were especially awkward, as the following examples illustrate.

The data needed for individual customer calculations was only available from several different sources, including the customer files (in paper form). In addition, at least four separate computer printouts were sent to bank branches every quarter. These provided customer information on international loans, foreign currency bought and sold, short-term investments and the volume of credit transactions. Not all customers were on these lists – one of many reasons why the calculations required a number of 'guesstimates'. Users had to write down information from all these sources on a special form before keying the data into the program. In this way preparing to use PC-CAPA was like preparing for a batch run on a mainframe computer. In its favour, however, the system was truly interactive, allowing the user to make unlimited changes for 'what if?' trials, and providing almost instantaneous results.

THE MANAGEMENT OF CHANGE

In the Spring of 1986 I began a research project to study the implementation of PC-CAPA. Bert, an economist at NCB's headquarters, had been involved in the preliminary specifications for the new system. He told me:

> PC-CAPA is nothing more than a dedicated calculator. You put income and expense items in, and out comes the contribution on the customer account for the calculation period. And it's easy as pie to use. Much easier than the old mainframe system. I really don't see why it's worth doing a big study about the system's development and implementation.

However, Larry, Marty, and Tom, who had taken over responsibility for the project at headquarters, felt differently. They had given me access to NCB because several members of the project group were concerned about possible adoption problems at the branch offices. They felt frustrated because the executive 'sponsor' for the project was only interested in distributing the program as quickly as possible so that the other top executives could see 'results'. Version 1.0 was released in April 1986 – and by September it had already been necessary to replace it with a debugged version 1.1.

PC-CAPA was one of a handful of applications used to introduce stand-alone PC-based programs to different user populations accustomed to large, integrated mainframe systems. For branch office bankers with business customers, it was usually the first of its kind they had encountered. Most members of the project group predicted barriers to adoption such as:

- a lack of sufficient 'business sense' for them to be able to undertake profitability analysis;

- an inability to transfer skills acquired on large, time-sharing transaction systems to stand-alone PC applications, whether through a fear of PCs, a fear of change, or plain laziness.

The project group had worked on PC-CAPA for 13–14 months before the release of version 1.0. Tom was a project manager with a business school training. His very first project at NCB was to get PC-CAPA designed, programmed and distributed. It was his job to make the requirements operational, and communicate them to programming staff in the new user information centre at headquarters. Larry and Marty were old hands at NCB. Both were university-trained economists with rather broad, flexible jobs: they assisted executive working groups, prepared analyses and plans, and coordinated various projects. Marty became the project's champion, and worked to integrate it with other NCB activities aimed at improving the business customer portfolio.

The project group also included a programmer from the user information centre, as well as three branch office bankers and three credit officers acting as user representatives. In practice, it was often hard to distinguish between the attitudes of user representatives and those of headquarters staff. The latter, perhaps, were less inclined to sound like hackers! The camaraderie within the project group was often in striking contrast to their irritation with colleagues back in the branches. Their annoyance was not so much with users who had problems with the application, as with potential users who never even got started.

Credit officers were used to doing CAPAs, and had often had prior exposure to PCs. They worked in large, open offices which were very seldom visited by customers and where they could help each other continuously. Adoption of PC-CAPA at the credit offices was achieved pretty easily through 'learning by doing' with varying (and sometimes rather large) amounts of assistance, by telephone or in person, from various members of the project group.

There was wide acceptance of a plan by which credit officers would introduce branch office bankers to the program. It was seen as part of a larger process that would make credit office work more consultative and more educational. In April–June 1986, credit officers organised a series of 2–3-hour introductory sessions with a large number of potential branch users. A second series was organised in September–November. There was no attempt to involve NCB's Rationalisation and Organisation Department, which usually designed and carried out training courses. Most of the time in the introductory sessions was used to discuss the calculation model, the sources of data (including 'guess-master') and the interpretation of results. The program itself was demonstrated briefly.

There were two types of user in the branches:

- those making decisions about the terms to be given to a customer;
- those actually using the program.

These two functions were rarely carried out by the same person; yet many introductory sessions were only open to the first category – 'indirect' users such as branch and assistant managers. Most of the project group, and the credit officers responsible for the introductions, assumed that potential direct users had the necessary skills to use the program on a personal computer, or would easily acquire them by using PC-CAPA. They also seemed to assume that all potential direct users had daily contact with local experts who would have the time and the interest to teach them, or that local experts would simply do all the calculations. Only one of the credit officers responsible for introducing the new system hit upon the idea of using an entire day to train direct users in PC-CAPA.

Between November 1986 and February 1987 I interviewed 19 potential users at seven branch offices. Often this interview provoked the first serious look at the program at the branch office. There were many signs that early users did not fully understand the application, and were making serious mistakes in using it and in interpreting its results. Reaction on the grapevine had already suggested to the project group that the situation was pretty much the same everywhere, so they and I supplemented each others' detailed observations and analyses. These analyses were especially eagerly discussed in project meetings towards the design of Version 2.0. In addition, Marty selectively fed results to PC-CAPA's executive sponsor and to the network of executives who were particularly interested in building up the business customer portfolio.

I finished my project in August, 1987, but called Marty in March 1989 to see what had happened. He told me that Version 2.0 would be released in a few days. Branch office adoption of Version 1.1 had never really got off the ground. He was feeling optimistic, however, because a good deal of progress had been made to develop the business sense of branch office bankers so that they would be properly motivated to do profitability calculations.

"What about computer skills and resources for using PC-CAPA?" I asked. "Have there been any improvements?" He had to admit that he didn't know, and that he still wasn't really sure that the issue was relevant for him. Besides, printouts from PC-CAPA would probably be made a mandatory part of loan and other applications sent by branch offices to credit offices for approval. I certainly agreed with him that highly motivated potential users would willingly adopt any kind of improvement over the old system, and that compulsion would be one way to ensure adoption among the others! But there were lessons to be learned from the 'banal' problems experienced by earlier adopters and potential users.

PROBLEMS FOR THE USERS

Terry was considered the perfect local PC expert at one of the branch offices. He explained that he was a PC hobbyist, and that he also had used quite a bit of overtime. He had a couple of hours he could use at the office before going to evening classes twice a week. Unlike many of the people at headquarters, Terry had a great deal of sympathy for those who were having a harder time of it. He was quite sure that he understood the application; but as it turned out, there had been an important change in the register of interest rates, which even he had never discovered.

Terry was not unique. Many of the men who had taken to using PC-CAPA were hobbyists. Local experts often became 'byte-freaks', using more and more time on the details of computing and less on being a banker. This phenomenon seemed to contribute to the almost disdainful disinterest in the application shown by many indirect users of PC-CAPA (typically bank managers). There were, however, a few bankers (especially women) with a very matter-of-fact attitude towards the technology. These also got started quickly, especially where they had hobbyists to help them move over a few rough spots.

Quite aside from these computer-related problems, there was evidence of two conflicting subcultures. Bankers at the branch offices, and many of the headquarters staff, tend to side with the customer and want to take some risks. In contrast, credit officers are trained to give top priority to avoiding risks and securing high levels of profits.

As an example, the users of PC-CAPA were required to enter the time spent servicing a customer's account, so that the cost of labour could be determined. But it was quite difficult for some bankers to keep track of the time they spent on an account, and discussions of this problem often bordered on the bizarre. As it did not seem reasonable to attribute this to stupidity, laziness or general rebellion, I could only suspect that it must be harder for bankers to look at themselves in cost terms than it was for credit officers.

'Forgetting' time spent on a customer could, of course, be one way to make the account look better, yet many bankers were anxious to be as cautious as possible. At one branch office I visited, bankers logged time carefully and rounded up liberally if they were uncertain. As a result, this branch's customer costs tended to look worse than those from other branches. At the same time, however, this branch achieved very high levels of overall profitability, partly because the cautious account analyses were used to increase aspiration levels.

However, the credit officers tended to ignore the total, subtle picture when exercising their authority in connection with individual customers. Indeed, a number of them attempted to prevent branch offices giving 'outrageously favourable' conditions for single products, even if the analysis of the total account's profitability showed good results. The tendency to focus on single products was reinforced by the structure of the program; when working on one type of product in the menu hierarchy, the user couldn't see the effects on the overall profit for the customer account without moving up the hierarchy again.

It also seems that some credit officers felt very uncomfortable that bankers were no longer being 'forced' to consult them about all accounts requiring a profitability analysis. As a result they resisted attempts by branch managers to raise the account threshold that required credit office approval. By preventing this, the credit officers could maximise the number of profitability analyses they would have to examine as a routine part of the approval process. As a result, the decentralisation that PC-CAPA had been intended to create appeared to be a chimera. Perhaps there would be more decentralisation of authority, but only after there was proof that branch officers had adopted the norms and values of credit officers.

In addition, the profitability model embedded in PC-CAPA created considerable difficulties. The cost of funds was said to represent the 'opportunity cost' of capital, yet it was not the same rate used in the branch office accounting system. In fact it had been set so high that it discriminated against business customers. This was a half deliberate, but not widely explained, attempt by the designers to ensure that the growth in the business portfolio would be profitable.

The cost of labour (bankers' time) was also set at a very high rate. The argument was that the bank could sell services to outsiders at a rate of 300 kroner an hour, so the market had determined the price. If a customer's account couldn't match the 'opportunity cost' of the banker's time, then the account would have to be improved or dropped. The underlying assumption was that the market price gave a more than adequate contribution to meeting overheads. Otherwise the bank would not continue to sell labour at that price. By interpreting the high costs of funds and labour as including fully allocated overhead, a user could use a positive bottom line as an aspiration level. Many bankers, at least initially, assumed that high rates simply reflected sound fiscal conservatism.

However, there was no way of telling if a customer was just acceptable (ie making a positive contribution in the short term) or even making an adequate long term contribution which just happened to be less than the aspiration level dictated by 'opportunity cost'. In fact a number of users became alarmed when the high labour rates seemed to make many of their customers look like a net expense for NCB. This suggested the unthinkable for many bankers, that bankers should cease selling capital and financial services to their customers because it does not pay!

To some users, this means of spreading customer-account profitability analysis was a subtle signal of the bank's commitment to survival and growth as its main goals, with customer service merely a means towards these goals. Some bankers were quite happy to admit this, even thinking it was quite a good competitive manoeuvre, which at times could include attempts to squeeze or even cheat customers. Others found this thought distressing; they might use PC-CAPA anyway, but they also seemed resigned or cynical about fighting a losing battle. This was rarely discussed openly.

TASKS

1 What went wrong with the management of the PC-CAPA project and the adoption of PC-CAPA at the branch offices?

2 What should Marty do to improve the adoption of version 2.0?

3 Imagine that you were employed at headquarters in 1986, and made responsible for the adoption of the first release of PC-CAPA in branch offices.

a) How would you have organised the provision of technical co-requisites for using PC-CAPA without changing the technology radically?

b) What kinds of organisational interventions might have helped? (You should also consider interventions within the design group itself.)

c) How would you have planned and organised introduction, training and follow-up?

In areas (b) and (c), think about branch office bankers' skills, motivations, decision-making authority and other resources relevant to doing a CAPA, regardless of the medium.

4 Imagine that you are responsible for improving NCB's project management for the development and revision of decision support

applications for branch office bankers.

a) What kinds of procedures and organisational structures would you recommend?

b) What kinds of technological improvement might be appropriate for a new release of PC-CAPA and other support systems?

ESSENTIAL READING

Cleland D I, King W R, *Systems Analysis and Project Management*, McGraw Hill, 1983 (or another basic text on project management)

Kling R, Defining the boundaries of computing across complex organisations, in Boland R, Hirschheim R, eds, *Critical Issues in Information Systems Research*, John Wiley, 1987, pp307–362

Otley D, *Accounting Control and Organisational Behaviour*, Heinemann, 1987

ADDITIONAL READING

Bjørn-Andersen N, Kjaergaard D, Choices en route to the office of tomorrow, in Kraut R, ed, *Technology and the Transformation of White-collar Work*, Erlbaum, 1987, pp237–251

McCall M W, Kaplan R E, *Whatever it Takes: Decision-makers at Work*, Prentice-Hall, 1985

Salaway G, An organisational learning approach to information systems development, *MIS Quarterly*, 1987, vol 11, no 2, pp244–264

Sprague R H, Watson H G, eds, *Decision Support Systems: Putting Theory into Practice*, Prentice-Hall, 1989

15 Organisational change and information systems: Airfuels Ltd

Geoff Lockett

COMPANY BACKGROUND

Airfuels Ltd supplies fuel to aircraft across the world, and is one of six major suppliers. Until the past year it has been very closely allied to its parent oil company Petroleum Products (PP) and has depended very much on its larger brother for many of its operational services. It has therefore been very much the junior relation among a series of larger partners in the corporate structure.

One of Airfuels' major products is sold in large volumes with a small profit margin, making the selling price all important. Although the quality of the fuel is vital (like petrol), price and quality of service are the main determinants of success. Recently there has been enormous growth in air traffic involving both large and small aircraft. This has also involved an increase in the number of smaller airports in remote areas. Fuel has become a growth industry, but there is increasing complexity and difficulty of control. Deregulation has added further complications by creating smaller airlines and increasing the number of bankruptcies, with the associated credit risks.

PREVIOUS ORGANISATIONAL STRUCTURE

Until recently the organisation was run as a series of small subunits within the companies of Petroleum Products Ltd. These subunits, known as associates, were organised on a country basis (see Figure 15.1). Each of the country-based units was, in essence, managed separately.

Monthly figures were sent to head offices which produced accounts and management information (MI) using their own minicomputer and associated systems. Most of the services for these units (eg accounting, personnel, etc) were provided by the larger organisations in each country. In France, for example, Petroleum Products (France) would handle the computerised accounts for Airfuels (France), and they would be charged for data processing etc.

This created a workable system, but one that was not really designed for

197

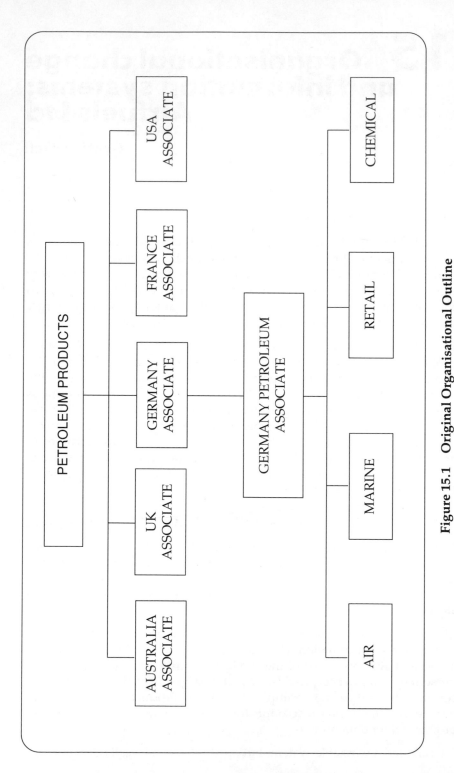

Figure 15.1   Original Organisational Outline
(*This is a simplified illustration which does not show all the complexities and countries*)

their use. More importantly, Airfuels regarded it as inflexible and very costly, especially when totalled across the differing countries. In some countries the sales were large enough for Airfuels to be given dedicated staff; in other countries they shared services. This meant that Airfuels' chief accountant was often unable to have direct control. Customer interfaces were unsatisfactory: airlines are truly international, whereas Airfuels was country based.

ORGANISATIONAL CHANGES

In 1988 the parent company (PP) decided to alter the way the whole organisation was managed. Its strategy was to form a series of separate businesses which cut across countries and regions. For tax and fiscal purposes the country organisation might still exist, but managerially they would be powerless. Instead, a small number of business streams were created (eg Retail, Chemicals, Airfuels, Marine, etc) and given the opportunity to behave in an autonomous manner. The new structures are shown in Figure 15.2.

Some of the units are highly interrelated and transfer a great deal of information to each other. Their separation has been fairly gradual. This process is continuing and its final form is hard to predict. For Airfuels the changes have been more dramatic.

A new managing director called Brian Smith was appointed, who was given the task of creating a new enterprise. He was asked to run Airfuels as a single business, and given the choice either of using central services or developing new ones for Airfuels alone. Judgement would be made on financial performance, and the business was not to be constrained either from the centre or by particular countries.

AIRFUELS: THE NEW COMPANY

When the new company was formed, it was no different from the original sum of its parts. The people were all the same; only their reporting structure had changed. For example, the chief accountant for Belgium worked on a number of business streams, eg chemicals, retail, marine. Something had to be worked out so that there was someone working directly for Airfuels rather than for Petroleum Products (Belgium). It was a difficult process, and it is still going on. All the main services are similarly affected, and the management and control of the various professional activities (eg personnel, accounting, etc) has raised issues which need resolution.

Brian Smith took a long look at his problem and visited most of the major regions of the world. He concluded that there was a tremendous profit potential if only he could weld the organisation together. After some deliberation he decided to organise the company on regional lines,

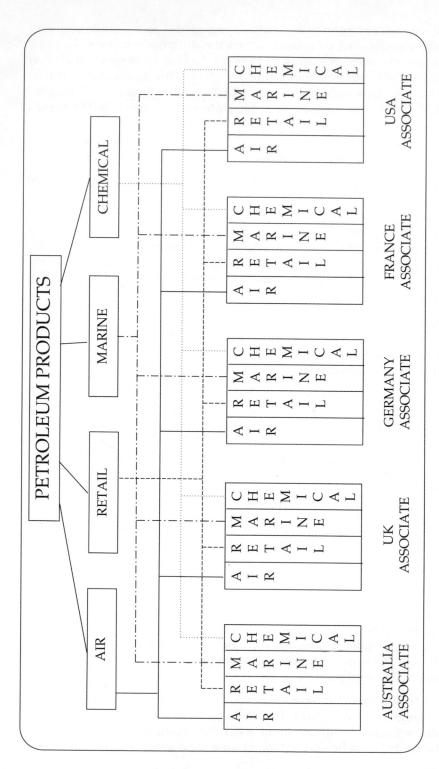

Figure 15.2   The New Organisational Structure

rather than manage from the centre. The time differences across the world could be as much as twelve hours, and most problems would have to be settled regionally. Therefore the proposed structure is as shown in Figure 15.3.

At this point the location of each regional centre was not fixed; more importantly the regional managers had yet to be chosen. Overnight, therefore, a worldwide company of only 1100 people had been created. Could it be run easily, and what would be its new relationship with Petroleum Products? These were some of the questions that had to be addressed. Brian Smith stated:

> This is a fast-growing business on a worldwide scale. Aircraft have no barriers, and a Jumbo can move from London to Paris to Australia to Los Angeles and back in a few hours, picking up our fuel on the way. We need to somehow manage that globally. The margins are small, the volumes high, and the profits can only be improved by having access to fast information. At present I find out what is going on when it's too late. The other growth area is in the small aircraft sector – there is a lot of money to be made and the growth is coming. We must be in a position to capitalise on our international dimension using the strength of the group's quality image.

> This is the background to my problem, and I have to make improvements, but at present I have no control of the information systems; I'm between a rock and a hard place. But I've just been asked for over £1 million to update the old computer system at our head office. I have told them to think again and give me what I want, and what the managers need to run the business. It should be possible to have one simple system worldwide which is cheaper to run. I have got to spend money anyway, and the systems need a shake up. We have got to make it work.

The chief accountant took a similar view. He would be the main person responsible for the day-to-day operation of the new system and was happy at the prospect:

> The initial initiative came from Brian Smith – for replacing expensive and aged systems. We are on too many systems. The plan to replace accounting and invoicing systems has been scrapped and we have just started again. It's a good idea but we have not sorted out our problems yet. The final concept grew out of the new organisation – ie regionalisation. They will be more accountable – we will be able to show them that Airfuels exists. It will be a business. At the moment we just get the local system costs killing us without any control, and we should be able to do it cheaper. The present system is mainly batch processing, and we

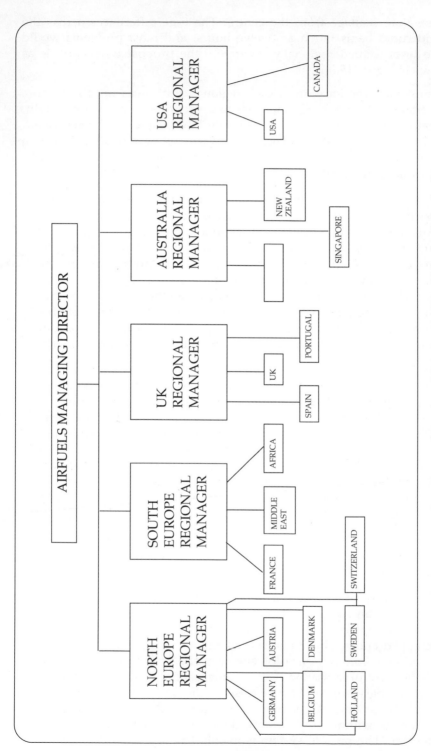

Figure 15.3   The Proposed Regional Structure, Showing the Principal Countries

need an adaptable, flexible, real time system. I want to get rid of programmers and get the tables I want when I want. We now have influence but not command. I am responsible but do not really have control. It will be an interesting experience and give us a much bigger, newer system. I am looking forward to getting the new tools and getting the benefits.

THE COMMERCIAL ENVIRONMENT

The company is one of a few large suppliers, and each company has certain regions where it is strong and others where it is weak. Like all organisations this is due to a mixture of history and differing company strategies. Most fuel suppliers have a presence at the larger airports, and from time to time cooperate in delivery mechanisms. They may even share the same fuel tanks.

One area where cooperation has increased is in data retrieval at the aircraft itself. There are a number of examples where information is typed directly into a workstation and passed through dial-up to a central computer system. So the minute the fuel is pumped into an aircraft, this information is passed into the central computer system to update stocks and accounts. Things like this tend to be happening at the larger throughput centres. However, although the volumes are large, the profitability of the sales is much smaller on a pro-rata basis. The competition is fierce, and each contract may be reviewed fairly regularly.

With the major carriers (eg BA, TWA, etc) the tendency is to form an agreement for a limited period such as one year. Attached to this agreement will be a number of clauses which allow the prices to be amended, for instance after an oil price change. Exchange rates, similarly, are dealt with on a complex but agreed system. There is no lack of data between the major customers and suppliers in the industry. But as stated earlier it is an interesting and volatile industry. It is comparatively easy for someone to 'hire or lease' a jumbo jet and start up an airline on what almost amounts to a franchise system. A few companies like this have grown and are now important; others collapse with the accompanying debts. Some of the developing countries similarly follow these kinds of extremes, and the liberalisation of the skies suggests the problems will increase.

Another problem is the vast distances between airports, and the remoteness of many of them. Much of the largest growth comes in holiday travel to exotic places. As a result, aircraft land in many places that have little infrastructure, and it becomes difficult to maintain an information communication system. Should you serve such trade, or concentrate your efforts? If you don't have a presence, will this affect your other sales? It is an interesting dilemma.

The other growth area is the sales to light aircraft. Its characteristics are almost a mirror image of the holiday travel market – there are numerous small customers who are not very price sensitive, and service is the key. But there are also risks in this field, notably in the handling of money, credit cards and cheques. The two types of business do not really mix, but the customers have to be supplied. Supply logistics and communication difficulties are common, and managing such activities at a distance poses problems. However, there is an enormous profit to be made from this activity, especially in the USA. A large growth in the European market, with associated potential profits, has been expected for a long time.

THE INFORMATION SYSTEMS ORGANISATION

The information systems (IS) manager is Fred Brown, who has worked for the organisation for over ten years. He is well known within the parent company, is well liked and sees himself as an IS professional. His present staff of over 20 people has a budget of £2 million. Most of the people work in operations or maintenance, and there is little or no development work on new systems, apart from the growth in PC applications.

At present his main office is in the London headquarters, though most of the computing is done in one of the suburbs. The major components of the work are the accounting and commercial systems which ensure the smooth running of day-to-day operations. In the UK there is a large package which looks after the UK business and performs reasonably well. However, it is getting old and is mainly based on a Sperry computer which needs replacing. There is also a pricing module, which is run on a Hewlett-Packard machine. Like most systems, this has been gradually developed and improved until it is reasonably sophisticated. Feeding into their systems are airfield systems. These take fuelling data via terminals from the airports through a dial-up system using standard telephone lines, and send data into the centre. Again this is technologically an old system.

The countries round the world have similar systems which are normally part of the much larger associated systems. A small country in fuel terms (eg Belgium) will use the services of the Benelux associate to look after the accounts, invoices, etc, and will pay for this service. The people working directly for it will be mainly talking to customers and generating business. For 'rations' (eg payroll, pensions, office accommodation) they look to the associate. As we have seen, however, they may have to look to their own devices in the future.

This means that there is a central IS organisation which does not really look after most of the computing. It handles the UK, and provides management information on a monthly basis. But what is done outside the UK is not really under the direct control of the London office. There have, however, been some attempts to standardise the international systems: for instance, they are trying to have the same computer package used at all the airfields. These systems are so specialised, and of such little interest to the associate companies, that there is a clear need for a central Airfuels policy if any significant progress is to be made. The IS manager sums up the present position this way:

> Brian Smith, the new MD, said he didn't have all the information he wanted. He cancelled the central systems development project – £1 million on a new IBM. They said it would modernise the procedure. What did he get internationally? Nothing. He wanted information about the worldwide company. Previously only the technical bits had been managed internationally. They did a business requirements specification in August 1986 – it took five months. I was then interviewed for the Airfuels job, after reading the requirements. I said I would build a distributed system on a clone basis, ie build a system for the UK and then export it to other countries. Consolidate accounts etc – because of volumes this does not warrant an on-line central system. We used the requirements specification as a tender document – it wasn't good enough to get a tender. Within a few weeks we realised we should put a tender out for a functional specification in two to three months. The Internal Systems Group gave a fixed cheap price deal. This then became the tender document for the prototype system plus development.

> We now have to decide the software and hardware. There are at present only three of us and it's fun running a multi-million pound project. All the indications are that it could be exciting. It is interesting to size the project – complex and big. Brian Smith and Ken Money, the financial controller, think there are no real problems about using the same package worldwide. We will have to implement from here (the centre) but we haven't come to grips with it yet. There are substantial benefits from being quicker and more accurate, more consistent. The systems should be cheaper to run both in the IS costs and clerical costs. We are presently being saddled with IS costs which are disproportionate to the services we use. A 20% saving on systems and accounts gives us a strong financial case. This may be a problem for small countries, but we are OK with large countries. Brian has just introduced the regional structure and it is enormously helpful.

INFORMATION DEMANDS

The organisation is clearly experiencing many changes, either forced or desired. It is competing in a global environment where there is increasing competition alongside considerable growth. It is likely, for example, that the company will move into the USA in a big way, and in a few years that could be their largest market. Similarly, with the advent of 1992 in the EEC there could be dramatic changes. It is therefore probable that, in common with many other industries, the demand for information of all kinds will grow substantially. An analysis by region of Airfuels' present information handling is given in Table 15.1. The projected air traffic growths are shown in Table 15.2.

AREA	REGION					
	CENTRE	UK	AUSTRALIA	USA	SOUTHERN EUROPE	NE
Number of monthly transactions	14000	1800	2100	3200	1500	7600

Table 15.1   The Number of Monthly Transactions (sales entry, repricing, etc)

At present most of the information handled by the systems ensures that day-to-day business is carried out, but there is little on-line information enabling management to act quickly. A major item that is often quoted is credit control. In this business customers can run up large bills very quickly, and you can be left with large debts. How can you keep track of what is happening when the business you are dealing with is spread very thinly worldwide? Airlines come and go, and a stable industry seems unlikely in the foreseeable future.

In the short term the new business will have to manage by coordinating the separate systems, as at present. This means that management is often caught by not having the information in time to alter events. It has medium- to long-term control, but cannot have a great effect on short-term decisions. Most managers in the new environment want this to change, but have been used to being part of the parent company. They will be expected to 'manage' the business and will be judged on their performance. They know that this will require more and better management information, but have not had the time or experience to get a clear picture. This is probably best summed up in the words of financial controller Ken Money:

> Brian Smith came in and said, "Don't spend the £1 million from the Sperry on IBM. I don't see any real cost benefit to the business." After his tour of the world with our MIS, he said, "I do not wish to be in this position again. Our profitability figures are just wrong. Is it possible to do all the invoicing on one system?" We then

	Average Annual Growth (%)	
	1970–85	1985–2000
Europe–Asia	13.1	7.4
Intra-Orient	10.8	7.1
Trans-Pacific	9.7	7.4
TOTAL	11.0	7.3
US Domestic	6.3	4.3
North Atlantic	6.1	4.2
Intra-Europe	5.8	3.8
TOTAL	6.2	4.1
WORLD	7.2	5.3

Table 15.2   Boeing Forecasts of Air Traffic Growth by Region 1985–2000

discussed it around the organisation, and it grew into a common accounting system for Airfuels. The ideas of regionalisation were being brought to the fore by the Organisation and Planning Committee, who were looking into transfer pricing systems. The true profitability did not line up with management accounts; they were using different base lines. We have also just done an analysis of allocated overheads for 'systems and accounting'. It looks like £7 million, and we have no control of it. We also have offshore and onshore business dealings with the same customers. Clever games are being played, and we don't know how to control them. We agreed the concepts, and the senior managers agreed the new system. It will be simple, cheap and easy to introduce. We want to plug in and run the system, or plug out and go. It was suggested that I do it, but I told him he must take on a professional. I think we should put in a centre plus a pilot site and then sell it worldwide. For example UK and Belgium. Then let us look at it again.

THE PLAYERS

The organisation is therefore a new one, made up of parts of the old ones. This has created a greenfield site scenario tinged with the history of a large international organisation. Most of the people will be affected by the new environment, and it is instructive to consider their different perspectives. In turn they are the managing director, the regional directors, the remote associate office managers, the accounts clerks, and the IS manager.

The managing director has a clear picture of what he would like at his fingertips. He is new to the organisation, and therefore probably brings fresh insights to the problem. Previously he worked for a much larger part of the parent company, but like many senior executives he has never been very pleased with the systems provided. At present he is spending a large amount of time welding this new structure together, and he is rarely in the office. Exciting developments are taking place in Australia and the USA, and he is required to spend an enormous amount of time travelling the world.

Each of the regional directors will be responsible for the performance of up to six countries, including one of the major ones as measured by sales. The areas are largely defined by geography, eg Australasia, but the fate of the most complex area – Europe – is still under discussion. Three regions are to be created, and three Directors have been appointed, but their office locations are still to be decided. This is a completely new role for the company, and its full implications have to be worked out. However, the managing director will use these people as his main management team, plus a few functional directors. Quite clearly they will take time to get a feel for the new job.

Each of the separate countries will now have a new Airfuels manager controlling what the company call Remote Associate Offices (RAO). Some of these country-based businesses are large, but many are very small. As stated previously, these parts of the company were managed by the associate company of Petroleum Products, but will now be largely on their own. It is mainly in these offices that it has been difficult to track down information on a timely basis, and it is here that a new approach is needed. Some job restructuring will be necessary, but the details so far have not been worked out.

At the data entry level we have the accounts clerks, and all the points mentioned above apply. In some places there may be as few as two people looking after an office and maintaining all the administrative procedures. They will have to deal with all the normal activities of sales, enquiries, etc, plus all the unusual ones such as supply logistics problems, document loss, etc. Given the environment, the system will have to be reasonably simple to operate and manage if it is to work. However, regional centres have been brought in without too much difficulty, and it is thought a similar learning period should be sufficient.

Finally the person who will have to carry the project is the IS manager. He is new to the business but has experience of putting in some systems before, although not quite of this international dimension. One of his major problems is managing the project, and this is currently uppermost in his mind. He is also turning his attention to supporting the final product when it is produced. Although he has little doubt that it will be successful, he is slightly worried about the amount of support he will get from the parent company. He knows that his career could take off if it was tremendously successful, and does not care to consider other possibilities.

CASE QUESTIONS

The IS manager has been asked to produce an IS strategy for the new organisation over the next five years, and present it to the managing director. Imagine you are faced with the same task. Certain issues and questions come quickly to mind.

1 What are the main options open to him?

  – Point out their strengths and weaknesses.

  – Suggest the best option, and decide the main presentation points.

2 What form of project management structure would you propose?

  – How would you control the system development?

  – How would you control the budget?

3 How would you implement the solution – in what order and on what timescale?

  – Would you develop the software in-house or use outsiders? Why?

  – Would you connect the computers together using leased lines or using a rented network on public telephone lines?

4 How would you prove to the strongly 'nationalistic' German group that the proposal was the best way to proceed – ie how would you overcome the 'not invented here' syndrome?

ESSENTIAL READING

Keen P G W, *Competing in Time*, Ballinger Publishing Co, 1985

Lockett A G, Palmer B, Organising for change: Managing an IS project across countries, in Thomas H, ed, *Managing Information for Competitive Advantage*, Blackwell, 1989

Mumford E, *Designing Human Systems*, Manchester Business School, 1983

Rockart J F, The changing role of the information systems executive: A critical success factor perspective, *Sloan Management Review*, Fall 1982, pp3–13

Slevin D P, Pinto J K, Balancing strategy and tactics in project implementation, *Sloan Management Review*, Fall 1987, pp33–42

ADDITIONAL READING

Child J, *Organisation*, Harper and Row, 1984

Clark F, Drake P, Kapp M, Wong P, User acceptance of information technology through prototyping, in Shackel B, ed, *Human–Computer Interaction: Interact '84*, Elsevier Science, 1985, pp703–708

Eason K D, The process of introducing information technology, *Behaviour and Information Technology*, 1982, vol 1, no 2, pp197–213

Hirschheim R, *An Analysis of Participative Systems Design: User Experiences, Evaluation and Recommendations* (LSE Working Paper), January 1985

Kanter R M, *The Change Masters*, Simon and Schuster, 1983

Land F, Hirschheim R, Participative systems design: rationale, tools and techniques, *Journal of Applied Systems Analysis*, 1983, vol 10

Morgan G, *Riding the Waves of Change: Developing Managerial Competencies for a Turbulent World*, Jossey Bass, 1988

Peters T, *Thriving on Chaos*, Harper and Row, 1987

16 Organisational and technological change in retail distribution: FoodCo

Greg Bamber and Russell Lansbury

BACKGROUND AND PROBLEMS

During the 1970s FoodCo, a large Australian retailer, increased its number of stores, its turnover and its volume of sales. As it aimed for further increases, it proposed to modernise its distribution facilities to cope with the receipt of goods, inventory control, storage and despatch of the 5000 different items of stock carried at any one time. The company decided to invest in two large dry food distribution centres (DCs) which would employ the latest technology.

The planning and installation of the two DCs took about three years to complete. Each of the new DCs would be among the largest (32,000 square metres) and most sophisticated retail distribution centres in Australia. They were designed to have a total capacity of 21,000 pallets. About two-thirds of these pallets were in conventional low-bay storage, with the rest in high-bay automated storage and retrieval. These DCs introduced several applications of information technology that were novel in the context of food warehousing.

The main features of each DC included:

- an automated pallet storage and retrieval system for holding reserve stocks;

- slow-moving full-case lines to be assembled using fully automated high-rise order selectors (order pickers);

- store orders to be assembled using radio-controlled double-pallet jacks (rather than manually operated single-pallet jacks);

- carton-line storage to be used for 'broken' lines, small or low-demand items;

- reduced air and noise pollution levels through good ventilation and the use of battery-powered mobile warehouse equipment;

- comprehensive fire protection, tunnels and other safety arrangements;

– pleasant lighting, and restaurant and relaxation facilities for employees.

Computer systems were used to locate stocks and provide 'pick lists' for truck loads. Forklift drivers were given scheduled instructions from the computer; these advised of let-downs and pick-ups. All pallets received into the DC were addressed to a specific location. Although not completely automated, each DC was highly computerised.

The first stage of distribution centre A (DCA) was opened in Sydney, New South Wales, late in 1981. Distribution centre B (DCB) was opened in Brisbane, Queensland, in 1983. These new DCs aroused a great deal of interest. DCA was described glowingly in a trade journal (*Materials Handling and Storage*, May–June, 1983, pp18–22):

> A milestone ... the most sophisticated computerised handling system available ... an example of 'total concept' materials handling on the grandest scale ... a very impressive facility and worthy of the awe with which its opening has been greeted in the materials handling industry.

What was the reality behind such hype? The technology used in the two DCs was virtually identical. In both cases the initial workload and the original employees were transferred from older, manually operated warehouses in the same city, which were much less capital intensive.

Their subsequent histories showed marked divergence. Despite the plaudits cited above (and many others in 1983) the company's management were even then seeing DCA as a 'disaster story'. Vexed disputes at DCA during the construction phase were a foretaste of things to come. In the words of one manager, trying to commission DCA was a 'nightmare'. It was plagued by industrial disputes and became a byword for inefficiency. It was the Achilles heel of FoodCo.

In Australia generally, 1984 was a year with unusually few stoppages. This followed the 1983 election of a new federal Labour Government. The company also saw 1984 as 'a better year by far' than 1982, given that the percentage of working hours lost in industrial disputes at DCA was reduced by nearly half.

Yet in 1984 there were 38 recorded stoppages at DCA, and more which were not recorded. There were also many inefficient practices among the managers and other workers, and some industrial sabotage. Industrial disputes became endemic at DCA, and employees used 'guerrilla' tactics to prevent particular stores (such as the company's main city centre store) from receiving supplies. In this context it is hardly surprising that DCA never even approached its planned levels of productivity during its first four years of operation; it was also heavily dependent on using overtime and casual workers to meet its orders.

The failings of DCA appeared especially acute in contrast with DCB, which the company saw as working 'like a dream'. Unlike DCA, DCB made full use of the new technology. Its productivity levels rose steadily, and it had virtually no industrial disputes. Using the measure of average rates of pick per person hour (ppph) DCB was achieving 145 ppph in 1984, compared with 98 ppph at DCA.

BACKGROUND TO THE DISTRIBUTION CENTRES

In 1985 there were 285 warehouse workers employed at DCA and 225 at DCB. DCA was located in Sydney's old western suburbs, a large and competitive labour market in which the available supply of workers was 'industrially sophisticated'. Many of the supervisors and workers were transferred from an old warehouse nearby, although the union had warned FoodCo about a few known 'troublemakers', some of whom had become workgroup leaders. By contrast, fewer of DCB's workers had an industrial background. (There is less manufacturing in Brisbane than in Sydney.) DCB's management were more selective about who was transferred from the old warehouse, especially into the supervisory team.

In both cities, FoodCo had outgrown its old warehouses. It continued to use them, however, but only for the slower-moving non-food stocks. More of the workers at DCA had second jobs, so were not dependent on a single employer. This was especially the case on the afternoon shift, which had many more stoppages than the morning shift.

DCA was in the same city (Sydney) as the company's regional and national head offices. Its management were subject to close scrutiny from various superiors who arbitrarily intervened in increasingly desperate attempts to try 'to heal this gaping wound'. But such interventions were counterproductive; they undermined the authority and independence of the site management.

By contrast, DCB (Brisbane) was over 600 miles from the national head office, and experienced less intervention from its regional head office. The DCB management had a strong sense of independence; they exercised their authority confidently in the workplace without fear of unwanted intervention.

MANAGEMENT IN THE DISTRIBUTION CENTRES

The company transferred a DC manager from a small, old warehouse to manage DCA. He had worked his way up into management and was neither specifically trained nor experienced in using information technology. Apart from him, DCA suffered a discontinuity of management, as FoodCo became impatient to find a remedy for the escalating problems of this DC. Managers were moved in to rectify DCA and sometimes moved on before they had time to tackle the problems thoroughly. Other managers left voluntarily. DCA acquired a reputation as a 'career destroyer'; its managers were caught in the crossfire of a power struggle between the regional and national head offices.

There was also considerable inter-functional conflict, especially between the supermarkets, distribution, and electronic data processing functions. The DCA managers became demoralised as their superiors interfered in local decision-making and quarrelled amongst themselves. Sensing the weak position of DCA management, the shop stewards demanded that their grievances be resolved by higher-level managers from either the regional or national head offices. This further undermined the authority of managers at the site.

No one individual associated with DCA was sufficiently competent and strong to be the 'champion' of change. There was confusion about who was in charge; the DC manager, the regional office, or the national head office. As one company executive put it, "DCA is a ship without a skipper." Especially in its early days, there appeared to be no strategy there; the various managers connected with it adopted short-term tactics, which were not always consistent.

By contrast, for DCB, the company recruited a professional DC manager already experienced in logistics and in computerised warehousing. As the company's best qualified person in this field, he was able to take charge as a strong leader from the start. He formulated a series of strategies to commission and subsequently to operate DCB. Not only did he become the champion of innovation, but he developed other managers with complementary skills who stayed with the project through its formative years.

At DCB, employees with promotion potential were identified using aptitude tests and then promoted into supervision. First-line supervisors were made responsible for managing their own workgroups. In an attempt to build a spirit of cooperation, DCB's management emphasised the importance of direct communications between managers, shop stewards, supervisors and individual employees. Periodically the DC manager would talk to a meeting of all employees on each shift.

THE WORK ORGANISATION

Warehouses are often blamed if the all-important stores become out of stock, and warehouse workers in general have relatively little scope for feelings of recognition or achievement. Warehouses are often badly lit and ventilated, and the working environment is often either too hot or too cold. Nevertheless, the environment in both of the new DCs was much better than in the older warehouses which preceded them.

Management claimed that the jobs in the new DCs required new skills, since people had to learn to operate the new equipment. However, the new tasks were not very difficult and workers were supposed to follow instructions from the computer, rather than rely on their own knowledge and experience. At DCA, the 'pick routes' seemed disorganised; workers complained that the computerised 'pick list' would sometimes instruct them to pick heavy goods to stack on top of breakables. Therefore they did not always follow the recommended pick route, nor unload goods exactly where the computer instructed. But once the goods were put in a different place, chaos could soon follow: the pick list might say to pick baked beans at a particular location when dog food had been left there instead!

People seemed to work inefficiently and slowly at DCA. In spite of its productivity failings, and in keeping with the prevailing custom, management did not discuss productivity or work targets with its employees. Although the unions opposed the notion of performance appraisal at both DCs, the DCB management displayed productivity charts and discussed performance with individuals. Those whose pick rates were consistently below average were counselled and retrained, or might return to the old warehouse.

The work organisation seemed to be more efficient at DCB, though one shop steward there assured us that the people did a 'fair day's work'. DCB workers were told to pick orders so that the stack of cartons remained as level as possible; they picked 'level layers'. At DCA, some workers picked around a pyramid of cartons, which was more likely to precipitate breakages as the pyramid collapsed.

A 'them-and-us' divide was apparent at DCA. "It was like a barricade between the workers and supervisors, who adopted an autocratic style". As one manager put it, "The supervisors used a piece of four by two [wood] when a feather was needed", resulting in confrontation with workers. Also, there were entrenched demarcation customs among the workers (for example between forklift truck drivers, order assemblers, checkers, packers and cleaners). Furthermore, there were allegations that recruitment and the allocation of jobs were determined by favouritism (or on the basis of religious or other links).

DCB, by contrast, was described by shop stewards as being like 'one big family'. Supervisors had a more consultative style and there was considerable flexibility among the workforce; everyone did their own cleaning. If a storekeeper broke a carton at DCB he or she would clean it up, but at DCA it might simply be left for the cleaners. Each of DCB's zones was managed by a supervisor, but with a quasi-autonomous workgroup approach. By contrast, at DCA there was no such clear association between zones and supervisors. Some said that the supervisors there had 'lost the ability to motivate', and had 'given up their managerial responsibilities'; there was 'no discipline'.

The DCB management designed an induction and training programme for all employees, who quickly became confident about operating the new technology. At DCA, by contrast, training had a lower priority, so neither the managers nor workers became competent or confident about operating the technology.

As DCA was being established, the workgroup leaders took the opportunity to win extra pay and generally to maximise the workers' advantage by further restricting the working practices which had prevailed at the old warehouse. At DCB management sought to maximise its advantage by increasing its control over the labour process and, where possible, changing the prevailing working practices which it saw as restrictive. Although the workers claimed extra pay for working with the new technology at DCB, management made no concessions.

INDUSTRIAL RELATIONS

All employees at DCA were members of the National Union of Workers (NUW), one of the most powerful and reputedly militant Australian unions. At both DCs the managers preferred to deal directly with the shop stewards rather than the full-time union officials.

However, the industrial disruption at DCA was exacerbated by managerial tactics which sought to separate the employees from their union officials. This approach was based upon management's view that the workers were being 'misled' by the union. The result of these tactics, however, was to strengthen the power of unofficial workgroup leaders at DCA, who frequently called for industrial action independently of their shop stewards and the full-time union officials. As one manager commented, there was industrial anarchy. And perhaps the stoppages at DCA were not solely to pursue serious industrial grievances. As many workers on the afternoon shift had second jobs, it was suggested that one reason for their instigating stoppages was to gain a much-needed break from work.

Retail warehouse employees in Brisbane usually belong to the Shop, Distributive and Allied Employees' Association (SDA). This has more members than most other Australian unions, but many of them are part-time and it is generally seen as a moderate right-wing union. Industrial disruption was negligible at DCB. There was some criticism by shop stewards that pay levels were lower there than at DCA, and about the high productivity levels (ie pick rates) which the DCB management demanded. In 1984, the DCB manager dismissed a worker who was seen as a 'poor performer'. The SDA contested this case successfully at an arbitration hearing. Even so, some workers at DCB complained that the SDA was too weak, but others claimed that this reflected the workers' fear that the DCB management would dismiss people whom they saw as troublemakers.

In spite of such claims, managing industrial relations at DCB was more akin to 'fire prevention' than the 'fire-fighting' approach at DCA. DCB management aimed to be 'firm but fair'. They made positive attempts to establish and maintain a high level of trust between all levels of their organisation, as a foundation on which to build industrial peace and employee commitment to corporate goals.

THE CRISIS AT DCA

Largely because of the increasingly apparent failings of DCA, FoodCo was losing market share in its most important market: Sydney (Australia's largest city). FoodCo shares were becoming the focus of takeover speculation. Managers were getting more and more nervous about the Company's survival (and their own job security). We asked a FoodCo senior executive if he had actually walked around DCA and talked with the workers and shop stewards. "Heavens, no," he retorted, "I wouldn't get that far down the hole." This was despite being plagued by complaints from irate customers and staff about FoodCo stores.

One day the personal secretary to one of the executive directors announced crossly to her boss, "I've wasted all my lunch hour shopping in your so-called flagship store, only to find that it's run out of the essentials: butter, eggs, sugar and Fosters. This company is hopeless. In future I'll be taking my custom across the street!" (If stores get a reputation for being out of stock of key products, then customers quickly take their trade elsewhere.)

Last Wednesday, for the sixth time in two months, the FoodCo Managing Director was woken by a phone call in the middle of the night to hear that there was "more industrial trouble at DCA. The busiest Sydney stores have run out of essential supplies and cannot be restocked again this week." He immediately summoned a well known management consultant to a working breakfast at the Hilton. He opened the conversation by saying:

> As usual, the damn storekeepers and packers at DCA have timed their disruption so that our best shops will lose much business on their busiest shopping days: Thursday to Saturday, before a holiday weekend! We're getting a dreadful reputation. I am at the end of my tether with DCA. What can we do to rid FoodCo of this recurring nightmare?

QUESTIONS/CASE STUDY TASKS

You are asked to take the role of the consultant and to advise on the strategies that the company should adopt to overcome the problems at DCA and raise its performance to the levels achieved by DCB. To help you in this task you should consider the following questions.

1 What are:

   a) the major factors contributing to the problems at DCA, and the interrelationships between these factors?

   b) the most critical factors?

2 What actions could management take to make DCA more like DCB?

3 Could management change the style of employment relationships at DCA?

4 Could subcontracting DCA to a third-party operator provide a satisfactory solution to the problems? What would be the pros and cons of such an approach?

5 At DCA, could the 'social' and 'technical' systems be changed to suit each other more closely than hitherto?

ESSENTIAL READING

Bamber G J, Lansbury R D, eds, *New Technology: International Perspectives on Human Resources and Industrial Relations*, Unwin Hyman, 1989 (especially chapters 1, 8 and 9)

Braham P, Marks and Spencer: A technological approach to retailing, in Rhodes E, Wield D, eds, *Implementing New Technologies: Choice, Decision and Change in Manufacturing*, Blackwell, 1985, pp123–142

Buchanan D A, Boddy D, *Organisations in the Computer Age: Technological Imperatives and Strategic Choice*, Gower, 1983 (especially parts 1 and 3)

ADDITIONAL READING AND REFERENCES

Bamber G J, Some 'knowns' and 'unknowns' about management, industrial relations and technical change, in Williams B R, Bryan-Brown J A, eds, *Knowns and Unknowns in Technical Change*, Policy Studies Institute/Technical Change Centre, 1985, pp131–151

Bamber G J, Lansbury R D, eds, *International and Comparative Industrial Relations: A Study of Developed Market Economies*, Allen & Unwin, 1987 (especially chapter 5)

Child J, Loveridge R, Harvey J, Spencer A, Microelectronics and the quality of employment in services, in Marstand P, ed, *New Technology and the Future of Work and Skills*, Frances Pinter, 1984

Lansbury R D, Technological change and employee participation in the retail industry, in Lansbury R D, Davis E M, eds, *Technology, Work and Industrial Relations*, Longman Cheshire, 1984, pp120–132

Martin R, *New Technology and Industrial Relations in Fleet Street*, Oxford University Press, 1981

17 Ergonomics training: Headco

Tom Stewart

ORGANISATIONAL SETTING

Headco is the London-based head office of a large retail chain which has over 200 stores in the UK. The company has a good reputation for looking after its staff. Its extensive staff welfare policies stem partly from historical paternalism, and partly from a long-term view of the importance of human resources in a successful business.

The company is a pioneer in the field of occupational health. Each location has well-equipped first-aid and medical facilities. In the head office there is a full-scale medical facility with treatment rooms, physiotherapist, dental surgery, fitness gymnasium and a team of medical officers and nurses. This team looks after head office employees, but also has responsibilities for the company's other employees up and down the country.

The concerns of the occupational health department have grown considerably over the years. Much effort now goes into preventative medicine and the active promotion of health and safety, and not just the avoidance of illness and injury. The medical officer has been instrumental in applying ergonomics to problems in the workplace. Projects have been as diverse as designing new tills in the stores and developing new stock handling equipment in warehouses.

The organisation is highly centralised, with major decision making concentrated at the head office. It is also organised along quite narrow functional lines, with relatively senior managers responsible for specific areas of the business. This makes it difficult to justify and implement changes which degrade one area in order to improve another, even if the overall benefit to the business is positive.

One of the few functions which does cross the traditional lines of authority is the occupational health department. They also have relatively senior staff, given their size, and are not regarded as threatening to other managers. However, like other areas of the business they are under increasing pressure to justify their existence.

They must also demonstrate that the current policy of preemptive occupational health is commercially worthwhile. Their unique position allows them to make an impact across functions in ways which other departments cannot. However, their sphere of influence is limited to health and health-related issues. These include:

- ergonomics;

- health and safety;

- some aspects of staff welfare.

There is a separate personnel department.

PROBLEM NUMBER 1: ORGANISATIONAL CHANGE

The first problem is that the organisation is changing rapidly, and old mechanisms for absorbing technical change can no longer cope.

In recent years, there has been a growing awareness that change is necessary in various aspects of the business. The forces for change include a recognition that continued growth in existing sectors cannot be sustained indefinitely. This is compounded by increasing pressure from traditional competitors and from new entrants into the retail market.

Head-office costs have also escalated, because:

- office costs in the south-east have rocketed;

- the rapid growth in staff in the 1960s has created a 'bulge' in the senior staff population, and they are expensive.

Like most of the retail sector, the company acquired information technology relatively late. It relied on traditional reporting procedures and structures long after other industries were investing in data processing.

However, the company soon came to appreciate the potential benefits of information technology (eg as a means of improving stock ordering and managing costs). When it did, there was tremendous pressure to catch up, and technology has been introduced with dramatic speed.

Indeed, the late conversion to information technology has created an almost naive view of technology as the answer to all the problems of the existing operation. This, in turn, has created unrealistic expectations, and some hostility towards the rapidly growing computer systems department at head office.

It has also led to the development and introduction of systems at such a pace that there has been little thought about practical implementation problems. For instance, no one has considered how to introduce clean, quiet VDU-based office work into a noisy warehouse environment without causing problems for staff expected to use the system.

The working environment at head office is far from ideal, and the building is oldfashioned. It was never designed with technology in mind – or, more accurately, the technology its designers had in mind was limited to typewriters, adding machines and other simple, stand-alone items. None would make much demand on the working environment. The furniture is also oldfashioned and there were problems with poor ventilation and overcrowding even before VDUs began to flood into the offices. VDUs and personal computers (PCs) have added to the existing problems and made their own contribution in terms of noisy printers, trailing wires and even more clutter. As more and more integrated systems are developed, so the hardware multiplies and the cabling and interconnection seems to take on a life of its own.

PROBLEM NUMBER 2: OFFICE TECHNOLOGY

The second problem is that office technology does not fit existing office design (or more accurately, lack of design).

During the rapid diffusion of VDUs and PCs throughout the organisation, Headco, like most large users, has often found difficulties in integrating them with current office design and furniture. Head office has seen a proliferation of all types of computer equipment, from mainframe systems with VDUs to word processors (WPs) and PCs, both stand-alone and integrated into networks. This has created a large number of ergonomic, health and safety problems for staff.

Traditionally, ergonomics has been concerned with the design of equipment and the working environment to take account of the strengths and limitations of the people who are expected to use them. Although originally limited to the design of equipment used at work, its techniques can be applied to any product used by human beings. These products may be as personal as a hand tool or as communal as a ticket barrier, or the working environment in an office.

Ergonomists use a wide range of techniques from a number of disciplines to ensure that products and systems can be used comfortably and efficiently. Anthropometry allows them to anticipate the size and shape of potential users. Biomechanics helps them understand how forces may be exerted. Physiology provides information on energy expenditure, and the effects of the environment on the body. But increasingly, as equipment becomes more complex, they use psychology (to understand how people process information, interpret displays, make decisions and perform skilled tasks) and social psychology (to understand how people communicate with and relate to others).

Getting the best out of people and equipment is becoming increasingly important for most organisations in today's highly competitive commercial world. Headco is no exception. Improving the ergonomics of equipment and the workplace can be a highly cost effective way of increasing staff morale and productivity.

Today's office provides ample scope for such activity. Much productivity is lost in the office as a result of poorly designed equipment and inappropriate workplaces. However, by far the most widely publicised issue concerns the alleged health hazards associated with VDUs. Various risks have been identified including eyestrain, postural problems, repetitive strain injuries, facial dermatitis, adverse pregnancy outcomes and other dramatic and frightening maladies. Many of these are unproven, but a significant number are well established and clearly involve ergonomics. The question of whether such problems are health problems or 'merely' ergonomic ones is rather arbitrary, though in some organisations it may well have profound legal implications.

Even so, discomfort, temporary fatigue and other similar conditions are unpleasant, unnecessary and unacceptable in the modern office. There should not be differences of opinion between management and staff or their representatives on this point (although in many organisations there are), and this leads to ergonomics and health issues being brought into the forefront of industrial relations. There is no benefit to be gained from staff who feel uncomfortable at work, and Headco's occupational health policy is a recognition of this.

However, some of the claims made in the name of VDU ergonomics are clearly ridiculous. Work is tiring, and it is entirely normal to feel tired after work. No mysterious radiation or postural link is needed to explain this phenomenon. After all, the office is a place of work, and much of the advertising hype about ideal environments and user-friendly equipment seems to overlook this fact. Comfortable working conditions are not the same as comfortable resting conditions.

Nonetheless in Headco, as in many organisations, VDUs have often had a far more negative impact on the workplace than necessary. One reason is that office tasks performed on a VDU may be quite different from their paper-based equivalents.

Firstly, the VDU becomes much more of a focus than the equivalent paperwork or manual records. For example, even with shared manual filing systems staff can usually choose how to work – whether to refer briefly to a file on the spot, to take it back to their desk, or to take it to a colleague or supervisor. With VDU tasks, far more attention focuses on the VDU, and the tendency is inevitably to bring the work to the screen. This makes it all the more important that the VDU working conditions are right.

Secondly, there is an interaction between the VDU and various aspects of the environment, and some of these interactions pose problems for users. Most current VDUs (those used in Headco are standard industry models from a major supplier) use cathode ray tube (CRT) displays which present a bright image on a dark background. To view this comfortably, the characters on the screen must be sharp, stable and clear. Good VDUs should be able to achieve this, although some routine adjustment may be necessary to keep the display clear.

Because the display itself generates the bright characters, light from the environment reduces the contrast between the characters and the background, making them less legible. However, for reading documents, the more light on the document, the greater the contrast. This creates a conflict: there must be enough to read the document, but not so much that the screen becomes difficult to read. More recent displays with dark characters on a light background offer one solution, at the cost of greater susceptibility to flicker.

Paper-based workers with similar problems in reading a particular document have several options. For instance, they can move the paper about and change the viewing conditions to improve the visual task.

VDU users have much less scope to move the equipment especially when they also have to operate a keyboard. They tend to move themselves rather than the equipment if they need to change their viewing angle, or avoid reflections on the screen. These awkward postures can become fatiguing and uncomfortable, especially if they are maintained for a significant period of time.

But it is not just the visual environment which interacts with office equipment. More and more printers and other noisy equipment are being installed. These can cause significant distraction, and raise the level of perceived stress in the office.

Electrical equipment generates heat, and this adds to the thermal load on the ventilation system. As more and more offices use mechanical forms of ventilation, with no opportunity for fresh outside air, so the quality of the air itself can become a major issue. At Headco, opening the windows simply increased the noise level and introduced traffic fumes from the busy road outside. This added to the problem of creating an effective working environment for staff who make regular or intensive use of VDUs.

PROBLEM NUMBER 3: BUSINESS COMES FIRST

In Headco the importance of health and safety is recognised at a senior level, and the company sets and maintains high standards. In practice, however, there can be conflicts between safety and the high levels of productivity which are also demanded. Indeed, some staff argue that it is not possible to meet the company's productivity targets and comply with its health and safety policy. In the warehouses, for example, there is an explicit policy that proper steps and ladders must be used when working at height. However, staff and supervisors know that when an item is just out of reach, it is quicker to use the racking as a step than to get down off the ladder and move it along.

Thus there tends to be an unwritten connivance between supervisors and staff, allowing the safety rules to be infringed in order to meet productivity targets. This places a twofold burden on staff. If they stick to the rules, they fail to meet productivity targets. If they bend the rules, and an accident happens, they take the blame themselves because they did not follow management rules.

Nonetheless, ergonomics is taken seriously. The occupational health department has helped to introduce improved equipment, workplace and environment design throughout the organisation in warehouses, stores and offices. Other parts of the organisation have embraced the concept less wholeheartedly, but over the last few years it has become a recognised issue in new workplaces or when old workplaces are being revised.

INTRODUCING ERGONOMICS TO IMPROVE WORKING CONDITIONS

The company doctor at Headco was concerned about continuing problems experienced by some staff when working intensively with VDUs. Ergonomics consultants were brought in to work with the facilities manager responsible for buying furniture in head office. One of their first projects was to select appropriate furniture for WP workplaces for secretaries. They interviewed staff, made measurements and observations of working practices, and produced an appropriate specification for a suitable workplace. This involved a single level L-shaped configuration, with a low shelf on one leg of the L to carry the bulky processor unit and disk drives.

This simple design solved the main problems of equipment location. In conjunction with suitable adjustable chairs, it allowed the staff to maintain a comfortable and efficient posture. The furniture was compatible with existing company standards, was similar in cost to existing furniture, and could be introduced as required with WP equipment. Similar workplaces were also planned for the growing army of VDU users at head office as part of a continuing refurbishment programme.

As the programme continued, more and more VDU users gained the benefit of better workplace design and an improved working environment. This, however, left two problems. One was that it takes time to refurbish a large working office and some of the existing furniture and offices were not due to be upgraded for some time. Secondly (despite considerable investment in ergonomically designed furniture, better chairs, etc) some staff were still suffering visual and muscular discomfort. It was clear to the company doctor that the staff themselves were not making the best use of what was being provided.

At about this time the company doctor and the ergonomics consultant were speaking at a conference on the ergonomics and health implications of office automation. They heard a presentation by a US-based training company on the Dataspan Ergonomics Skills Programme. This was developed by the Joyce Institute for Boeing Aerospace in Seattle, and had shown some success in providing VDU users themselves with the skills to take responsibility for their own workplace.

This appeared an ideal complement to the traditional ergonomics consultancy activities of System Concepts (the author's company). After visiting the Joyce Institute in Seattle and examining the training materials in detail, System Concepts decided to introduce Dataspan into the UK, and Headco agreed to become an early trial site. Headco's personnel department now became involved through their training section, and agreed to set up a pilot course to assess the costs and the benefits of such training.

ERGONOMICS TRAINING AT HEADCO

Dataspan training is provided on site, and takes just two hours per day during one week. Staff are taught basic ergonomics and given a real understanding of what causes the problems they experience. They are taught exercises and techniques to reduce stress and discomfort. Using special projection equipment they are trained to be quicker and more accurate when handling data and text. They are also given a do-it-yourself ergonomics checklist, and helped to apply it to their own workplace through consultations with the trainer.

The results of the pilot course were favourable and a second course was held to assess how the training could be customised to meet Headco's particular requirements. This, too, was well received. A programme concentrating on issues of ergonomics, health and comfort was developed in collaboration with the training specialist and the occupational health department, and designed to fit in with existing courses on text and data skills.

The course was targeted towards staff who made intensive use of VDUs. At that time, there were approximately 300 such staff in Headco.

CASE STUDY TASKS

Imagine you are a consultant evaluating ergonomics and training at Headco.

1 List the ergonomics issues at Headco.

2 Training is only one of a number of different mechanisms for improving the ergonomics of existing workplaces within Headco. What makes this approach particularly attractive to the company?

3 Why might the approach not work? What could go wrong, or reduce the success of the scheme?

4 Who should be responsible for ergonomics? To which level in the organisational hierarchy should they report?

5 What can be done to prevent the ergonomics initiative becoming caught up in interdepartmental disputes? How can a sufficiently broad perspective be maintained?

ESSENTIAL READING

Cakir A, Hart D J, Stewart T F M, *Visual Display Terminals: A Manual Covering Ergonomics, Workplace Design, Health and Safety, and Task Organisation*, John Wiley, 1978

Dainoff M J, Dainoff M H, *A Manager's Guide to Ergonomics in the Electronic Office*, John Wiley, 1987

Damodaran L, Simpson A, Wilson P, *Designing Systems for People*, NCC, 1980

Shackel B, Ergonomics in information technology in Europe: A review, *Behaviour and Information Technology*, 1985, vol 4, pp263–289

ADDITIONAL READING

Grandjean E, ed, *Ergonomics and Health in Modern Offices*, Taylor and Francis, 1984

Oborne D J, *Computers at Work*, John Wiley, 1985

Scalet E A, *VDU Health and Safety: Issues and Solutions*, Ergosyst Associates, 1987

Stewart T F H, Ergonomics of the Office, *Ergonomics*, 1985, vol 28, no 8, pp1165–1177

18 Management strategy and technological change in British Telecom: From Strowger to TXE4

Ian McLoughlin and Jon Clark

ORGANISATIONAL SETTING

This case concerns the management of a major technological change in British Telecom (BT): the introduction during the late 1970s and early 1980s of a new telephone exchange system called TXE4. BT provides a national network of local and trunk telephone exchanges and transmission lines for both business and residential customers.

For much of the century, the provision of this service was the responsibility of the General Post Office (GPO) which was part of the Civil Service. However, the past 25 years have seen an increasing emphasis on the provision of telephone and other telecommunications services on a commercial rather than public service basis. For example, in 1969 the GPO was renamed the Post Office and established as a public corporation split into a number of semi-autonomous businesses, one of which was telecommunications. Then in 1981 the Post Office was split into two separate independent businesses, and British Telecom was created. In the same year the Telecommunications Act opened up some areas of BT's activities to competition from the private sector. Finally, in 1984, BT was 'privatised', and 51% of its shares were sold to private investors.

The increasing emphasis on commercialism was reflected in changes in internal organisation. After 1969 the business was divided into a three-tier structure comprising:

- a national (corporate) headquarters;

- ten regions;

- 61 local telephone areas, which control the operation and maintenance of telephone exchanges.

During the 1970s, the structure remained the same, but after 1979, the emphasis within it has shifted markedly. Prior to 1979 the business was run on a functional basis biased towards engineering. By 1981 it was market-orientated and market-led. However, these changes initially took effect at national level. They were not introduced at local telephone area level until after 1983. In addition to these changes, advances in information and computing technologies permitted major new developments in the provision of telecommunications services. For managers, unions and staff, the late 1970s and early 1980s were therefore a period when traditional approaches and practices were beginning to be challenged by rapid commercial and technological developments.

Most of the events described here occurred before privatisation. The tasks, however, ask for:

- an evaluation of corporate strategy in the light of the new commercial environment following privatisation;

- an assessment of the implications of any recommended changes for industrial relations.

In 1983 BT had well in excess of 200,000 employees. Two unions were involved:

- the Post Office Engineering Union (POEU) – now the National Communications Union – which organises senior and junior engineering grades (the latter forming the majority of the membership, although not amongst maintenance electricians);

- the Society of Telecom Executives (STE), which organises management grades, including exchange maintenance supervisors.

The POEU had around 130,000 members and represented approximately 97% of engineering grades. The STE had around 23,000 members, representing around 85% of potential members and over 94% of first-line supervisors.

BACKGROUND TO THE CASE

The revolution in computing and information technologies means that the telecommunications infrastructure is now as vital to business as were the rail, road and shipping networks in earlier times. For the private consumer the telephone is also an essential service, with over 80% of households connected to the network. It is something of a paradox, therefore, that in the early 1980s the task of connecting calls – the function of the telephone exchange – although fully automatic was in most cases still accomplished by technology dating from the late 19th century. The inventor of this system was a Kansas City undertaker, Almon Brown Strowger. The story has it that Strowger had a strong motivation for designing an automatic exchange. The local switchboard operator was the wife of his main competitor, and she had been diverting calls meant for his business to her husband! Whatever the vagaries behind its invention, the Strowger system was still being installed in Britain as late as the mid-1960s. However, because it was

based on electromechanical technology that switched signals in ana-
logue form, it was universally regarded as an unsuitable basis for a
modern telecommunications infrastructure.

However, the task of finding a suitable replacement for the Strowger
system was both lengthy and complex. An early attempt to develop a
viable all-electronic exchange failed in 1962. Much of the 1960s was
therefore spent developing a semi-electronic system, and early versions
were introduced into small local exchanges in the mid-1960s. It was not
until 1972, however, that the Post Office decided to replace all large local
Strowger exchanges with a new 'TXE4' semi-electronic system. The scale
of this modernisation made completion before the end of the 20th
century very unlikely. Moreover, TXE4 was seen as a stopgap until a
viable fully electronic system, 'System X', could be developed. In the
event the first TXE4 exchanges were introduced in 1976, but by 1979
only four were in operation. The pace of change increased rapidly in the
1980s, and by 1985 342 units had been brought into service. By this time
the original plan had been changed. BT anticipated that fully electronic
System X exchanges would be available from the mid-1980s onwards. As
a result, the TXE4 modernisation programme was curtailed in 1985. The
exchanges involved served nearly five million customers, or 25% of all
exchange connections.

THE PROBLEM

The Post Office's decision to adopt TXE4 had been based on the
following objectives:

- to meet the growing demand for telecommunications services and
  improve service quality;

- to reduce the cost of exchange maintenance;

- to cut exchange maintenance staffing levels and improve productivity.

Having set these corporate objectives, national management were then
faced with two tasks:

- negotiating a national framework for the introduction of TXE4 with
  the trade unions, within which TXE4 could be introduced;

- developing a strategy so the corporate objectives behind modernisation could be achieved within the local telephone areas where the
  new exchanges would be introduced.

The first task was partly simplified by the fact that the STE regarded the
introduction of new technology as a 'management issue' and therefore
did not seek to negotiate over change.

There was, however, an immediate difficulty. The business objectives behind modernisation increasingly emphasised commercial aspects, but corporate labour relations policy tended to lag behind, following a more traditional public-service ethos. For example:

- seniority was the accepted basis for selection and promotion;

- terms and conditions were established by national bargaining with very little room for local discretion;

- strong emphasis was placed on job security.

Two objectives – reduced staffing and improved productivity – appeared to challenge this ethos. Even so, the process of national negotiations during the late 1970s resulted in a framework of agreements that owed as much to the traditional labour relations approach as to the influence of a new commercialism. Moreover, in the event, this framework provided the basis for a smooth introduction of TXE4 without any industrial disruption and with the maximum possible support of staff.

The first step was a nationally agreed standard to determine staffing levels in the new TXE4 exchanges. The new agreement was a substantial industrial relations innovation for the business. It provided a precise, quantitative formula to determine staffing levels. This related the level of maintenance work to be done to the number of customers connected to the exchange and the level of traffic it carried. Using this formula it was possible to read off the staffing level for any given exchange from a simple chart.

Next, the tradition of employment security in the business was formalised in 1980 through a national 'job security agreement'. Management agreed to make no compulsory redundancies. The POEU, in return, accepted the new technology and other changes.

Finally, although not a subject of specific negotiations, management recognised the staff's acceptance of new technology with across the board productivity payments. These had been a regular feature of collective bargaining in the business since the 1950s.

In fact the framework provided by these national agreements left local area managements with considerable scope for discretion, as much by non-decision as by conscious choice. For example, the national standard for determining staffing levels offered a precise formula relating them to the volume of available work. Even so, there was enough leeway in its 'small print' for levels to be raised as local areas saw fit. In practice local management had a considerable discretion in relation to this issue, especially when considering exchanges where the standard formula could not be applied. For example, if an area was at the beginning of its modernisation programme management might 'overstaff' the first exchanges to be converted to help build up expertise. This gave some insurance against the occurrence of serious technical problems.

In addition, the staffing level agreement gave no indication of the criteria that were to be used when staff were selected for retraining, although general reference was made to both senior and junior technicians, with the implication that both grades were eligible. Interestingly, the agreement did require local management to consult with staff and the local POEU 'at an early stage' over proposed staffing levels.

The corporate objectives behind modernisation also left considerable scope for local discretion. This was especially important when the areas were developing strategies for the operational control of maintenance in TXE4 exchanges. For instance, one major objective behind the adoption of TXE4 was a more efficient use of labour. However, little guidance was given on how to achieve this, or what changes were to be made in the organisation and supervision of maintenance work. Without a clear strategy at corporate level, management in each area were left to resolve these issues at local level.

The jobs of maintenance technicians and supervisors were also directly affected by the change from an electro-mechanical to a semi-electronic system. The Strowger system was driven by electrical contacts and contained several thousands of moving parts, all of which were affected by dirt, wear, breakage and misalignment. It therefore required:

- a high level of routine maintenance to prevent progressive deterioration of the equipment;

- a significant amount of corrective maintenance to locate and rectify faults after they had occurred.

The job of maintenance technician required considerable manual dexterity as well as a good understanding of the engineering principles behind the system. The necessary skills and expertise were often gained after many years' experience – often in the same exchange, and even on the same area of equipment! Junior technicians usually assisted senior technicians, especially in routine maintenance, and also gained experience in corrective maintenance on-the-job. Traditionally, junior technicians had a good chance of being promoted to senior technicians by their mid- to late twenties.

Supervisors were typically promoted from the ranks of senior technicians after several years of maintenance experience. They therefore had an intimate knowledge of the work of their subordinates. However, work was usually organised so that senior technicians took an (often strictly demarcated) individual responsibility for both routine and corrective maintenance of a specific area of exchange equipment. In effect this meant that as long as performance targets were met senior technicians enjoyed considerable individual autonomy in the day-to-day organisation of their own jobs. In the course of time a series of bureaucratic guidelines had been developed at national level. These governed maintenance procedures and the use of computers to monitor exchange performance. It was these guidelines, rather than the exchange supervisor, which set the parameters of day-to-day decision making. As a result, the Strowger supervisor's job had been reduced to mainly administrative tasks, such as:

– collecting and collating performance information;

– completing time-sheets;

– scheduling days off.

However, the fact that all the supervisors had previously worked themselves as maintenance technicians, was an important symbol of their authority. If there was a major technical problem they could understand the nature of the difficulty and advise on solutions. They could also counsel junior technicians, and advise on their progress.

The TXE4 system, however, had relatively few moving parts; these, moreover, were more reliable, requiring little routine maintenance. However, the operation of the exchange was controlled and monitored by complex electronic equipment, which provided information on faults. To correct faults, maintenance technicians no longer required the manual skills and understanding associated with Strowger mainten-ance; instead they needed:

– a systems approach;

– highly developed diagnostic skills in order to interpret information and correct faults.

The retraining requirements for maintenance technicians emphasised this complexity. Over a two-year period they had to complete 17 weeks of formal courses at BT's national technical training centre. This training was supplemented within telephone areas by post-course 'hands-on' experience in operational or nearly operational TXE4 exchanges. Significantly, national management did not envisage any changes in the skill requirements or job of exchange supervisors. As a result, they were given only a short technical appreciation course.

THE INTRODUCTION OF TXE4 IN THREE TELEPHONE AREAS

The remainder of this case describes how management in three separate *telephone areas* – 'Coast', 'Metro' and 'Town' – tried to achieve more efficient use of labour, in pursuit of the corporate objectives behind modernisation. It also shows how managers, unions and maintenance staff set about applying the national agreement on staffing. The following examines how the outcomes of change as experienced by maintenance staff in a *single exchange* within each telephone area were affected by these local decisions.

The Coast Area

The Coast Area, on the south coast of England, included one medium-sized town, a number of smaller towns and a spread of semi-rural communities. In this area, staffing levels for new exchanges were decided unilaterally by management without consulting staff or unions. Levels were set in accordance with the national agreement, but were increased at local discretion (where appropriate) to take account of the actual circumstances at specific exchanges. The issue of selection for retraining was negotiated with local POEU representatives. The result was a formal agreement on selection by the 'sitting tenant' principle, ie the existing maintenance staff in the exchanges would be given first option to retrain according to their length of service as a senior technician. In effect this meant that only senior technicians were offered a chance to retrain.

The Coast Exchange was situated in a small seaside town. Before modernisation the staffing level was two senior technicians. A junior technician (shared with another exchange) carried out peripheral maintenance work, mainly connecting and disconnecting customers. This work was not affected by modernisation. There was no change in staffing level after modernisation. This was partly because the exchange was one of the first in the area to be converted and management chose to 'overstaff' in order to build up maintenance expertise. In line with the local agreement, the 'sitting tenant' senior technicians were selected for retraining.

Choosing a supervisor for the new exchange was rather less straightforward. At first management planned to choose one person to act as supervisor for all planned TXE4 units within the area. This policy was changed because of a need to reorganise management structures throughout the area in line with the commercial orientation already becoming clear at national level. The requirements of organisational change therefore took precedence over those of technological change. As a result, the Coast Exchange saw four changes of supervisor in the four months before modernisation and the eleven months after it, thanks to successive changes in area management responsibilities!

Naturally maintenance supervisors were left rather confused about their responsibilities in the new TXE4 exchange, and had little influence on the senior technicians' work organisation or the subsequent day-to-day running of the exchange. In fact the senior technicians adopted a form of self-supervised team working. This was similar to the methods they had used as Strowger technicians in that particular exchange, although they now tended to carry out more tasks collaboratively. The job of the junior technician, on the other hand, remained confined to peripheral maintenance work.

The Metro Area

The Metro Area was situated in London. It covered a geographical area best described as an urban sprawl with a touch of greenbelt suburbia. In this area, too, management decided staffing levels unilaterally without consultation, but according to the national guidelines. However, as in Coast Area, criteria for selecting staff to be retrained were agreed at local level with POEU representatives. Again the key criterion for selection was seniority as a 'sitting tenant' senior technician; and again there was no clear policy on the exchange supervisor's role in the new TXE4 exchanges. In many instances the existing supervisors took responsibility with no clear idea of what their role would be either before or after the exchange was brought into service.

The Metro Exchange stood in the High Street of one of the area's main urban centres. After the national agreement had been applied, staffing levels in this exchange were reduced. This was partly because the exchange was among the last in the area to be converted; there was no need to overstaff in order to build up expertise. Before modernisation there had been four senior technicians and two junior technicians, who spent some of their time assisting their senior colleagues in routine and corrective maintenance. After modernisation there were three senior technicians (the fourth had retired) and two junior technicians. However, the juniors could no longer help their senior colleagues with maintenance because – thanks to the seniority principle – they had not been retrained! However, just before the new exchange was brought into service, management found that one of the senior technicians was unable to cope with the new technology. His place was hurriedly taken by the next most senior technician in the area wishing to retrain.

An additional problem was the effect of modernisation on the role of the supervisor. The supervisor at Metro Exchange had worked as a Strowger technician for 14 years, and had spent another 17 as a Strowger supervisor. However, as the modernisation went ahead, and his senior technicians gained the new skills they needed for TXE4 maintenance, the supervisor increasingly withdrew into his administrative role. Once the new exchange was brought into service he left the technicians to allocate and organise their own work, and felt unable to offer any technical support. As he commented:

> TXE4 has, if anything distanced me from the (exchange) floor. Being an old Strowger man, I've only the sketchiest outline of the technology. I can't make a useful engineering contribution. If you've got troubles (ie a technical problem), you feel much happier if you know what you are talking about. I am now purely a paper engineer. On the old exchange system I definitely influenced the actions taken by the technicians. I could look at a problem and say, "Take that course of action", and I knew if it was done properly it

would work. Now I can't say that.

In fact, much as at the Coast Exchange, the senior technicians organised themselves as a self-supervising team, working far more collaboratively than they had on Strowger. However, there was now a strict division of labour between the senior technicians and the junior technician, whose job was restricted to peripheral maintenance work such as connections and disconnections. Indeed, within a few months of the conversion one junior technician resigned. He felt that TXE4 modernisation had downgraded his work and reduced his career prospects.

The Town Area

The Town Area was situated in southern England. Although it contained a number of rural communities, this area was dominated by a large town. In contrast to the Coast and Metro Areas, retraining criteria and staffing levels were both established by unilateral management decision, and accepted *de facto* by the local POEU – there was no consultation or negotiation with staff or unions about selection criteria for retraining. Management decided that the determining factors were to be experience and maturity rather than seniority. Seniority would only become a factor if candidates were otherwise of equal merit. In practice it still tended to be 'sitting tenants' who went for retraining. This, however, reflected the area management policy on manpower. They tried to ensure that exchanges which were likely to be modernised would have appropriate staff even before selection became necessary.

The Town Area, unlike the other areas, developed a clear and coherent policy on the supervisor's role in TXE4 exchanges. In effect this plugged the gap left in the national policy. First, one individual was to take charge of all the new TXE4 exchanges in the Area – and this person took the same retraining course as the technicians he was to supervise. This included hands-on experience, after the course, in new exchanges that were being tested and debugged before coming into service.

The Town Exchange was situated in a residential district of the area's major town. Staffing levels here were unchanged, with a complement of three senior technicians and one junior technician (who was not retrained). The supervisor's experience of change was very different to that of his colleagues in the other two telephone areas. The emphasis on supervisor training meant that he was not distanced from operations on the exchange floor; instead, he found that he could make a larger contribution to the maintenance effort, drawing on his own TXE4 retraining to assist the technicians with complex faults. As he put it himself:

With Strowger it was more of a paperwork and organisational

exercise, whereas in TXE4 that element still exists, but there is more of a technical content as well.

In this case the senior technicians also developed a team approach to work organisation. Although the supervisor took part in initial discussions as to how work should be organised, day-to-day work was still entirely a matter of self-supervision. Again there was a strict demarcation between the largely shared work of the senior technicians and the peripheral tasks of the junior technician.

THE TASK

Your task is to act as a team of management consultants (with four to six people in each team). You have been employed by BT in the light of privatisation to evaluate corporate strategy and national agreements by looking at the effect of TXE4 introduction in the Coast, Metro and Town areas. Your recommendations should take account of the increasing corporate emphasis on commercialism, and include an assessment of any likely implications for industrial relations.

You have been asked to focus on:

1 The industrial-relations aspects of the corporate strategy behind implementation at area level, in particular the national agreement on staffing levels and the job security agreement. In the new commercial environment should management end these agreements and delegate decisions on staffing and selection to local management? If so, what criteria should now be used to select staff for TXE4 retraining?

2 The corporate assumption was that the skill requirements and the job of the maintenance supervisor would not be changed by the introduction of TXE4. In particular, in the new commercial environment, should the job of the supervisor now be redefined? If so, specify the options that corporate management might consider in developing a strategy. Indicate any implications for the pattern of work organisation that has developed in TXE4 exchanges, and any implications for industrial relations.

ACKNOWLEDGEMENT

The authors would like to thank the editors and John Foster for comments on earlier versions of this case.

ESSENTIAL READING

McLoughlin I, Clark J, *Technological Change at Work*, Open University Press, 1988, chapters 2, 3, 5 and 7

ADDITIONAL READING

Batstone E, Ferner A, Terry M, *Consent and Efficiency: Labour Relations and Management Strategy in a State Enterprise*, Blackwell, 1984

Boddy D, Buchanan D, *Managing New Technology*, Blackwell, 1986, chapters 5 and 8

Buchanan D, Management objectives in technical change, in Knights D, Willmott H, eds, *Managing the Labour Process*, Gower, 1986, pp67–84

Child J, Managerial strategies, new technology and the labour process, Knights D et al, eds, *Job Redesign: Critical Perspectives on the Labour Process*, Gower, 1985, pp107–111

Clark J, McLoughlin I, Rose H, King R, *The Process of Technological Change*, Cambridge University Press, 1988, chapters 2, 3, 4 and 6

Dawson P, McLoughlin I, Organisational choice in the redesign of supervisory systems, in Boddy D et al, eds, *The New Management Challenge: Information Systems for Improved Performance*, Croom Helm, 1988, chapter 9

McLoughlin I P, Rose H, Clark J, Managing the introduction of new technology, *Omega*, 1985, vol 13, no 4

Rothwell S, Supervisors and new technology, in Rhodes E, Wield D, (eds) *Implementing New Technologies: Choice, Decision and Change in Manufacturing*, Blackwell, 1985

19 New technology and bargaining: The *Evening News*

Mike Noon

BACKGROUND

The *Evening News* is a large provincial UK newspaper with a daily circulation of over 140,000 copies. It was established in the late 19th century, and in the early 1970s was bought up by the media giant Combined Publications plc. In common with most of the regional daily press, the *Evening News* operates as a local monopoly – it has no daily competitors, but does face competition from several paid-for weekly newspapers and numerous free newspapers (one of which it owns itself). This weekly competition has been increasing over the last ten years, largely as a result of cheaper production methods becoming available. Consequently, the *Evening News* has seen its share of the market being slowly eroded on two fronts:

- Fewer people are buying the *Evening News*: they can read most of the stories in at least one of the free newspapers, or the paid-for weekly titles.

- Many advertisers have become more cautious of their advertising budgets over recent years, and are now looking at other sources to advertise their products, for example the free newspapers, radio commercials, posters, leaflets, and magazines.

These two factors have led to a decline in sales of the *Evening News* and a drop in revenue from advertisers – the two sources of income for a newspaper.

The changing market experience of the *Evening News* is far from unique: other newspapers across the country are facing similar problems. The solution that many have adopted is to alter the production process by introducing new technology. This has two outstanding advantages:

- It streamlines production by reducing the need for print workers, thereby saving labour costs.

- It improves the efficiency and effectiveness of the existing staff, by getting them to learn new skills and accept new working practices.

239

Most newspapers have some form of new technology in operation, but the latest development is the computerised editorial system. It is called *direct input*, because once information has been typed into the system it is altered, edited, rejigged, set and otherwise processed via VDU screens. Under the old system, print workers would input the stories, font sizes, typefaces, headline sizes, and so forth. Direct input makes many of their traditional craft skills redundant.

The managers of the *Evening News* saw direct input as the way forward, and they have invested £1.5 million in the technology. In 1983 a research working party of managers and production supervisors was set up. They investigated a number of systems in operation in Europe and the United States, and recommended the Newstext direct input system. The board of directors of the *Evening News* accepted the recommendations, but because of the size of the investment they had to get approval from the directors of Combined Publications in London. When the project received the official go-ahead, the managers placed an order with Newstext and set out a timetable for a phased introduction of the system. Phase one was the computerisation of the production department (1984), phase two was the introduction of a front-end direct input advertising system (1985), and phase three the addition of a front-end direct input editorial system (1987). The first two phases went as planned, and included preliminary negotiations with the print unions about future staffing reductions. Phase three proved to be problematic.

THE INTEREST GROUPS

The employees most affected by phase three are the journalists and the print workers. Journalists will be expected to operate the new technology, so they will have to learn new skills and adapt to new working practices. The print workers, on the other hand, will be faced with huge job losses because the new technology makes most of their jobs redundant.

The journalists

There are 103 journalists at the *Evening News*; 100 of them are members of the National Union of Journalists (NUJ), and the other three are members of the Institute of Journalists (IoJ) – a tiny professional association that rejects all forms of industrial action. The NUJ structure is rather quaint: it divides its membership into 'chapels' at the various workplaces. Thus the journalists at the *Evening News* are members of the *Evening News* NUJ Chapel. The shop steward is called the Father of the Chapel (FoC) or Mother of the Chapel (MoC).

The NUJ at national level has devised a set of policies to help the chapels negotiate the introduction of direct input, and suggests that each chapel negotiates a new technology agreement (NTA) with the management. It has also published a number of booklets to enlighten members about the hazards and the advantages of direct input. As a result, the *Evening News* chapel was very well informed, and early in 1986 they invited the regional NUJ officer to one of their meetings to give them a talk on what to expect from new technology. He warned them how managers at other newspapers had tried to introduce direct input 'on the cheap'. He told them:

> The one thing you can be sure of is that they'll cut corners. They're spending over a million on the equipment, so they'll make every saving possible when it comes to installing it. If you want extra money for using the new system, a good working environment with specially designed office furniture, ventilation and lighting, and good working practices, then you've got to be ready for some hard bargaining, and you've got to stand firm.

After this pep talk the chapel was generally more optimistic about the advantages that direct input could bring. The journalists saw the opportunity of getting management to refit the office, and so improve their surroundings. More importantly, they felt that new technology provided them with an ideal opportunity to improve their pay. There was discontent about the wages at the *Evening News*, not least because the editorial staff were low down the Combined Publications' league table of journalists' average pay, yet the newspaper was near the top of the profitability league table.

The print workers

If the journalists were optimistic, then the print workers were clearly pessimistic. Direct input could mean only one thing for them: redundancy. They realised that their skills were no longer needed, and knew that the halcyon days of yesteryear, when the print workers could demand high wages through their pervasive influence over the production process, were finally over.

In the past their power had stemmed from the fact that they were a pre-entry closed shop, with a long apprenticeship system and control over a crucial part of the production process. For example, stopping work for an hour to hold a chapel meeting would delay the newspaper, cause disruption and possibly lead to the loss of an edition – and a consequent loss of profit for the company. The new technology was therefore attractive to managers. Besides streamlining production by eliminating the need for most print workers, it also wiped out the powerful print union: the National Graphical Association (NGA).

The print workers at the *Evening News* were relying on handsome redundancy payments. They were confident about getting good redundancy terms because management needed the cooperation of the printers in the transition to full direct input. The system was being introduced gradually, so they would be needed during the bedding-in period. At least a residual group of printers would have to be retained to provide a backup until the system had been debugged.

The management

The *Evening News* has its own board of directors who are responsible for all decisions at local level. However, financial constraints are set by the provincial newspapers division of Combined Publications, and three members of the group board are also on the *Evening News* board. The hierarchy is illustrated in Figure 19.1.

THE UNION JOINT ACCORD

Traditionally there was no love lost between the two unions; both had accused the other of crossing their picket lines in the past. However, at national level the unions' executive officers decided that it would be in the best interest of all members if the two unions forgot their differences and worked together over the issue of direct input. They were convinced about the wisdom of this by events at the UK's first two provincial newspapers to introduce direct input: in both cases the managers had exploited the unions' differences by playing one union off against the other. So in October 1985 the general secretaries of the NUJ and the NGA signed a joint accord, advocating that NUJ and NGA chapels at provincial newspapers negotiate jointly with management over new technology.

The *Evening News* chapels decided to hold a joint meeting to see how to interpret this at local level. After some initial mistrust from both sides, it was decided that when negotiations began over new technology, both chapels would insist on being involved at every stage of negotiations. In short, they would be following the national joint accord to the letter.

NEGOTIATIONS BEGIN

In August 1986, management sent an internal memo to all staff members saying that they were aiming to have a direct input editorial system 'going live' on Monday February 9, 1987. On October 10 the NUJ and the NGA were invited by the managing director to a preliminary meeting with all the management to discuss the introduction of the system. They were briefed by the editor and production director on how they envisaged the system would be used, the dates at which various stages would become operational, and the overall plan of how it would affect the production process. The union representatives were encouraged to put forward their views and bring their concerns about the use of the system into the open. The NGA raised the issue of redundancy, while the NUJ raised questions about the working practices and new skills they would be expected to learn.

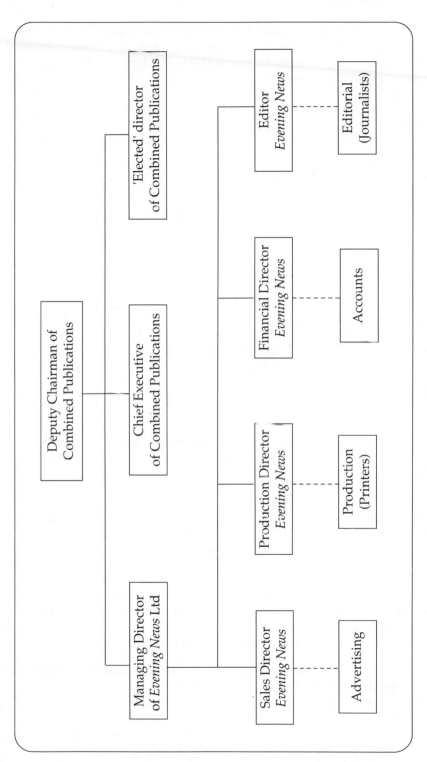

Figure 19.1 The *Evening News* Board of Directors

As all sides expected, nothing was resolved at this initial meeting. The unions, however, were particularly pleased, and at a joint meeting afterwards reported to their members the issues that had been raised. The NUJ FoC later commented:

> We felt that the joint approach had got off to a good start. We [the union representatives] were backing each other up in the meeting, and it was a good way of getting an overview of what management were doing.

Indeed, this satisfaction also appeared to be shared by the editor. The next day he wrote a memo for the noticeboard, saying that he felt the meeting was productive, and a useful start to the discussions about direct input.

Six days later, however, after a board meeting, the union officers received a letter from the managing director, which stated:

> Although the preliminary meeting provided a useful basis for discussion, I feel it would be in the interest of all concerned if in future separate meetings take place between the NUJ and the editor, and between the NGA and the production manager. I was persuaded to hold the initial joint meeting against my better judgement, and feel that such an arrangement will cause future negotiations to be unnecessarily cumbersome and time-consuming.

The union officers were astounded by the letter, especially since a few days earlier the editor seemed in favour of joint meetings. The FoC commented:

> It was obvious what had happened. The managers were being told what to do from above. The joint meeting had obviously not been okayed by the bosses at Combined Publications. We then realised that they were the ones we were really negotiating with.

The two unions held an immediate joint chapel meeting, and the members voted against agreeing to separate negotiations. They were determined to stick by the accord. Their decision was forwarded to management, and the editor told the NUJ FoC that he would not countenance joint meetings. He later commented:

> The initial joint discussion was useful, but it would have been hopeless to conduct negotiations jointly. It would have introduced complications where none need have existed. Our management view was that it was a silly situation – why should we honour the accord between the NUJ and the NGA, since we were not party to it in the first place?

DEADLOCK

Over the next few months communications were exchanged but there was no movement from either side. Meanwhile journalists in the IoJ agreed to start training on the new equipment, and in December they began to use VDUs. The NUJ position was that no training should start until a new technology agreement had been signed covering all aspects of direct input; any NUJ member who agreed to start training would be disciplined by the union. This situation infuriated the editor, and on January 9, a month before the system was supposed to go live, he wrote to all the NUJ members at their home addresses. The letter emphasised that the deadline was fast approaching, that journalists would be expected to use the new technology on February 9, and that any individual refusing to use the system after that date would be in breach of contract and could be dismissed.

A special chapel meeting was called, and a number of the journalists expressed concern that the negotiations had not yet started. Some suggested that the chapel abandon the joint agreement with the NGA, fearing that it would scupper their chances of getting a good deal from management. After the meeting the union officers contacted their head offices, and after further meetings they were advised to suggest a 'compromise' solution to management: that separate negotiations should be held, but that an 'observer' from the other union should be present. This was acceptable to all sides, and the first negotiations began on February 2.

NEGOTIATIONS RESTART

The NGA–management negotiations progressed very rapidly, largely because the redundancy payments offered were very generous and the chapel was not prepared for a fight. Within two days an agreement had been reached.

The NUJ–management negotiations were far more problematic. The first two days went fairly smoothly, and although there was some hard bargaining, agreement was reached over many of the health and safety issues connected with direct input, and the modifications to existing working practices. However, deadlock was reached over the two crucial issues for journalists operating a direct input system: screen breaks and new technology pay.

The screen break issue was concerned with how long a journalist should be expected to work on a VDU screen before being allowed to take a break. The NUJ argued that research in other countries had shown that working for long periods on screen was detrimental to health in a number of ways:

- It was damaging to eyesight, because it involved staring into a bright screen at a fixed focal length.

- It led to various aches and pains, because journalists had to remain sitting at the desk in a fixed posture.

- It created feelings of isolation, because a VDU obscured a large part of a journalist's field of vision, and therefore reduced eye contact and verbal exchange.

According to the NUJ, the remedy for these potential hazards was to allow journalists a 15-minute break away from screen after every 75 minutes of continuous work.

The managers accepted the NUJ's concern over these issues, but felt the research evidence was far from conclusive. They argued that statutory breaks were unnecessary, because the work involved 'natural breaks'; however, they did suggest a statutory break after two hours of continuous screen work. Privately the editor was particularly worried about the potential disruption to production deadlines if journalists were given the right to leave the screen at regular intervals. He feared that screen breaks might be used by the NUJ as an industrial sanction designed to disrupt the newspaper, much as the NGA had done when they had held chapel meetings at key production times.

The second issue was technology pay. The NUJ saw the introduction of new technology as a chance to negotiate significant increases in the basic pay of journalists. The *Evening News* was a particularly 'low payer' among the provincial newspapers, so the NUJ chapel members were keen to take the opportunity to improve their wages. NUJ policy was that all journalists in the chapel should receive the same new technology pay. Although photographers would not be using the new technology, they were also to receive new technology pay because they would have to comply with any changes in working practices that the new system might bring about (eg the introduction of new deadlines). The journalists were therefore looking for an across-the-board payment of £32 per person per week.

The editor accepted that the journalists should receive an increase in salary for learning new skills and operating the new technology, but could see no reason why the photographers should be given technology pay, since they would not be touching the new equipment. He therefore agreed to negotiate a sum of money for the journalists, but said that such negotiations would not cover the photographers.

The NUJ officers felt that they needed extra support, so they requested a negotiator from NUJ head office. The next day (February 4) the deputy general secretary of the NUJ arrived and led the negotiations. After some hard bargaining, the editor decided to reappraise his position, and offered £19 per week extra technology pay for journalists and £13 per week extra for photographers.

This was a clear improvement, but was still not acceptable to the NUJ. After further negotiating sessions tempers began to rise, and deadlock was reached as both sides refused to budge. The NUJ called a chapel meeting for 6 pm on February 6, when the officers were to advise the membership not to accept the management's offer. However, ten minutes before the meeting the editor gave the FoC a revised new technology pay offer: £21 for journalists and £13 for photographers. This came as a complete surprise to the union officers, who had been told by the editor during the negotiating sessions that there was no possibility of more money than had already been offered.

The chapel meeting lasted for over three hours, with some very heated exchanges between chapel members. Eventually a vote was taken and the members rejected the offer by 93 votes to 6. The FoC later commented:

> If anything, the new pay offer aggravated the chapel. They saw it as an attempt to split the chapel and buy off the journalists. The offer should have been put during the negotiations, not slipped in afterwards. The editor failed to see our point of view; he just wanted to save as much money as possible to impress the bosses at Combined Publications head office.

> We were happy to accept the new technology, we weren't Luddites, but we wanted a share in the benefits it would bring, especially since it was us who would have to alter our working practices and accept new working conditions. If management hadn't been so obstinate about the joint negotiations then things could have been sorted out long before the training deadline. We had signed a joint accord with the NGA, so it really became a matter of principle for us.

The editor saw things in a very different light. He commented:

> Essentially it all boiled down to greed. The journalists wanted as much money as possible and were determined to go to whatever lengths. Even when I offered them extra money as a final gesture of goodwill to avoid a confrontation, it was twisted by some of the more unscrupulous union members to give the impression I was attempting to undermine the chapel. It was the NUJ's fault for refusing to negotiate. Months were wasted before they saw reason.

D-DAY: FEBRUARY 9

The deadline for the system to go live arrived, and five people were selected by the editor to start training: the two assistant editors, the features editor, the chief subeditor and the deputy chief subeditor. Next to the editor, they were the most senior members of staff. They received letters by the internal mail informing them that they were to report for training at 2 pm that afternoon. The FoC claims that these five people were selected for political reasons. He commented:

> The editor knew that these people would have the most to lose in terms of their careers. He selected them hoping they would all start training and break the solidarity of the chapel.

The editor denies there was any ulterior motive in selecting the journalists:

> The most senior members were selected because we needed the heads of departments to know from the start how the system operated. This was important, because as soon as a journalist walked away from the desk to start training, a VDU was installed so they never reverted to the old system.

The two assistant editors immediately resigned from the NUJ and began training to use the new technology. The other three refused to start training, and were all given letters by the editor which warned them that, if they did not agree to begin training within 48 hours, they would be given the sack. The NUJ called an immediate mandatory disruptive meeting to offer moral support to the three members selected for training, and began to consider industrial action.

The FoC contacted the editor at the end of the meeting, and they both agreed to a 24-hour 'ceasefire' to let tempers cool. They set up a meeting for February 10 to try to resolve their differences.

QUESTIONS

Questions 1 to 5 are suitable for discussion sessions lasting one to two hours. Question 6 needs far more detailed consideration with reference to theoretical material. It is suitable for small group discussions or individual written answers.

1 Suggest possible compromises over technology pay, screen breaks and training that might be acceptable to both sides when they meet on February 10.

2 What measures earlier on could have taken by (a) management and (b) the unions to avoid the deadlock and imminent confrontation?

3 The editor and the FoC have very different interpretations of the situation. With whom do you agree more? Why do these interpretations differ? Consider the pressures and constraints that they were under, and to whom they were accountable.

```
1986
August        —   Unions told of new technology deadline
October 10    —   Joint meeting between NUJ, NGA and
                  managers
October 11    —   Editor writes memo to noticeboard
October 17    —   MD writes letters to unions re: joint
                  negotiations


1987
January 9     —   Editor writes to NUJ members at home
                  addresses
February 2    —   Negotiations begin
February 3    —   Provisional issues settled
February 4    —   NUJ Deputy General Secretary brought in
February 5    —   Deadlock over screen breaks and pay
February 6    —   Deadlock: Chapel meeting rejects offer
February 9    —   Editor writes to first five people to train
              —   Two of them begin training, three refuse
              —   Editor threatens 'refuseniks' with sack
              —   NUJ Chapel meeting supports 'refuseniks'
Febuary 10    —   24-hour 'cease fire'
              —   Meeting set up between NUJ and Editor
```

Figure 19.1   The Chronology of Key Events

4 From your impressions about the attitudes of the two sides, try to predict what happened during the next 24 hours.

5 The *Evening Clarion* is also owned by Combined Publications plc, and it too is about to invest in a direct input system:

    (a) Imagine you are a management consultant. What advice could you give to the *Clarion*'s management team from your knowledge of the *Evening News*?

    (b) Imagine you are the NUJ regional officer. How would you attempt to conduct negotiations at the *Clarion* in the light of what happened at the *Evening News*?

6 How would you describe the management style of the *Evening News* editor? Suggest alternative styles of management that could be adopted in introducing technical change. Explain the circumstances under which each of your suggestions would be most and least appropriate.

ESSENTIAL READING

Child J, Managerial strategies, new technology and the labour process, in Knights D, Willmott H, Collinson D, eds, *Job Redesign: Critical Perspectives on the Labour Process*, Gower, 1985

Daniel W W, *Workplace Industrial Relations and Technical Change*, Pinter, 1987

Dodgson M, Martin R, Trade-union policies on new technology: Facing the challenges of the 1980s, *New Technology, Work and Employment*, 1987, vol 2, no 1

McLoughlin I, Clark J, *Technological Change at Work*, Open University Press, 1988

ADDITIONAL READING

Buchanan D, Boddy D, *Organisations in the Computer Age: Technological Imperatives and Strategic Choice*, Gower, 1983

Marginson P, Edwards P K, Martin R et al, *Beyond the Workplace: Managing Industrial Relations in Multi-plant Enterprises*, Blackwell, 1988

Purcell J, Sisson K, Strategies and practice in the management of industrial relations, in Bain G S, ed, *Industrial Relations in Britain*, Blackwell, 1983

Willman P, *New Technology and Industrial Relations: A Review of the Literature* (Research Paper No 56), DoE, 1987

20 Negotiating the introduction of digital exchange systems in British Telecom

Jon Clark and Ian McLoughlin

ORGANISATIONAL SETTING

This case examines how the introduction of electronic telephone exchanges in British Telecom was managed and negotiated in the late 1980s and early 1990s. BT provides an integrated network of local and trunk (national) exchanges and transmission lines for both business and residential customers. For much of this century this service has been the responsibility of the (General) Post Office, but in 1981 the postal and telecommunications businesses were split. BT was established as an independent public corporation to provide the basic telecommunications infrastructure service. At the same time the Telecommunications Act 1981 opened up some areas of BT's activities to market competition. Then in 1984 BT was 'privatised': the government sold 51% of its shares to private investors.

For many years now, and particularly since privatisation, BT's corporate management has attempted to introduce a more commercial, market-orientated approach to the business. Among other things this has involved giving greater priority to the demands of its large business customers. BT is now under permanent public scrutiny. Since 1984 its activities have been regulated by a national Office of Telecommunications (Oftel), and it is known that influential members of the Conservative Party wish to open it up to further competition, and even break it up into regional companies if it fails to increase efficiency and improve customer service. BT national management is therefore subject to a number of conflicting pressures: from government, Oftel, the media, shareholders, customers and, of course, from its trade unions and staff.

BT has well over 200,000 staff. There is a long-established tradition of centralised bargaining over basic terms and conditions of employment, high trade union membership, and management–union cooperation over the introduction of new technology. The tradition of cooperative industrial relations was clearly reflected in a 1980 national agreement with the largest union in the industry, the Post Office Engineering Union (now the National Communications Union). Under the

251

agreement, management agreed there would be no compulsory redundancies, and the union agreed to cooperate with the planned introduction of new technology and the provision of high-quality customer
service.

In 1984, however, the director of personnel announced a major shift in
the corporate approach to industrial relations. This included:

- a restructuring of pay and grading;
- the devolution of wide areas of bargaining and consultation
  (excluding basic pay) to the local level;
- a reduction in staffing levels.

In 1985 BT abolished one major tier of its management structure,
reorganised its 61 telephone areas into fewer than 30 'districts', each
with greater autonomy, and cut down the numbers of staff working in
national headquarters. Later that year, district general managers were
urged to reduce staff numbers, examine all existing arrangements with
the unions and change any practices they felt were no longer consistent
with running the business efficiently. These changes in commercial
structure and management approach coincided with important innovations in information technology, which permitted new developments in
the management of telecommunications services. In short, for managers
and staff in BT, the 1980s were a decade in which traditional approaches
and practices were under almost continuous challenge.

BACKGROUND TO THE CASE

The theme of this case study is the introduction of a new electronic
telephone exchange system known as 'System X'. The exercise for
students which follows the case study concerns the implementation of
the System X modernisation programme at district level in BT, looking
in particular at negotiations over the design and organisation of System
X maintenance work.

The term 'System X' was coined in the early 1970s by a team of engineers
from the Post Office and the three main exchange equipment suppliers
(GEC, Plessey and STC) engaged in designing a viable, fully electronic
exchange system. 'X' represented the problem to be solved. The System
X design, completed by the mid-1970s, uses a modular approach. Each
exchange unit is assembled from a selection of hardware and software
'building blocks'. This means that the system can continue to evolve
over time, and use can be made of new technologies as they become
available and cost-effective. For example, with advances in micro-
processor technology the physical size of the processor area within the
overall system was reduced by a factor of 13 between the mid-1970s and
mid-1980s, and its processing power was increased fourfold in the same
period.

The use of microelectronics and computer processing techniques in the design also means that the program running the exchange system can be stored in the form of software. This makes it possible to alter many functions performed by the exchange from a remote computer terminal. The flexibility provided by the software components of the system means that new voice and non-voice services (text, data, graphics) can be added and connected without major changes in the exchange hardware. It also allows information about the performance of the exchange and faults in the system to be accessed from remote terminals outside the exchange building. All this has major implications for exchange maintenance.

Maintenance is an essential activity within the exchange network. For calls to be switched effectively, the equipment which effects the switching must be kept in satisfactory working order. The main exchange system which System X is intended to replace was named after its designer, Almon Brown Strowger, a Kansas City undertaker. Until his design was patented in 1891, telephone calls had to be switched manually by switchboard operators. Legend has it that Strowger was driven to find a way of automating the process when he learned that a corrupt local switchboard operator, the wife of his main competitor in Kansas City, had been systematically switching calls meant for Strowger to her husband!

In the 1920s Strowger's design was adopted by the Post Office as the standard automatic exchange system for Britain. By 1970 it completely dominated the network. The Strowger system is driven by electrical contacts and composed of several thousand moving mechanical parts, all of which are affected by dirt, wear, breakage and misalignment. It thus requires large amounts of routine maintenance to prevent progressive deterioration of the equipment. When faults do occur, their location and diagnosis also demand substantial amounts of detective work. Over the years automatic equipment has been developed which can be bolted on to the Strowger system to assist maintenance technicians in 'faulting'. Even so, the system still requires regular, sustained, skilled human intervention in diagnosis and repair.

About 50% of Strowger maintenance is of a routine, preventive kind, so most work can be done during a single daytime shift, with emergency cover and overtime at nights and weekends if required. For some technicians, call-outs and overtime are a useful and regular source of supplementary income, amounting to 15–20% on top of basic pay. Most of this work goes to senior technician (technical officer) grades; in terms of pay, qualifications and status, these people are the elite of BT's engineering technician workforce, and constitute the vast majority of exchange maintenance technicians. Within general guidelines and targets senior technicians are used to working autonomously on their own block of exchange equipment without direct supervision. Junior maintenance technicians (T2As) do much of the less complex engineering work in the exchanges, such as connecting new customers to the network, but they have traditionally had a good chance of being promoted to the senior technician grade by their late 20s.

Since the early 1970s, a number of new semi-electronic exchange systems (called TXE2 and TXE4) have been introduced. These reduced the amount of necessary maintenance; even so, corrective and preventive maintenance were still carried out almost exclusively by technicians working full-time in individual telephone exchanges. So were other activities, such as connecting new customers and reading meters. The working practices of maintenance staff are a direct product of this long-established tradition of exchange-based, labour-intensive daytime maintenance. So is the role of exchange supervisors, who are somewhat remote from day-to-day maintenance and chiefly occupied with administrative and staff management duties. However, there are now several important challenges to this traditional system of exchange working:

- The System X exchange design has new technical capabilities.

- There is strong political pressure on BT to improve efficiency.

- Corporate management aims to be more commercial in its approach.

Management are also committed to a substantial reduction in their very high maintenance costs – and these costs chiefly arise from the large numbers of maintenance staff.

In fact, the programme of System X modernisation was intended to come full stream in the early 1980s. It was delayed because of a series of major technical problems with the system software. During this period British Telecom decided to hedge its bets by placing orders for a second source of digital exchange equipment (immediately dubbed 'System Y') from the Swedish company Thorn Ericsson. By late 1985, however, the software problems had been solved. By 1987, after a major production effort by the equipment manufacturers (GEC and Plessey), the new exchange equipment was available in large numbers. This put strong pressure on district managements to introduce an accelerated programme of System X (and some System Y) implementation so that all the remaining Strowger systems could be replaced by the early 1990s.

The speedy and successful implementation of the System X modernisation programme is crucial to BT's future commercial strategy. Digital exchanges promise to provide a better quality of exchange line with many fewer faults, but they are also the focal point of plans to create an integrated services digital network (ISDN), through which customers will have direct access to an ever-increasing range of data and voice telecommunications services.

THE PROBLEM

District A is about to begin a major programme of System X exchange modernisation. The aim is completely to replace the district's 75 staffed Strowger local exchanges within five years.

At present there are around 250 maintenance technicians (mainly senior technicians) based in these exchanges. They work a nine-day fortnight on a day shift, with emergency call-outs when required. There is a significant amount of overtime. This, together with standby payments and emergency call-out payments, amounts to an average of 15% of total earnings for senior technicians. Despite union pressure, there are no national staffing standards for System X exchanges. However, everyone expects that staffing will be massively reduced by comparison with all other existing systems. A report by stockbrokers Scrimgeour, Kemp-Gee and Co has predicted that the maintenance requirements for System X exchanges will be between four and five times less than for an equivalent Strowger unit.

Exchange staff and their unions generally accept that System X maintenance will be controlled centrally, through an operations and maintenance centre (OMC). Two OMCs are planned for District A. All the district's System X exchanges will be technically linked to one of these OMCs, and information about faults in particular units will be conveyed automatically to a kind of 'mission control room' in the OMC. It has not yet been determined who will interpret and use this information. However, it is likely that a trained engineer (either a senior technician or a first-line manager) will make an initial diagnosis of the cause of the fault, and decide whether it can be rectified automatically or requires a site visit.

District management has not announced whether or not they feel that the larger System X exchanges should be permanently staffed by maintenance technicians. However, it is generally accepted that management will want to move control of maintenance operations away from the exchange floor to the OMC. The pooling of staff in the OMC would allow management greater flexibility in their deployment as, when and where required (on the fire brigade model). It is also expected that management will wish to staff the OMCs on a 24-hour basis, so reducing the need for emergency call-outs.

Finally, national management is known to be encouraging district managements to change the existing high ratio of senior to junior technicians in exchange maintenance. This assumes that many faults in digital exchange systems will be diagnosed automatically, so only low levels of skill will be required to put them right. (An example would be replacing a faulty plug-in unit and sending it off to a centralised repair centre.) Changing the ratio of seniors to juniors will clearly make an important contribution to reducing the maintenance costs.

The national union view is that System X maintenance jobs should be designed so that technicians are allocated responsibility for one or more exchanges, perhaps on a rotating basis. On-site maintenance should be allowed to the maximum possible extent. The union fears that centralised control of maintenance will lead to the deskilling of maintenance work: routine maintenance tasks will be carried out directly from the OMC, while more difficult faults will be diagnosed and rectified by sending the faulty piece of equipment to a specialised repair centre. This, it is argued, would reduce job satisfaction among technologies represent a challenge to the traditional divisions of labour into clearly demarcated work tasks, blurring distinctions between traditional occupational categories.

Q: What's the staffing level for a System X exchange?

A: One man and a dog.

Q: What's the dog for?

A: To make sure the man doesn't touch the equipment.

Q: What's the man for?

A: To feed the dog.

Against this background, the union is keen that System X maintenance jobs should be graded as highly skilled senior technician work, and it is likely to resist an increase in the proportion of junior technicians working on exchange maintenance.

One final problem is likely to cause some dispute. Apart from a 'control room' dealing with exchange maintenance information, the new OMC buildings will almost certainly contain other computer-based support systems operated by clerical and administrative staff. Parallel to exchange modernisation, BT is also introducing a computer-based customer service system (CSS) across the country. This is intended to provide a common database on all aspects of customer service, including bills, equipment sales and installations, fault records and maintenance. Technically it will be possible for clerical staff to have access to all aspects of the database, including fault, maintenance and meter records. This means that clerical staff using remote computer terminals will be able to carry out a number of activities that were previously carried out by exchange-based maintenance technicians. These include connecting and disconnecting customers, and taking meter readings. Management is known to want flexibility for clerical staff to carry out this work.

This is likely to present a major problem for the union. Until 1985 BT clerical staff were organised in a civil-service union – the Civil and Public Services Association. In that year, however, their membership was transferred to the engineering-dominated POEU. The POEU was then renamed the National Communications Union (NCU). On the positive side, the NCU now organises the vast majority of non-management grades in BT, and thus faces the challenge of new technology without the fear of inter-union rivalries so common in other sectors.

However, there is still some degree of distrust between engineering (known colloquially as the 'oilies') and clerical (known as the 'inkies') grades. Both may have legitimate claims to carry out a number of work tasks which were previously carried out by separate occupational groups (engineering technicians and clerical workers) in separate workplaces (telephone exchanges or offices). New computer-based technologies represent a challenge to the traditional divisions of labour into clearly demarcated work tasks, blurring distinctions between traditional occupational categories.

THE TASK

The class should be divided into management and union groups and draw up a negotiating strategy. They should outline their objectives for the new System X maintenance organisation and its introduction in District A.

In drawing up their strategy, they should make a clear distinction between what they would ideally like to achieve on a wide range of issues (which will form the basis of their opening position in the negotiation) and their most important priorities – the three or four minimum requirements they hope to achieve. The teacher's notes provide some additional information, which will be given to each group separately. If it is not possible to carry out a roleplay exercise, students should prepare background papers for management and/or union negotiators outlining a range of policy objectives (opening position) and identifying the most important priorities among them.

Some of the issues arising will be:

- the time scale for the full implementation of the System X programme;
- staffing levels, and how to deal with job losses;
- the senior/junior technician ratio on System X maintenance, and the question of skill distribution;
- location of technicians in OMCs and/or individual exchanges;
- shift work;
- the nine-day fortnight;

- loss of overtime, standby and call-out payments;

- job demarcations between engineering and clerical/computer staff;

- responsibility for work allocation in the OMC (first-line managers or designated senior technicians).

ESSENTIAL READING

Clark J, McLoughlin I, Rose H, King R, *The Process of Technological Change*, Cambridge University Press, 1988, chapters 2 and 7

McLoughlin I, Clark J, *Technological Change at Work*, Open University Press, 1988, chapters 2, 4, 6 and 8

ADDITIONAL READING

Batstone E, Ferner A, Terry M, *Consent and Efficiency: Labour Relations and Management Strategy in a State Enterprise*, Blackwell, 1984, chapters 7 and 9

Clark J, Jacobs A, King R, Rose H, New technology, industrial relations and divisions within the workforce, *Industrial Relations Journal*, 1984, vol 15, no 3, pp36–44

Dodgson M, Martin R, Trade-union policies on new technology: Facing the challenge of the 1980s, *New Technology, Work and Employment*, 1987, vol 2, no 1, pp9–18

Price R, Information, consultation and the control of new technology, in Hyman R, Streeck W, eds, *New Technology and Industrial Relations*, Blackwell, 1988, pp249–262

Salaman M, Negotiation, in *Industrial Relations: Theory and Practice*, Prentice-Hall, 1987, pp434–454

ACKNOWLEDGEMENT

The authors would like to acknowledge the advice and support of Philip Vernon and Howard Rose in the preparation of this case study.

21 Selecting a computer system for New Times Medical Centre

Mike Fitter

INTRODUCTION

> We've really got to make a decision by the end of the month. I'm fed up with all the dithering. We need a computer now, and we've got the opportunity to get one at a special price.

So spoke Dr Rush, general practitioner and junior partner at New Times Medical Centre.

The medical centre provides a service to 8000 patients in Peasborough, a medium-sized market town. It is staffed by Dr Rush and his three partners, a practice nurse, and six part-time administrative staff (clerks and receptionists).

The case study involves a roleplaying exercise about the possible introduction of a computer system into New Times Medical Centre. It is based on specific developments in primary health care computing. In this sense it is a 'generic' case study, reflecting many relevant current issues in general practice, and the process of introducing new information technology into small service organisations.

BACKGROUND TO PRIMARY HEALTH CARE IN THE UK

Since the establishment of the National Health Service in 1948, general medical practice has steadily shifted from single-handed GPs working from a surgery in their homes to purpose-built medical centres managed by a partnership of as many as twelve or more doctors. Four GPs is a typical partnership size. The increase in size provides the usual benefits of 'economies of scale', such as:

- shared resources (equipment, specialist and administrative staff, etc);

- the opportunity to share expertise and provide 'cover' to other partners' patients.

In fact, although each partner retains a formal list of patients who are registered with them, in practice patients can usually choose which doctor they consult.

The growth of organisational size also creates the usual potential difficulties, such as:

- the need to manage an increasingly complex organisation;

- the need for effective coordination of activities between GPs.

It is here that the introduction of a computer system has the most to offer, as a tool for supporting the management of information in the practice. As business partners, the GPs are responsible for the ancillary staff whom they employ (nursing and administrative staff). Thus GPs have dual roles as managers of the organisation and as doctors for individual patients.

Potential conflicts between these two roles have been brought into sharper focus by the 1989 government white paper on the Health Service, and by the medical profession's response to it. Taken together, the proposals in the white paper foreshadow a major transition towards a more performance-related financial assessment of the quality of health-care delivery. This requires quantitative measures of performance, and information management procedures suitable for carrying out clinical and financial audit. Computerisation is seen as a central plank in this strategy.

BACKGROUND TO INFORMATION TECHNOLOGY IN PRIMARY HEALTH CARE

The introduction of computers into general practice has followed a different path to that adopted in most areas of work. Unlike systems developed by computer specialists and introduced under the senior management patronage, GP enthusiasts have developed their own software to suit their own perceived needs. Most of the GP computer systems available on the market today originate from these early systems, although the development of many of them has been taken over by computer specialists working in close collaboration with GPs. As a result of this history, software design focuses on the needs of practitioners, rather than emphasising management or financial data, and early experience was established around the interests of doctors enthusiastic about computer technology.

Quite often the enthusiast would attempt to 'go it alone', and would be tolerated by mildly or strongly sceptical colleagues. This did not offer a sound base from which to develop information systems capable of integrating activities and improving coordination between the practice's members.

The government's Micros for GPs Scheme was introduced in 1982, and provided administrative systems with a 50% price subsidy. It was taken up with enthusiasm by the target number of 150 practices. However, when the author and some colleagues evaluated this project, the results were disappointing. They revealed that many practices did not use their system very effectively.

In 1987 schemes were launched by two companies, each of which offered 'free' computer systems to general practices in the UK. In return for the system the practices would supply the company with clinical data collected from individual patients. This data, suitably filtered to ensure the anonymity of individuals, would then be sold primarily to the pharmaceutical trade for post-market surveillance (checking the use of new drugs, particularly for any adverse reactions) and for market research.

These new schemes were of major significance in two ways. They stimulated the GP market in the obvious way of providing resources at no direct financial cost. Less obviously, they created an interest; but then (perhaps because of 'ethical' objections from one or more partners) some practices decided to purchase a system from another supplier. However, these schemes also required (and depended on the practices providing) good quality, marketable data. This in turn required, for the first time, that the systems be used effectively. And to get clinical data on drugs prescribed and the reason for the prescription, the computer had to be used routinely in the consulting room.

In 1980 the medical profession had produced a report recommending the use of computers in general practice, especially during the consultation (RCGP, 1980). They anticipated direct clinical benefits from the improved quality and efficiency of record keeping, but there was some concern about possible negative effects on doctor–patient communication if a computer was used during the consultation. Research on these issues concluded that there was little or no detrimental effect on doctor–patient communication, and that the quality of clinical care could be improved. However, the computer was not more efficient than the manual patient record for individual encounters, and took significantly longer to use in the consultation.

The most recent generation of systems have more advanced user interfaces, and are easier to use. Nevertheless, there is concern about the time they will require for regular use during consultations, and there is no convincing research evidence that they will not be a burden to the harassed GP. However, there is little doubt that computerisation can lead to more systematic and analysable records in the longer term.

Typical facilities provided by most of the systems currently available include:

- a patient register (names, addresses, age and sex, and basic demographic data on the patients within the practice);

- a facility for ordering and printing prescriptions for medication (including repeat prescriptions where the computer is used to regulate the number and frequency of repeats);

- a call/recall module for identifying, contacting and monitoring groups of patients for health screening and preventive immunisations;

- the consulting room facilities described above.

BACKGROUND TO THE CASE STUDY

The setting for this 'generic' case study is New Times Medical Centre, a purpose designed building owned by the four GP partners and providing a service to 8000 patients. The senior partner, Dr Senior, had the vision for the new building and worked closely on the design. However, s/he will retire in a few years, and for the last two years has been letting go of the reins. Dr Senior is happy to leave major decisions to the other partners, provided they seem to be sorting things out satisfactorily.

Dr Uno joined Dr Senior in partnership 15 years ago. S/he sees the provision of individual attention to patients as the first priority of general practice. Thus meetings are a distraction from the real task, and Dr Uno has been happy to leave major decisions in the capable hands of Dr Senior.

Dr Pewter joined the practice five years ago, when another practice closed down and the practice's list size expanded. S/he brought some new ideas to the practice, in particular the importance of preventive screening. It was Dr Pewter who initiated the decision to employ a practice nurse (Jean Plant), who runs a regular 'well woman' clinic that provides advice and carries out health checks on women of childbearing age.

Dr Rush joined the practice two years ago. S/he believes that, although the quality of care is generally high, and people's hearts are certainly in the right place, the practice could be better organised. This could reduce the occasions when things get overlooked (eg when patients' test results have not come back from the hospital after three months and no one has followed it up). Dr Rush sees a computer system as the obvious solution to such organisational inefficiency. S/he believes it could probably also be used to increase the practice's income by carrying out more preventive services (for which the practice gets 'item of service' payments), and by ensuring that they claim for everything to which they are entitled.

The practice also employs six part-time administrative staff, whose functions include booking appointments, receiving patients when they arrive, filing, preparing repeat prescriptions, booking home visits, and general clerical and typing tasks. Most tasks can be carried out by any of the administrative staff, though one acts as bookkeeper and wages clerk. She is older, paid a little more, and is generally seen as the senior staff member, although she has no formal responsibility for the supervision of other staff. Recently the partners have discussed whether they need a practice manager who would 'run the office' and be a formal link between themselves and the rest of the staff. No decision has been made, although it is recognised that none of the current staff would be suitable for the post.

Through the enthusiasm of Dr Pewter the practice has set up a patients' group – a 'talking shop' where patients get together, support each other and provide a forum for the practice to consult with its 'client group' over decisions it is considering. Dr Pewter has worked hard at establishing the group, and at the last four quarterly meetings the average attendance has been 20 patients. Typically there is a short presentation from one of the practice members, for example on the risk of coronary heart disease, and then a general discussion. Some of the active patients have been discussing the need to provide more social support to some patients, for example those on very low incomes or with poor housing conditions.

The income to the practice is determined mainly (60%) by the number and age of patients on the practice's list (ie capitation fees). About 30% of income derives from payments for fixed costs (premises etc), and the remaining 10% is income from 'item for service' payments. These are payments available for specific additional preventive services (eg inoculations and screening tests) which the practice is encouraged to provide. New Times Medical Centre could at least treble its income from these additional services if it chose to do so.

The payments are made to the practice by its family practitioner committee (FPC), which administers payments to 100 practices in the locality. Although traditionally the FPC has been essentially a 'pay and rations' organisation, it has recently been reorganised and given responsibility for monitoring the cost effectiveness of expenditure. In the near future it will be expected to oversee predetermined budgets for each of its practices.

The regional health authority (RHA) has recently assumed responsibility for family practitioner services (the FPCs), following a reorganisation initiated by the government. The RHA is keen to promote computerisation. In order to manage the service effectively it needs good data on service provision and operating costs. In the longer term it sees the implementation of a computer system in every practice as the only way of achieving the necessary controls over budgets.

To this end, the RHA has arranged a deal with a major pharmaceutical company to provide a basic computer system free to all practices that will agree to give the company data on medication prescribed and the reason it was prescribed. To conform with legal and ethical requirements, this data will be anonymous with respect to the patient, ie 'stripped' of any information which may be able to identify an individual, such as the name or address.

THE PROBLEM

The problem facing the practice is whether, at this stage, to accept the 'special offer' of a computer system. If it decides to go ahead, the practice should also consider specifically which of the available facilities it wishes to implement, how it will prepare itself to do so, and what the implications are for the organisation of the practice in general and for the roles of individual members in particular. If the practice decides not to go ahead then it needs to be clear about its reasons and to know, at least in outline, its future plans.

The details of the computer system, including essential and optional modules and an assessment of the likely costs and potential savings, are provided in the Appendix at the end of this section.

As Dr Rush's opening remark indicates, the practice has already had some discussions on whether to get a system. The following points were made at a recent partnership meeting:

Dr Rush:

> The computer will provide the organisation we need. It will more than pay for itself, and it will show we are really committed to moving forward. Without one we won't be able to cope with being responsible for our own practice budget for drugs and for treatment costs, which you all know deep down will be with us sooner that we like to think. The 'no cost' offer from Acme Medical Systems is too good to pass up.

Dr Uno:

> I don't think we should be railroaded into a rash and premature decision. We may find we've taken in a Trojan horse, providing the health authority with exactly the device it needs to monitor and impose changes which we know won't be in the interests of our patients. And what's more you shouldn't believe all that hype about making things easier for us, I reckon it will increase our work load.

Dr Pewter:

> I think we need to get a computer. It will be essential for the

preventive screening we are planning to do. But I'm not sure if we are quite ready yet. Perhaps we should get a practice manager first, who can help prepare for the changeover. We shouldn't underestimate the amount of work and disruption that will be involved.

Dr Rush:

Nonsense, if we delay we'll never get going. We can do it if we're really committed and I'm prepared to devote all my study time to this project if we go ahead.

Dr Senior:

It's important that we all move forward together, that's how we've always done things here. I'm a bit concerned about whether this offer is the right computer for us, but I can see that we need to make a clear decision rather than let it go by default. I suggest we call a meeting with the staff and the patients' group. We can also get those people from the health authority along to explain their side of things. Then on the basis of that we'll make a decision.

THE TASK

The task for the case study has been designed as a roleplaying exercise. The scenario is a meeting held at the medical centre to decide:

- whether a computer system will be acquired, and if so which specific facilities will be purchased;

- how the system will be implemented;

- what specific economic, organisational and individual consequences are likely for the parties involved (eg financial costs and benefits, job changes, service to patients, etc).

At the meeting four distinct 'stakeholder' groups are represented:

- the GPs;

- the employed staff (nurse and administrative staff);

- the Health Service management (from both RHA and FPC);

- the medical centre's patients' group.

The interests and perspective of each group are described below. Their role in the meeting is to negotiate with the other groups in an attempt to reach an agreed decision. It should be pointed out that in reality the employed staff and the patients' group would probably not be represented at such a meeting. However, they clearly have an interest in the outcome of the meeting and, in the exercise, are given an opportunity to present their points of view.

The overall purpose of the exercise is to identify the likely consequences of computerisation for each of the stakeholder groups, and to illustrate the overlapping and disparate interests of each group. A roleplaying exercise allows participants to understand the implications of computerisation in this setting for themselves.

The stakeholder groups

The participants can be seen as members of one of the four groups. The members of each group, although not having identical views and interests, share a common interest with other members of their group which distinguishes them from each of the other groups. The composition and perspective of each group is outlined below:

The general practitioners

This group comprises the practice's GPs. They are 'front-line' workers who spend most of their work time treating patients in their consulting rooms. However, they are also the 'owners' of a business partnership with an annual turnover of more than half a million pounds. Their income from the practice is not fixed: it depends on the income and expenditure of the business. Thus when they are making decisions about the development of the medical centre, they must consider both their clinical and their business/managerial roles.

The employed staff

This group comprises a nurse and up to six administrative staff, all employed by the practice. The nurse's role is to provide a support service for the doctors. She carries out minor clinical procedures (applying dressings etc), gives injections to patients referred by the doctors, and runs the 'well woman' clinic. The administrative staff include receptionists who book patients into surgeries, process requests for repeat prescriptions, and carry out general clerical tasks, including 'pulling' and filing patients' records and some typing duties. The senior receptionist is the practice's bookkeeper and wages clerk.

The patients' group

The practice set up the patients' group about three years ago. Its purpose is to enable the practice to consult with patients when it is considering important changes. For example, the surgery hours were changed a couple of years ago as a result of consultations with the group. The group comprises about six 'activists', who organise meetings approximately four times a year. Depending on the nature of the meeting, anything between 10 and 60 patients may turn up. In the past year the patients' group has had some success in setting up a parent and toddler group, and has begun a 'damp housing' campaign to improve conditions in a local block of flats. Recently the practice nurse addressed a meeting about the importance of health promotion and healthy lifestyles. Several patients said they would like advice and support in being more healthy (giving up smoking, better diet, etc).

The Health Service management

This group comprises officers from the RHA and the FPC. The deputy administrator from the FPC oversees the practice's finances. At the moment the FPC pays the practice on the basis described above. It also has to agree to any increases in the number of GPs or employed staff. There is no mechanism for limiting the cost of drug expenditure other than to 'inform and encourage' the practice if its expenditure exceeds the regional average. In the future the FPC will be responsible for setting a 'notional annual budget', and the practice will be expected to limit its outgoings accordingly. This budget will also include drug expenditure. The RHA officer is responsible for the FPC's budget and takes a strategic view of the development towards practices as cost centres. The RHA is also responsible for the overall standard of care provided, and includes within its team a health promotion officer, responsible for primary care preventive services.

Steps in the exercise

It is recommended that the exercise be carried out in the following sequence:

1 Prepare the groups

Participants should read the information provided above and the essential references listed at the end, so that they have a clear view of the issue being addressed in the case study. They should also clarify any questions of fact about the computer system on offer and its method of use. This may be done by group discussion, since some members are likely to have more technical knowledge than others. However, they should avoid jumping into the roleplay exercise itself at this point. The additional references at the end provide more information on primary care computer systems and their use.

2 Allocate a role to each participant

Each participant is assigned to one of the four stakeholder groups, with approximately equal numbers in each group. Within each group, where there are a number of different roles, participants decide who will play them.

3 Decide needs and strategy within groups

This is the first major stage of the roleplay session. Depending on the time available, between 30 minutes and two hours could be assigned to this task. At the end, each group should be clear about what it wants, what it does not want, and how it hopes to achieve its aims. Given the complexity of the situation, it may be appropriate to develop contingency plans dependent on the response of other groups. If the group has more than three or four members it is advisable for it to choose one or two members who will be its negotiators at the main meeting.

4 The meeting

The meeting, to agree a system and implementation strategy, is the main event of the case study. It will require between 30 minutes and one hour depending on time available. The meeting takes place at the medical centre and should be chaired by one of the GPs. The aim is to reach a consensus, though this may not be possible in the time available.

5 The partnership's decision

Having heard the arguments, the partners decide how to proceed (this should only take a further 10 minutes or so) and announce their decision to the other stakeholder groups.

6 'Post mortem'

A review of the process and outcomes. Remaining in role, all participants review the meeting and reflect on whether they got what they wanted, and discuss any insights into the relationships between groups. Then, coming out of role, participants examine what they have learned about:

- the use of computers in primary health care;

- questions of information and control;

- the likely consequences of computerisation for stakeholder groups;

- any other insights gained on technology and change in organisations.

An alternative to the roleplay

If there is not enough time, or if for some other reason the full roleplay exercise is not possible, we recommend that invidual participants consider how the problem might be tackled and then discuss their conclusions in the group. There are at least two possible ways in which they might do so:

- They could each adopt one particular stakeholder role, and then pool their conclusions in the group.

- They could focus on any differences in preference they would expect between stakeholder groups, and what they would expect to happen in practice.

ESSENTIAL READING

Fitter M J, The development and use of information technology in health care, in Blackler F, Oborne D, eds, *Information Technology and People: Designing for the Future*, British Psychological Society, 1987

ADDITIONAL READING

Ellis D, *Medical Computing and Applications*, Ellis Horwood, 1987

Fitter M J, Garber J R, Herzmark G A et al, *A Prescription for Change: The Longer-term Use and Development of Computers in General Practice*, HMSO, 1986

Fitter M J, Evans A R, Garber J R, Computers and audit, *Journal of the Royal College of General Practitioners*, 1985, vol 35, pp522–524

Herzmark G, Brownbridge G, Fitter M J, Evans A R, Consultation use of a computer by general practitioners, *Journal of the Royal College of General Practitioners*, 1984, vol 34, pp649–654

Smith P B, *Group Processes and Personal Change*, Harper and Row, 1980

APPENDIX

Note: The main purpose of the exercise is to discuss and negotiate the preferred system and method of use for the medical centre. Detailed financial balances are not required or expected; the financial information is simply a guideline to what is realistic.

Financial information

The practice is free to choose how it spends money, though the partners' personal income derives from the surplus of income over other expenditure. Thus the partners will wish to consider carefully any major items of expenditure.

Drug costs

The practice's annual expenditure on medication prescribed through the NHS is £260,000. At the moment this is not part of the practice's budget, being paid directly by the NHS. However, in the future practices will have a specific budget for medication, and over the next two years the RHA is hoping to reduce the overall allocation for medication by 2% in real terms.

Preventive services

The medical centre receives 'item of service' payments if it provides additional services. These include childhood immunisations, rubella and tetanus vaccination, and cervical cytology screening. Currently the practice receives an annual sum of £5000 from the NHS for these services. If the services were provided to *all* patients when a payment was available, the income could be £20,000, although it is unlikely that such a complete service could be justified clinically. At its upper limit, some of the service would be to patients who were not at any significant risk to the illness, though they would qualify for an item of service payment to the practice. Conversely, some at-risk patients, who could benefit from the service, do not entitle the practice to additional payments.

The computer budget

The FPC (Health Service management) has a budget of up to £5000 available to spend on the system for the medical centre. The practice and the patients' group have a budget of £2500 and £500 respectively. The aim should be to meet any expenditure over these amounts by equivalent savings. The GPs could take on additional facilities by reducing their own income from the practice.

The computer system

This well tried and tested system from Acme Medical Systems has recently received a major upgrade which makes new and exciting features available at a reasonable price. A special offer is currently open to medical centres. Thanks to an agreement with the regional health authority and a major pharmaceutical supplier, the basic system is available at no cost.

Additional functions may be purchased, although some of these are also available at no cost if the medical centre agrees to provide anonymous aggregate patient data to the pharmaceutical company for statistical analyses.

The basic system

The basic system includes a terminal (keyboard and screen), a printer, a processor and a hard disk, with software modules as follows:

- *Patient registration*. This provides a database of all registered patients, an essential core of all other modules, and is also useful for identifying patients' registration status, address, etc).

- *Repeat prescribing*. This enables legible prescriptions to be printed by computer for patients receiving regular medication from the practice without having to see the doctor each time. It also allows the practice to monitor and regulate the number of times medication can be repeated before the patient is required to see the doctor again.

- *Capitation and items of service*. This is an accounting facility that helps the practice to submit accurate monthly invoices to the FPC, and ensures it does not miss claiming for all that it is entitled to.

Additional modules

These may also be installed if the practice decides to do so, though some modules may involve extra expenditure. They include:

- *Appointment system*. This module, costing £4000, enables:

  • rapid identification of vacant slots and booking of appointments;

  • an analysis of each practitioner's workload;

  • an analysis of the frequency of patient attendance;

  • identification of regular non-attenders.

- *Consulting room use*. This module enables the full recording of patient histories and encounters, for example:

  • the reason for a consultation;

  • diagnosis;

  • treatment/prescription.

As well as collecting clinical information, a consulting room terminal enables direct access to computer-based patient records, and the direct printing of prescriptions. Before printing the prescription, the computer can check medication for contraindications (a possible negative reaction because of some other problem that the patient has) and for drug interactions (a negative reaction between the drug and another drug the patient is receiving). It would cost £8000 to provide terminals and other necessary equipment for all the practitioners. However, if the medical centre agrees to provide medical data (eg medication and reason for prescription) to the pharmaceutical company there is no charge for the equipment or for the associated software.

Before clinical information can be entered into the computer it must be classified using a coding system. This must either be done by the GP, (either during or after consultation) or it must be written down and entered later by a coder. Direct entry requires consulting room terminals. Indirect entry can be done without a terminal. In this case access to records is provided by a receptionist, who produces a printout of the patient record for the doctor immediately before a consultation. However, indirect entry requires a skilled coder, and it will cost £6000 per annum to provide data entry for all practitioners.

– *Decision aid*. If consulting room terminals are installed, 'patient management protocols' can be used. These are computer-based guidelines for managing patients with a chronic illness, eg diabetes, hypertension. For example, they enable the practice to set up a 'hypertension clinic' for patients who need to attend regularly. The clinic can be run by a nurse aided by the computer, and backed up by a GP who can be called upon if necessary. The module costs £2000, but if used can replace one GP with an additional nurse. This could provide a net annual saving of £6000.

– *Preventive module*. This module enables a comprehensive screening programme to be provided to 'at-risk' groups of patients. It costs £2000, but if used effectively it can increase the practice's income (see below) and should, in the long run, lead to a reduction in acute illness. This in turn will reduce workload, hospital referrals etc. Comprehensive use will also require an extra nurse and half a clerical staff post, at an annual cost of £20,000.

– *Patient services*. This module, costing £2000, can be used by patients at a terminal in the waiting room. It can provide:

- information on health education (diet, exercise, causes of illness, etc);

- welfare benefits information (calculation of entitlement etc);

- a database, membership and mailing-list service for the patient group to support self-help groups, etc.

– *Report generator*. This module, costing £1000, enables the audit of information such as:

- patient information (demographic and clinical; morbidity, etc);

- practitioner information (workload, prescribing patterns and costs);

- information on services provided by the medical centre (completeness of screening programmes, patient contacts, referral rates, etc).

  This information can of course only be analysed if it has been collected, and this requires the installation of the relevant system module.

22 Job design, work organisation and system design: Payfund

C. Wendy Olphert and Leela Damodaran

ORGANISATIONAL SETTING

Payfund is a large UK organisation with several thousand staff. One of Payfund's main tasks involves the calculation and issue of payments to its clients according to a number of rules. The case study relates to the design of a new computer system to support the administration of these payments. Payfund has a large, mainly London-based head office with sections responsible for personnel, finance, property, policy and procedures, and computer systems across the whole organisation. Payments are made to clients through a nationwide network of around 800 branch offices, organised into geographical regions. Branch offices (usually located in town or city centres, or suburban locations) will typically range in size from 20 to 50 staff. Most of these are in clerical jobs organised under section heads, who in turn are responsible to a branch manager.

The policy and procedures to be followed in each office are closely specified by head office. The main tasks carried out by the staff in branch offices are to collect personal details from clients (who may call at the office or send in an application form). If certain conditions are met, these details will be entered onto the computer. The computer will then determine the appropriate rate of payment and issue payments direct to clients on due dates. Once a payment has been set up, any relevant changes to clients' personal details or circumstances will be input to the computer as long as payments are being made. Clerical staff usually work in teams of six to eight, and section heads are responsible for managing the workload of the team, checking work, and advising both staff and clients in case of queries.

A number of different trade unions are recognised by the organisation, each of which represents staff at different levels.

BACKGROUND TO THE CASE

Payfund already has a mainframe computer system which processes and issues payments. This system was designed and installed in the

1960s, and is currently reaching the end of its useful life. Until quite recently (the mid-1980s), input to the computer was made from punched paper tape by specialist computer operators at each of the individual offices. Around 1985, however, the system was updated by the addition of VDU terminals in all offices. Using these terminals, clerical staff could input their own data relating to clients and payments, and make enquiries about payment records, though the data was still processed in batches. (The punch operators were redeployed within the offices.)

The design of a new, bespoke computer system began in 1986. The new computer was intended not simply to replace the functions performed by the existing system, but to improve the efficiency and effectiveness of the payments system and to create more rewarding jobs for staff. The design was to be undertaken in-house; a large project team was set up, headed by a project manager from the central computer department of the organisation. In line with all computerisation projects in the organisation, this project was required to adopt a modified version of the SSADM design methodology (see Damodaran, Ip and Beck, 1988).

SSADM (structured systems analysis and design method) was developed in 1980, and is in use both in the private and public sectors. In common with other system design methodologies, it formalises the steps or tasks to be undertaken during design, and contains techniques for performing those tasks. However it differs from many methodologies in recognising that users must be closely involved in development if a system is to meet their real requirements. Consequently users are given a formal role in the system design process.

SSADM addresses three major phases of the design process: feasibility study, systems analysis and systems design. But it does not attempt to address all aspects of system development. The three design phases are further broken down into stages, which in turn are subdivided into worksteps and then into specific tasks. Each task has an end product, and these are subjected to quality assurance reviews (see Longworth, 1989). The modified version of SSADM divides design activities into six stages, as shown in Figure 22.1.

To design the new system, project staff were drawn from Payfund's central computer department and from the branch offices. To ensure that users' interests were represented, the project team consisted both of staff trained in systems analysis and design (primarily drawn from the central computer department) and a number of staff drawn from other departments or offices. Most of the latter were management/supervisory staff from head office sections (eg policy) and branch or regional offices – although most had worked in branch offices at some point in their careers. The staff were divided into two teams, the design team and the user team. There were one or two clerical staff attached to the user team, but their task was to provide clerical support to the team rather than

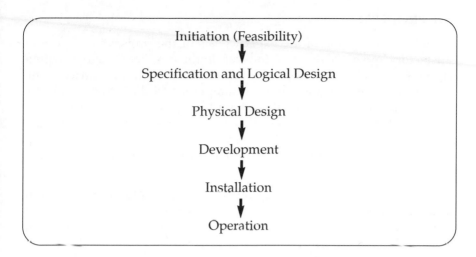

Figure 22.1   The Six Stages of the Project Design Methodology

represent the ranks of clerical users in branch offices.

Both the design team and the user team were headed by a manager (from a similar background but of a more senior grade) who reported to the project manager. Although some members of the project team were trade union members, there was no formal trade union representation on the project. A project steering committee was established, which included the project manager and design/user team managers and representatives from regional offices and head office sections. Consultation with trade union representatives was undertaken by the steering committee at formal meetings and by submission of certain project documents for trade union approval.

In the project design methodology, specific worksteps or tasks are assigned explicitly to the users to perform; in other worksteps they perform an advisory or quality assurance role to the design teams. In 1986, shortly after the project had been set up, the user team engaged the services of human factors (HF) consultants to advise and assist them in carrying out those tasks and worksteps in the design methodology which required user involvement or input.

The project was scheduled for completion by the early 1990s. The age of the existing system and concerns over its future reliability meant that timescales were critical, and the project could not afford much slippage. As a safeguard, management consultants were engaged to assist with planning and management and to provide additional technical expertise on the project, and each of the project teams (including the user team) had one or more management consultants attached to it to assist with these tasks.

THE PROBLEM

As stated earlier, one of the explicit goals of the project was to create satisfactory and satisfying jobs for staff. In the past, job design has often happened by default when computers have been introduced. The systems designers decide what the computer will do (usually with the goal of maximising use of the computer's power and consequently justifying the cost of the installation), and the remaining jobs are performed by the staff to the computer system – with costly consequences for the organisation (eg in staff turnover or underutilisation of the system).

Traditional systems design methodologies do not build in consideration of human and organisational issues such as job design. The modified version of the SSADM methodology being used by the project had been developed to try to ensure that such issues were addressed in the design of IT systems, and included a number of worksteps where job design issues were to be explicitly addressed.

In order to design a computer system which results in satisfactory job designs for eventual end users, the following procedures are necessary:

- To identify, early in the systems design process, what would constitute satisfying and effective jobs for users.

- To specify the users' requirements for the computer system accordingly.

- To ensure that these job design requirements are taken into account throughout the project.

The modified version of SSADM makes the user team responsible for all the worksteps/tasks related to job design in the methodology. (The design teams play no role in these activities; they are responsible for acting on the outcome of worksteps, ie creating system design options which meet the users' requirements in respect of job design.) However, the user team faced a problem. The methodology indicated when activities related to job design should be undertaken, and the kinds of task involved; however, it gave very little guidance on job design techniques, and none whatsoever on translating design decisions into system requirements.

Job design requirements clearly have an influence on the design of the technical system itself, but they also affect related areas such as user education, training and support. If users are to find a new computer system acceptable and usable, they must be properly prepared for its introduction. This preparation should include:

- 'education' activities while the system is being designed or selected (eg explanations of the objectives and timescales of the project, reasons for choosing one particular option over other options, etc);

- adequate and timely training in how to use the new system.

To help them overcome any difficulties they may experience in using the system, the users will also need ongoing support (eg 'help desks', access to specialist computer staff, documentation, etc). These factors become even more important when jobs are being changed at the same time as the introduction of a new computer – users will have to be given training and support for their new jobs, as well as for using the computer system.

The HF consultants who were engaged to help the user team with these issues faced a number of problems:

- How to tailor their experience and expertise in job design and related matters to fit the constraints of the systems design methodology.

- How to educate the user and design teams alike about the need for, and implications of, job design activities in the project.

- How to find an approach to the work which would make maximum use of a small amount of resources within very tight timescales.

IDENTIFYING USERS' REQUIREMENTS

From a human factors perspective, a crucial first step in any systems design process is to carry out a series of analyses, complementing those carried out in conventional systems analysis. This activity, known as 'user analysis' in the revised methodology, is a much simplified form of sociotechnical systems analysis. Its aims include:

- analysing the general work context in terms of priorities, pressures, communication patterns, etc;

- identifying the full range of potential users;

- establishing crucial task demands which will continue to exist once the new system is in place (eg the need to respond to customer queries);

- analysing work roles;

- establishing the extent to which users are prepared for the introduction of the new system.

The aim of user analysis is to provide baseline data which will contribute to a number of subsequent system design steps. For example, it should help to create a user requirements specification (one of the major outputs from the specification and logical design stage; see Figure 22.1) which is much more closely matched to users' real needs than would be possible using conventional systems analysis procedures. The data collected during user analysis would also form the basis of evaluation criteria. These could be used to test the proposed system design, and to see whether it really matched users' requirements.

The modified version of SSADM used on the project set user analysis as a workstep early in the project's initiation stage (see Figure 22.1). Unfortunately, however, the project had already begun before the modified version of the methodology was released for use by the head office's computer department. Instead of user analysis, the earlier version of the project's methodology began with a more general workstep called 'current system survey'. This was aimed at identifying problems with the current system and turning them into requirements for the new system. The user team (along with other user representatives, including branch office staff) had already started this work before engaging the HF consultants to advise and assist them.

Initially a lengthy list of problems (more than 200) was generated by groups of end users. These were being evaluated by the user team. Many problems experienced with the existing system had to do with:

– turnaround speed;

– updating of information on the computer (because data was processed in batches);

– finding information in response to queries from clients (since only partial client information was held on Payfund's computer).

It was clear, therefore, that the new computer system could improve efficiency and effectiveness by:

– automating a much larger proportion of branch office work;

– processing client information more quickly (preferably in real time rather than in batches);

– holding a much larger database of client information.

Thus the user team was beginning to derive the users' requirements for the new computer.

However, there was no systematic user analysis. At the same time as the HF consultants were appointed, the revised version of the methodology was released to the project. Some of the later activities it specified were dependent on user analysis. To deal with this problem, the HF consultants advised the user team to extend their current system survey to include some form of user analysis. The consultants were particularly concerned to gain data on existing levels and sources of job satisfaction. Without this data, the new system would be unlikely to achieve its target of creating better jobs for staff.

The user manager (the head of the user team and responsible for managing the HF consultancy contract) agreed. A significant part of the first year's HF consultancy budget would be used for a survey of work organisation and job satisfaction in a sample of branch offices. Twelve offices were selected, representing the range of offices by size and location. In all 162 staff representing all levels and roles in these offices were interviewed by the HF consultants.

The majority of staff interviewed for the survey were reasonably satisfied with their jobs, although there were some common points of contention. Table 22.1 lists the main sources of satisfaction and dissatisfaction in order of frequency.

1 Clerical Staff

Main Sources of Job Satisfaction		Dissatisfaction	
Being able to go home leaving an empty desk each day	57%	Interruptions	50%
Contact with clients	55%	Repetitive tasks	41%
Being effective in dealing with clients	42%	Not dealing with all information on cases	40%
Being busy	25%	Uneven workload	40%
Having responsibility	22%	Computer unreliability	26%
Ensuring payments are made on time and accurately	20%	Problems with colleagues or superiors	25%
Problem solving	17%	Inaccurate or delayed payments to clients	13%
Interaction with co-workers	13%	Performing ancillary/ support tasks	9%
Using the computer	12%		

2 Managerial Staff/Section Heads

Main Sources of Job Satisfaction		Dissatisfaction	
Dealing with people	66%	Staffing problems	50%
Increasing devolution of responsibility from Head Office	45%	Coping with policy changes from Head Office	40%
Ability to make organisational changes	45%	Insufficient devolution/ control over own Office	30%
Office running smoothly/meeting objectives	45%	Accommodation quality	30%
Staff being co-operative	15%	Computer unreliability	15%
Challenge/learning	15%	Poor communications with/ from Head Office	15%
		Lack of challenge/variety	15%
		High workload	10%

Table 22.1   Sources of Satisfaction and Dissatisfaction for Clerical and Management Staff

ORGANISATIONAL VARIATION

The survey findings gave the user team and the HF consultants plenty of ideas for improving job satisfaction. However, it was difficult to draw any conclusions about the types of job design that the majority of staff would find most satisfying.

All twelve offices taking part in the survey were doing exactly the same work; however, they differed to a greater or lesser extent in their work organisation, and in the way individual tasks had been combined into jobs for staff. The survey found two underlying reasons for this:

– Office managers had a certain amount of discretion or autonomy with regard to organising their offices.

– Although the offices differed in size and location, each also faced a different combination of local circumstances in terms of the number and type of payments dealt with per annum, staff quality and turnover, and type of premises.

These factors led managers to seek the most effective form of organisation for their own local conditions.

Most office tasks could be performed in different sequences or by different individuals; for example, under one form of work organisation, all the initial work on new cases would be done by one section of clerks, who then passed the cases on to other sections to be maintained. This meant that individual clerks usually dealt with only one subset of the whole range of tasks, and could be seen as specialising in that particular function. Under another form of organisation, individual clerks took responsibility for a section of the alphabet and dealt with all aspects of any cases in their alphabetical range. In this case, clerks needed a wide range of knowledge about all aspects of the work – ie they were 'generalists' rather than 'specialists'. The demands on section heads would naturally also differ according to whether they managed teams with specialist or generalist knowledge.

The autonomy of branch office managers gave them a degree of flexibility which was seen as essential for the efficient running of Payfund's operations. It was also an important factor in the managers' own job satisfaction. But it presented a knotty problem for the user team, consultants and design teams alike when trying to tackle job design issues for the new system.

THE JOB DESIGN PROCESS

As we have seen, the project began without any attempt to discover what changes might be necessary to ensure more job satisfaction for staff. From the 'current system survey' the user team had identified the major functional requirements of the system – ie the office tasks that should be performed (in whole or in part) by the new computer. To achieve improved efficiency and effectiveness, the user team had also specified a number of features for the new system. Data input, for instance, was to be in plain English rather than by numerical codes, and data was to be processed in real time rather than in batches.

At this early stage of the project the user team believed that because these proposed functions and features of the new system would enable staff to do their work more easily and more effectively, they would automatically lead to improvements in job satisfaction for staff. (They did, however, recognise that some sources of staff dissatisfaction related to organisational procedures and Payfund's policy, and felt that there was little that could be done with the design of the new computer system to remedy those types of problems.)

Despite the late start, the HF consultants completed the survey of job satisfaction in offices in time to feed into the first workstep in the revised methodology (now being used). This methodology allowed Payfund's job design and work organisation requirements to be formally considered (ie, towards the end of the project's initiation stage). However, at this point, problems began to arise. The project timescales had begun to slip quite considerably. The 'first pass' at job design and work organisation was a new workstep included in the amended version of the methodology. It had not appeared in the original methodology, so its implications for the initiation stage had not been taken into account. However, the next stage of the project (specification and logical design) included a workstep aimed at taking a 'second pass' view of job design and work organisation. Since resources had already been allocated to this, the project manager suggested that consideration of job design could be postponed until after the initiation stage.

The user team, backed by the HF consultants, argued against this suggestion. They felt it was essential to have at least an overview of job design and work organisation goals for the new system before proceeding to the next stage of the methodology. The project manager made some concession to this. He released some resources for a superficial study of the proposed new system's impact on end users. In fact the initiation stage was completed before any systematic consideration was given to job design or work organisation requirements. The data regarding job satisfaction was carried forward to the next stage of the project.

Later in the year the user team, assisted by the HF consultants, started the 'job design' workstep in the specification and logical design stage. However, they immediately ran into difficulties. At the end of the initiation stage they had completed a feasibility study outlining the requirements for the proposed new system. Some technical design work had already begun, and the design team had already taken a number of decisions with implications for job design and work organisation. For example, they had already decided which office tasks would be computerised and which would not. This meant that the interface points (where staff made input to or received output from the computer system) could already be determined, and work had begun on designing the dialogues and screen formats for the interface.

Although the user team had been consulted on these decisions, and even involved to some extent, they were making judgements about technical design issues without an opportunity to specify job design objectives. Once the design teams had completed this work, the time pressures on the project meant there was little hope of getting them to repeat it.

Under the revised methodology the job design process could have begun during the initiation stage, before any technical decisions were made. The user team could have taken data about job satisfaction during user analysis (eg taking account of users' requirements for greater responsibility and variety in their work etc; see Table 22.1). This data could then have been used as the basis for generating one or more job design options to meet those requirements. In turn, the job design requirements should have weighted the choice of tasks to be performed by the computer, and the choice of specific system design solutions. This, however, had not happened, so an alternative approach had to be found as quickly as possible so that the user team could come up with a statement of job design requirements.

As well as the job design workstep, the user team was responsible for another workstep. This involved producing evaluation criteria for later stages of the design, when system tests would be carried out. The HF consultants used the job satisfaction data to create some 'population-specific' job design criteria for this workstep. Many well known lists of good job design criteria already exist (see Davis and Taylor 1972; these describe the general characteristics of good jobs such as autonomy, variety, etc). It is important to establish what levels of these factors will be appropriate to different groups of workers.

The HF consultants suggested these criteria could be used for a 'bottom-up' approach to job design. When the user team were helping the design teams to decide which tasks could be computerised, they had spent some time drawing task allocation charts. These charts showed different options for allocating non-computerised work between staff at different levels. (Figure 22.2 shows an example of a task allocation chart.) The user team and consultants applied the specific job design criteria from the job satisfaction survey to the task allocation options, trying to choose those which offered the greatest potential for job satisfaction.

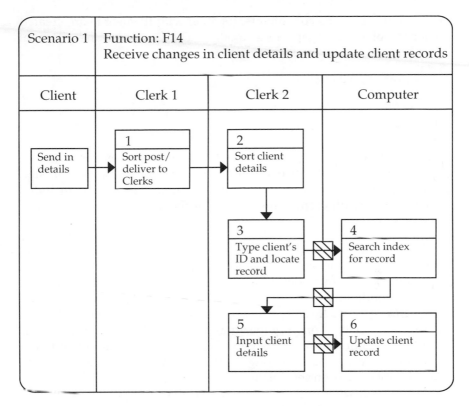

Scenario 1	Function: F14 Receive changes in client details and update client records		
Client	Clerk 1	Clerk 2	Computer

Figure 22.2 Example of a Task Allocation Chart

The process made it possible to choose a preferred approach to performing individual tasks. This would offer the greatest chance of job satisfaction for the different levels of staff involved. However, the individual tasks could then be combined in an almost infinite variety of ways to create whole jobs, and there was no time to evaluate all these permutations to choose a preferred set. Furthermore, one aim of the new system was to improve job satisfaction – but the job designs would have to be assessed to prevent conflict with the other aims of the new system, improved efficiency and customer service.

As previously stated, branch offices had adopted many different forms of work organisation. This had led to a wide variation in the way tasks could be combined into jobs. All, however, aimed to achieve efficient and satisfactory work within the constraints of that particular office. It seemed sensible at this point, therefore, to try a 'top-down' approach to job design. This would identify as many ways as possible of organising work in the office, and evaluate them against the three aims of the project. If this produced organisational options that might improve one or more of these aims, it would be worth looking at the job design options within those organisations more closely.

Pursuing this idea the consultants, together with the user team, created a number of work organisation models. They explored the potential consequences of each model in terms of:

- organisational efficiency;
- customer service;
- job design/job satisfaction.

These models included both the 'extreme' versions of specialisation (separate sections/staff for every function) and generalisation (all staff performing all tasks but grouped into sections). They also included options offering different combinations of the specialist and generalist approach.

However it transpired that all the models had both advantages and disadvantages. Some would work well in certain types of office location, or with certain staffing conditions. Others would work better when the opposite conditions applied. Since the offices in Payfund's network varied in respect of these characteristics, the conclusion had to be that no single form of work organisation would suit all offices. As has already been noted, the flexibility of branch offices to adopt different organisations was in fact a strong contributory factor to their efficiency. It would not have been sensible to eliminate this flexibility by imposing a specific form of work organisation when introducing the new computer system.

IMPLICATIONS FOR SYSTEMS DESIGN

With the consultants' agreement, the user team decided it was vital to keep the existing branch office autonomy in work organisation and job design. They believed the additional features of the new computer, which they had already specified, would go some way towards improving job satisfaction in the offices. It could also be improved if branch office managers were given extensive guidance and training on the principles of office organisation. This would allow them to apply sound principles when evaluating and selecting different job design options.

Unfortunately, but perhaps not surprisingly, the design teams were somewhat dismayed when the users' requirements began to emerge from the job design and work organisation workstep. They were proceeding apace with the logical design of the new system, including the design of interfaces and dialogues. It would have made life considerably easier for them if the user team had been able to recommend one specific work organisation and job design option to apply in all offices. However, the HF consultants' survey at the initiation stage had already shown that local office conditions varied quite widely, and that a work organisation pattern suitable in one situation might be completely inappropriate elsewhere.

Since branch office managers would keep some autonomy over work organisation in their office, the computer system would have to support a number of different job design options, including both the specialist and generalist patterns. Furthermore, many offices tended to change from one form of organisation to another. Sometimes these were no more than small variations, but at other times they became major reorganisations. The scale of change depended on changes in local circumstances (such as the loss of experienced staff to other organisations paying higher wages for clerical staff). This meant that many, or even most of the different combinations of task allocation might be appropriate somewhere, at some point in time.

This was not a great problem with the existing computer system – only a small subset of the office's work was computerised. However, under the new system many more tasks would be computerised. If there was more than one way to do each job, it would be much more difficult to arrange the computerised tasks (and the paths from one to the next) in a sensible sequence.

At first the design team tried to convince the user team and the project manager that a single job design option was a much better solution. However before the workstep was completed, the HF consultants carried out a rapid evaluation of the system design proposals as they stood at that time. They checked them against the two extremes of work organisation/job design variation (specialist jobs versus generalist jobs) and felt that the design proposals as they then stood would be sufficiently flexible to support both.

The consultants went on to identify some additional features for the system – features which could enhance organisational effectiveness and flexibility. For example, one major problem for section heads was to ensure an even workload for any member of staff who had to deal directly with clients. At any given time there might be a glut or a dearth of clients coming into the office. Most offices ran an appointments system to ensure that staff were not overloaded. It was normally a junior member of the clerical staff who scheduled appointments and kept the appointment book up to date. However, this was often a complex process, demanding sensitivity to clients, awareness of clients' personal circumstances and an understanding of the length of time each client was likely to need for an appointment. The consultants suggested that electronic diaries accessible to all relevant staff members might facilitate the booking process. They would also help staff to keep track of their own appointments.

The HF consultants produced a report which included both the requirement for the new system to support existing variation in work organisation and job design, and described the additional features which would contribute to organisational flexibility. However, by this time, the project was drawing to the end of the specification and logical design stage. Subject to sanction of the user requirements by the user committee, the next stage of the project would be to commence the physical design of the new system, ie to procure the necessary hardware and generating software programs.

Both the design team and the user team were under pressure from the project manager and the management consultants to keep closely to the project timetable. The design team had been worried that the job design exercise might make it necessary to redesign the proposed new system to accommodate the users' new requirements. They were relieved to find that no major rethink appeared to be necessary. They also persuaded the user team that the HF consultants' suggestions for extra facilities were 'niceties' rather than necessities, and would delay the project if they were incorporated. As a result, the user requirement for job design and work organisation (which subsequently went to the user committee for approval) stated that the new system would have to be flexible enough to support the existing variation in work organisation. The workstep had served to confirm that this would be the case, but had no direct influence on any features of the proposed new system.

CASE STUDY TASKS

Imagine you are responsible for advising the project on job design

1 As part of the user analysis process, draw up a checklist for a semi-structured interview with users. You are to investigate their current levels of job satisfaction and the factors which affect this. Would the same checklist be suitable for all types of user?

2 On the basis of Table 22.1, list the job design evaluation criteria which you think would be most important for:

a) routine clerical jobs;

b) the branch manager.

3 What would be the advantages and disadvantages (both for management and individual jobholders) of:

a) specialist jobs (where work is allocated according to functions)?

b) generalist jobs (where work is allocated by combining functions across some other grouping, eg by splitting clients alphabetically)?

4 What are the implications (eg for training and support, both of clerical staff and of branch office managers themselves) of allowing

job design decisions to be made at branch office level?

5 What actions would you recommend to the project manager if new job designs were brought into branch offices by head office before the introduction of the new computer system?

6 What arguments could have been used to persuade the project manager to skip the first pass at job design and work organisation in the initiation stage of the project?

7 List and describe the sequence of steps that you think should be built into the systems design process to ensure that job design and work organisation issues are considered and resolved at the appropriate times.

8 What ongoing actions are required during the project and after implementation to ensure that good job designs are achieved when the new computer system is introduced?

REFERENCES

Damodaran L, Ip K, Beck M, Integrating human factors principles into structured design methodology, in *Proceedings of Eurinfo '88: First European Conference on Information Technology for Organisational Systems* (Athens, May 1988), North Holland, 1988, pp235–241

Davies L E, Taylor J C, eds, *Design of Jobs*, Penguin, 1972

Longworth G, *Getting the System You Want: A User's Guide to SSADM*, NCC Publications, 1989

ADDITIONAL READING

Butera F, Thurman J E, eds, *Automation and Work Design*, North Holland, 1984

De Keyser V, Quale T, Wilpert B, Antonio Ruiz Quintanilla S, eds, *The Meaning of Work and Technological Options*, John Wiley, 1988

Drenth P J D, Thierry H, Willems P J, De Wolff C J, eds, *Handbook of Work and Organisational Psychology*, John Wiley, 1984

Eason K D, *Information Technology and Organisational Change*, Taylor and Francis, 1988

Emery F E, ed, *Systems Thinking*, Penguin, 1981

Klein L, *New Forms of Work Organisation*, Cambridge University Press, 1976

23 Design matters: The Oasis Palm Project

Heather Hopkins

THE ORGANISATIONAL SETTING

The window of the hotel revealed a scene of brooding cloud and relentless rain. Somewhere beyond the car park, Lake Coniston was lost in curling mist. A chill dampness hung in the air. In the recently converted conference suite of the Ghyll View Hotel the members of the Oasis Palm Project finished their coffee and settled themselves for the plenary session of the sixth project workshop.

The Oasis Palm Project was in its third year, and had two years to run. The project, jointly funded by industry and the research councils, had been set up to foster collaboration between university research groups and their industrial counterparts. It had the following brief:

- To establish expertise in the construction of large knowledge-based systems.

- To concentrate research efforts in the areas of:

  - intelligent knowledge-based systems (IKBS);

  - human–computer interaction (HCI);

  - software engineering.

- To develop appropriate methodologies for applying findings in each of these areas.

- To investigate the commercial viability of hardware and software outcomes.

Oasis Palm brought together research teams from the three universities of Halifax, Bracknell and Bognor. Each university had a different specialism:

- *Halifax*: systems analysis and design;

- *Bracknell*: sociotechnical aspects of systems and interface design;

- *Bognor*: logic programming and system development.

There were also two leading companies:

- the leading partner TRF: a computer manufacturer with an interest in exploring new areas for commercial exploitation;

- Aude Sapere: a progressive, research-oriented software house.

Researchers from these companies and from the university departments had spent the previous three years bringing together the benefits of their diverse experience, and applying it to the development of a demonstrator expert system for air traffic control operations.

Air traffic control had been chosen for this study because it presented an opportunity to explore the range of issues identified in the project brief, and had a range of exploitable outcomes beyond the scope of the study itself. Access to existing systems and operations had proved difficult, although some limited access to military installations had been made available. This had not been considered a problem at the conceptualisation stage nor for the identification of research issues. The project represented a challenging and innovative research and development opportunity.

The first year of the project had been characterised by a spirit of adventure and pioneering zeal. Talents from a range of disciplines – computer sciences, philosophy, languages, law, psychology and so on – provided the germinal ideas for a conceptual framework that would be equal to the task. Frequent meetings of collaborators dazzled with debate and a multiplicity of concepts. The project aspired to an organic unity that would be conducive to a high level of creativity and output.

However, the nature of the collaboration had its drawbacks:

- 'Pet' ideas came and went as interests changed with the balance of power.

- Geographical isolation produced duplication of effort and conflicts over approaches.

- Ambition brought people and ideas into prominence in disproportion to project needs.

- There were interminable meetings and exchanges of electronic mail.

Changes in the structure of the project occurred with some frequency. Teams were created and disbanded, team leaders found themselves in charge of a range of researchers in different locations and with different interests; different groupings with responsibility for controlling parts of the project flourished as the project management committee tried to coordinate resources to best effect, and to respond to different styles of working in the collaborating groups.

The project management committee, Promcom, was made up of one senior representative from each of the collaborating groups. There were six in all. Two were from the market sector targeted as potential customers, one was from the Research Council funding the university research and three were advisory members brought in on an ad hoc basis to contribute to specific discussions and decisions.

THE PROJECT MANAGEMENT COMMITTEE

Figure 23.1 shows the structure of the project management committee.

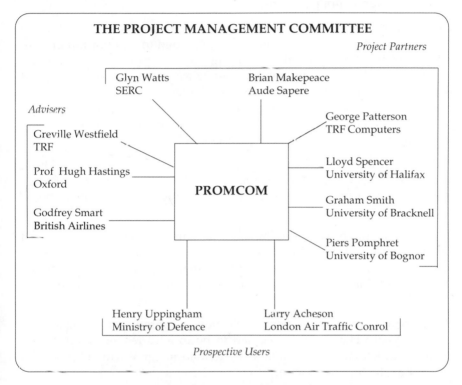

Figure 23.1   The Project Management Committee

Piers Pomphret of the University of Bognor had little patience with committees. An Oxford philosopher by training, he was rather introverted and more at home with the abstract than the concrete. He had no special allies on Promcom, and no interest in exploitation beyond its immediate implications for funding.

By contrast, Graham Smith from the University of Bracknell was an ambitious young academic. He was less interested in the project than in the personal opportunities it afforded him in terms of career advancement. He was therefore anxious for a successful outcome to the project, and his politics reflected this.

Lloyd Spencer of the University of Halifax was bright and charismatic. He had sufficient relevant experience in industry to be credible to both academics and industrial collaborators. His great failing was a tendency to promise more than could reasonably be fulfilled. Consequently, he was often an enthusiastic but unreliable ally.

Brian Makepeace of Aude Sapere was an intelligent and sensitive young man. He had been very successful in carving out a niche for his work and was generally respected. Brian and Lloyd were friends, and saw eye to eye on a number of problems.

Glyn Watts of the Science and Engineering Research Council (SERC) attended Promcom from time to time. He tended to monitor rather than intervene in the day-to-day running of the project. He was an administrator by style, and being rather conservative disliked Lloyd and Brian. He tended to favour George Patterson, the down-to-earth manager from TRF. George had no time for academics and an impatience to get on with the job. He loathed what he called the jawing of the innumerable meetings this project involved.

The three advisory members, Greville Westfield of TRF, Professor Hugh Hastings of the University of Oxford and Godfrey Smart of British Airlines, were each invited to contribute as appropriate to their special interests.

Greville Westfield was intelligent and shrewd, resented by Lloyd Spencer because Westfield's charm and diplomacy tended to eclipse his own. Westfield was considered to be a man with a good eye for the market, and this talent was not underestimated by the committee or his company.

Professor Hastings was a benign old boy, a retired archaeologist well past his peak. His function seemed to be to lend respectability to the project. Affectionate and fatherly, he tended to agree with all positions and to be reluctant to criticise.

Godfrey Smart of British Airlines was too serious and aggressive for his own good. Invited onto the committee to represent concern for passenger safety, he had welcomed the opportunity to keep the academics under control. He resented graduate selection and advancement in his own organisation, and felt he had missed promotion himself because of his lack of a degree. He was determined to demonstrate the superiority of his experience, whether or not it was wanted.

Henry Uppington of the Ministry of Defence was a civil servant in every respect. His primary concern was that appropriate procedures were observed. Sadly ignorant of many of the issues under discussion, Uppington would express concern over forms and formalities. Nonetheless, he was a valuable ally and could open a number of doors on opportunities for future research and funding.

The final member of Promcom was Larry Acheson of the London Air

Traffic Control Centre. Unfortunately he had suffered a serious heart attack during the first year of the project. It was hoped that he would be able to resume his position in the near future. This had not been seen as a problem, because it was generally thought that the relevance of his contribution would come at a later stage.

This, then, was the composition of Promcom. Early in its history, timetabling of objectives and target setting became a primary preoccupation as the need to measure progress, particularly for external evaluation, became a perceived priority. The advantage of establishing objectives was that it gave focus to the project as a whole and permitted the identification of common performance criteria. On the other hand, pressure applied by the industrial collaborators to establish industrial standards of appraisal and measurement had a discernible impact on the morale of the university groups. Broadly, the feelings of the university groups hinged on their suspicion that new ideas and methodologies had been relegated to a secondary role and, in effect, subordinated to the pursuit of 'deliverables'. The initial enthusiasm had become somewhat soured by experience.

Although there was little ill will between the industrial collaborators and the university groups, it was clear that each had different perceptions of their respective roles.

The university researchers, as rigorous in their methods as their industrial partners, sought to break new ground and to publish initial findings and discussion papers; however, the terms of their collaboration precluded this. Inevitably the industrial researchers were looking towards commercial goals, and their employment positions were very different. University researchers in the main were poorly paid and employed on fixed term contracts. Their counterparts, by contrast, were relatively well paid and secure in their jobs, and could see tangible benefits from producing commercially viable results. The rewards for university researchers depended on possibilities of further research and the largesse of funding bodies. These issues were invariably drawn into focus whenever the pressure of deadlines or conflicts over working methods came into prominence.

By the end of the second year, power to define the scope of the project lay securely in the hands of the industrial collaborators, and the university groups sought to meet targets, to exert influence on design considerations and to secure their own futures. By the middle of the third year a series of presentations had been given to demonstrate the technical sophistication of the system and the feasibility of the full scale version. These presentations had been very well received, and generated considerable interest. As a result, the project had a potentially influential lobby within the targeted organisations, and looked forward to exploring appropriate strategies for exploitation.

THE PROBLEM

Project workshops were held every six months. Their purpose was to review the work which had been completed in the previous six months, to plan the next, and to achieve a common understanding across the disparate activities and groups.

The pursuit of common objectives across the project had led the project management committee to structure project workshops with no concession to the diversity of interests of the participants nor, indeed, any acknowledgement of the disparity of their expertise. All sessions were to be attended by all participants. Absences tended to be noted. There were no parallel sessions or meetings of special interest groups unless these occurred informally at the bar. So for four days the workshop sessions had held captive an audience whose feelings ranged from the bored, to the fascinated, to the bemused.

On the Thursday evening, the last night of the workshop, participants had celebrated their survival in traditional workshop fashion. The following morning, few had braved breakfast, but by mid-morning most people had managed to struggle down to coffee to prepare themselves for the winding-up session.

When George Patterson rose to speak, he was confronted by a tired and lacklustre assembly. Patterson, the project coordinator, was a man of some considerable industrial experience – an engineer by training and inclination. He had worked for TRF for nearly twenty years. The previous evening he had retired early, and unlike many of his audience betrayed no sign of debility. Now in his mid-fifties, he was possessed of an affable disposition, comfortable with his paternalistic role, and a competent, no-nonsense style of management. He was good at his job, and knew himself to be a 'leader of men'. If this meant that at times he could be extremely sexist, then this was other people's problem; he was too old to make allowances. Shrewd and down to earth, he was not inclined to look kindly on those who might generate problems, or point to issues which he had already considered and, probably, rejected.

In this respect, he had a particular difficulty. Two years earlier the company had headhunted a 'high flyer' from the electronics industry, Greville Westfield, and created the new post of strategic planning manager. Westfield had been given a senior position with considerable responsibility for planning and policy making, and the task of 'bringing some vision' into the planning function. To his chagrin, Patterson had to report directly to Westfield. However, this had raised few difficulties for Patterson, because he tended to ignore Westfield's instructions and suggestions, and get on with doing things his own way. Westfield was well aware of this, but needed a specific issue to bring the situation into the open. George had no intention of giving him this satisfaction.

George cast an indulgent eye over his audience as he began to speak:

> Well, another project workshop draws to a close, and I think we can say that we have addressed many of the pressing issues that confronted us at the beginning of the week. We have made some progress towards establishing appropriate criteria for the evaluation of the system – its reliability and its interface design – and by the next workshop we must turn our attention to the ways in which we can best exploit our findings . . .

Patterson talked for about twenty minutes. He reviewed the workshop, thanked those people who had contributed, made a few clever remarks at the expense of the speakers, totally without malice, and opened the session to discussion.

Somewhere near the front of the room a question was asked: "Recently we had a review by the funding body. Have you any knowledge of that report?" The voice was that of Ian Grundy of TRF, who worked in a team reporting directly to George. Grundy was in a dead-end job and embittered. He held George responsible for his lack of promotion. George had no time for Grundy – 'that old sourpuss' as he called him.

Patterson curled his lip and rubbed his chin as he nodded:

> Yes, yes. All in all, it was very favourable, but there were some damn fool remarks about us not paying enough attention to job design. It's all very well, but it isn't in our brief, leastways not as I understand it. I can't see how it has any relevance to the type of work we're doing. We can't take on everything.

Clare Waterman was loath to speak at these sessions, but could not let this remark go without comment. In her late thirties, she was an organisational psychologist with the research team at the University in Halifax, where she had been working on the organisational context of the proposed system. In the midst of so much technical expertise, she had always sensed her own work to be very much a marginal concern, at best perceived as a matter of applied common sense. However, to her job design was an integral part of the system and, moreover, one which enhanced its exploitability.

> George, you've talked about evaluation of the product. I can see that it's fundamental, but as we move towards exploitation I think it's important to recognise that there are other areas of our activity that deserve attention. For example, our research design is, in itself, very unusual – the fact that we've drawn on so many different disciplines. We should find ways of evaluating the outcomes of collaborative research, and integrating the findings in any exploitation of the product. Likewise, I feel I must say that job design cannot be put beyond the scope of the project without

considerable detriment to the potential for exploitation. It can only be to our advantage to say that we've paid careful attention to the social context of the system.

While she was speaking, George fixed his gaze on the ceiling, then turned with a look of studied benevolence and said pointedly:

Our primary concern is with the technical aspects of the design. It's our job to see that it works. We want to build a system which does the job it is intended to do, and as cost effectively as possible. Obviously, we have to take factors concerned with human–computer interaction into account, but we can deal with those issues when we've got a machine we know is going to work. It's not our business what the customer does with the machine once they've got it. Our boys will help them all they can. We can tailor our systems to meet the needs of the individual customer. It isn't up to us to start telling organisations how to run their business.

At this point Clare found she had some unexpected support. Stephen Hunter, a Research Fellow at the University of Bognor, was new to the project. He had a first degree in production engineering, and had recently completed a PhD thesis on the limitations of ergonomics. He commented:

I've made a detailed study of several organisations trying to introduce new technology. It's fairly easy to show that the design and development of new technology is problematic. Social and organisational factors are crucial, but designers consistently fail to understand the significance . . .

Patterson was clearly irritated by these interruptions. His plans for a neat and uplifting concluding session had been disrupted. He replied with a dismissive yawn:

Yes, yes, yes – that's all very well, but when you've had as much experience as I have, you'll realise that even with the best will in the world you can't take into account the quasi-scientific ramblings which social psychologists put forward as arguments. Give me something I can measure and I'll do something with it. Show me how taking job design issues into account will help us sell more machines and I'll do it, but I'll need figures to back it up. It's no use me going to my boss and saying, "If we take account of organisational factors the workers will feel better!"

Patterson smiled indulgently at Stephen. It was a look which said, "You'll learn."

Clare Waterman listened carefully to this exchange. She knew her chances of making any impact on the debate were slight, and she groaned inwardly at the "there, there, little girl" line she knew Patterson would take, but she could not let these remarks go unchallenged.

> Clearly, design is concerned with form, function, suitability for purpose and aesthetics. Most of us would agree with that. The point is that this applies to all types of design. So broadly, design is concerned with a systematic and detailed evaluation of the problem, the alternatives and the final solution. I appreciate your argument: you believe that design should aim at finding solutions at an economic cost and with minimum complexity. But the system we're working on involves the relationship between functional design issues and social and organisational factors. It's the human factors that determine the success of the system. If we don't address these aspects, then a degree of failure in the system is inevitable.

Sensing the opportunity to become part of the debate Ian Grundy – 'old sourpuss' – was quick to get to his feet. He was not interested in human–computer interaction, but he was certainly interested in attacking George:

> This whole project was badly conceived from the outset. If we'd had better management and direction, we might have seen the need to take some of these issues into account. I've argued time and time again for – but no, a voice crying in the wilderness, that's what I've been. If we're coming under attack from our paymasters, I want it known that I've always believed that these areas have been sadly neglected.

"Thank you for those comments", retorted George sarcastically. "I'm sure we'll not forget your contribution." Turning to Clare and then to Stephen he smiled, and his eyes moved warmly over his audience as he addressed them again:

> You may think that we don't take these issues into account – but we do. We understand the importance of considering human–computer interaction, social and organisational factors and job design; and we do it automatically. You people seem to see it as a separate activity. Just ask any designer here and he'll tell you – well, you just do it. Designers are people too, you know. and if they've got a problem then their way of solving it is as good as anybody's. You don't need to be a psychologist to solve these problems. A lot of it is plain common sense.

Stephen Hunter's expression was one of exasperation, and he sighed as he sank back into his chair:

> Yes! – which explains why so little new technology is truly user-friendly, despite all the manufacturers' claims. We seem to have a problem *knowing* what's obvious. I mean what's obvious to

the man – I'm sorry – *person* in the street.

George was just gathering together his papers when Clare interjected again:

> The point you're inclined to forget is that social and organisational factors are fundamental to commercial success. At least we should give ourselves some credit for the effort and resources we've put into this area. If we did, we could capitalise on what I've been calling an integrated design package. In my last project paper, *Organisations and Design*, I argued for making our evaluation criteria broad enough to be exploited. What I'm saying is that when we know what our strengths *are*, we'll be in a better position to make use of them. So far I've had no feedback at all. We've reached the stage where people only read what relates to their own area. I'm as guilty as anyone else. The opportunity for collaboration in any real sense has long since passed. We just don't speak the same language. If this were a marriage we'd be consulting solicitors.

Before George had time to reply, Clare's point was taken up by Greville Westfield, George's boss, who had slipped in unnoticed and was crouched by the door:

> You know, I think there's a lot of truth in what's been said about the importance of job design within the overall conception of the system. I've been giving a lot of thought to these issues over the past few months. I can assure you that we will most certainly discuss them at our project management meeting next month and try to develop some kind of strategy for the consideration of organisational factors. Does that reassure you?

The sound of a coffee trolley came from the corridor. The plenary was at an end.

CASE STUDY TASKS

Imagine you are Greville Westfield. Your role on the project management committee (Promcom) is advisory. However, you are acknowledged to have a good eye for the market and an enviable reputation for commercial 'vision', both within your own company and the industry in general. The position you hold in TRF as Strategic Planning Manager is a powerful and influential one, with considerable power to define corporate priorities.

The next meeting of Promcom is in three weeks' time. You have been asked to attend to discuss the commercial exploitation of the system. The questions and references below are intended to help you to locate your ideas in a theoretical framework, and to identify some of the key issues.

Questions 1–3 are suitable for a teaching session of one hour. Question 4 requires some further personal research and consideration.

1 What would you do to resolve the conflict on Promcom? Would you support George on the job design position? What information do you need and from whom? How will George react? Relate your answers to theories of organisational politics and the politics of evaluation.

2 What would be the impact on the commercial exploitation of the system if the project continues to ignore job design and wider organisational considerations?

3 Is it too late for action to be taken to address job design issues on this project? Justify your answer by considering the input social scientists can offer to technical specialists.

4 Why should the Oasis Palm Project concern itself with social and organisational factors? What should Greville do to determine an overall strategy for TRF to prevent the same situation occurring in the future?

ESSENTIAL READING

Blackler F, Brown C, Alternative models to guide the design and implementation of the new information technologies, *Journal of Occupational Psychology*, 1986, vol 59, pp287–313

Clegg C, Corbett M, Research and development into 'humanizing' advanced manufacturing technology, in Wall T, Clegg C, Kemp N, *The Human Side of Advanced Manufacturing Technology*, John Wiley, 1987

Perrow C, The organisational context of human factor engineering, *Administrative Science Quarterly*, 1983, vol 28, pp521–541

ADDITIONAL READING

Blackler F, Brown C, Evaluation and the impact of information technologies on people in organisations, *Human Relations*, 1985, vol 38, pp213–231

Damodaran L, Simpson A, Wilson P A, *Designing Systems for People*, NCC Publications, 1980

Eason K D, Job design and VDU operation, in Peace B G, ed, *Health Hazards of VDTs?* John Wiley, 1984

Kakabadse A, *The Politics of Management*, Gower, 1987

Legge K, *Evaluating Planned Organisational Change*, Academic Press, 1984

Mumford E, *Designing Human Systems*, MBS, 1983

Rhodes E, Wield D, eds, *Implementing New Technologies: Choice, Decision and Change in Manufacturing*, Blackwell/Open University, 1985

Taylor J C, The sociotechnical approach to work design, in Legge K, Mumford E, eds, *Designing Organisations for Satisfaction and Efficiency*, Gower, 1978

24 User-centred design: Training Access Points

Gordon Allison

ORGANISATIONAL SETTING AND BACKGROUND

The Training Access Points (TAP) initiative was launched in July 1986 by Lord Young of the DTI. It was controlled by the Manpower Services Commission (MSC), now the Training Agency.

The idea behind TAP was to use the latest computer technology to provide fast and easy access to information about learning opportunities, thus easing the way for people to undergo retraining. These learning opportunities were numerous – an estimated 4 million or so – but information about courses was scattered and often difficult to obtain. Comprehensive information is held on large databases that can be accessed using Prestel. PICKUP, for example, holds information on work-related short courses in England and Wales. The plan was to supplement this information with smaller databases of local opportunities. Both national and local databases were to be accessible through the same terminal.

Local databases were developed by TAP agents subcontracted by the Manpower Services Commission. By the end of February 1988 there were 28 agents covering the UK, and the TAP service was available from the Highlands of Scotland to the Isle of Wight. Each TAP agent was in charge of a small team of workers responsible for:

- collecting information about learning opportunities;

- inputting data onto the computer system;

- providing support and advice to its clients, ie the employers and the public at large.

To ensure a high degree of consistency between different TAP sites, agents were required to implement the local databases on IBM PCs or compatibles using a proprietary database system.

TAP agents controlled a number of terminals in their areas. The MSC also supplied them with a specification document, detailing the structure of the database and the various codes used to index information. One of the most difficult tasks in compiling the database was allocating a particular course to a suitable subject category: a classification of subjects and their database codes supplied by the MSC contained more than 1200 entries arranged in a three-tier hierarchy (see Figure 24.1).

At a typical TAP members of the public could sit down at the computer. By answering a series of computer prompts they could get information about courses that met their particular requirements in terms of:

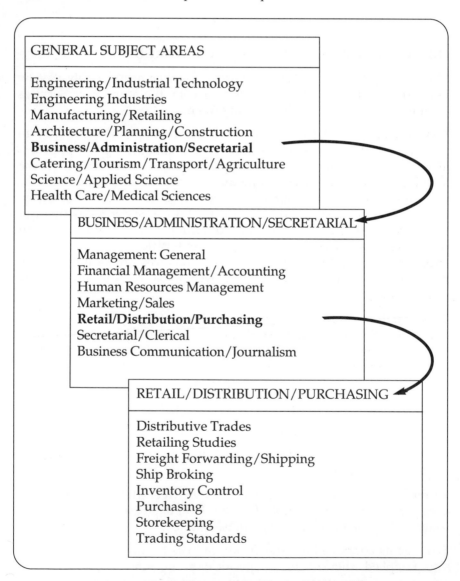

GENERAL SUBJECT AREAS

Engineering/Industrial Technology
Engineering Industries
Manufacturing/Retailing
Architecture/Planning/Construction
Business/Administration/Secretarial
Catering/Tourism/Transport/Agriculture
Science/Applied Science
Health Care/Medical Sciences

BUSINESS/ADMINISTRATION/SECRETARIAL

Management: General
Financial Management/Accounting
Human Resources Management
Marketing/Sales
Retail/Distribution/Purchasing
Secretarial/Clerical
Business Communication/Journalism

RETAIL/DISTRIBUTION/PURCHASING

Distributive Trades
Retailing Studies
Freight Forwarding/Shipping
Ship Broking
Inventory Control
Purchasing
Storekeeping
Trading Standards

Figure 24.1   The Three-tier Hierarchy of Course Topics

- subject;

- location;

- type of study (timetabled full-time, distance learning, intermediate or advanced).

Users chose a subject to study first, then went on to specify preferred location and so on until the number of 'hits' – records matching the search criteria – had been reduced to a small number. At this point users could obtain a hard copy printout of the details simply by pressing a key. An extract of a specimen record is shown in Figure 24.2.

Abstract		P/time Introductory course held at C/field Coll of T&A
Title		C&G 726 INFORMATION TECHNOLOGY WORD PROCESSING (evening class)
Start		September 1987
Name		C/FIELD COLLEGE OF TEC. AND ARTS
Address		INFIRMARY ROAD CHESTERFIELD S41 7NG
Contact		C/FIELD 31212 DAVID LEE
Price		Contact College
Outcome		C&G EXAMINATION
Subject	4670	word processing/keyboarding
Mode	1	LESS THAN 21 HOURS PER WEEK
Level	1	INTRODUCTORY
Location	7NG	TOWN CENTRE
Duration		Contact College
********	ENTRY	**********************************
. . .		
. . .		

Figure 24.2   Part of a course record (note codes for subject, mode, level and location)

The service was well received. Statistics showed that by February 1988 30,000 users a month were using the service. An independent survey of TAP users suggested nine out of ten would use it again.

There were problems, however. TAP agents complained that the database software made updates and revisions difficult, and was very slow when searching a large number of records. Many of the agents' complaints centred around the system's user interface, which was poorly laid out and offered very little advice to the user. It was also inconsistent: the same function key operated in different ways according to at which point in the enquiry process it was pressed. As a result of these deficiencies, some TAP agents were reluctant to let members of the public use the system except under supervision. This ran counter to the aims of the initiative, which sought to develop systems that were easy to use and capable of being installed and left unattended in public places such as libraries, community centres, job centres, and even shopping precincts.

It is worth noting that TAP agents held widely differing views about targetting and supplying the TAP service. Some agents saw the service as aimed primarily at disadvantaged sectors of the population (eg ethnic minorities and the unemployed). As such they sought to provide a free service located at points of greatest need, such as community centres and job centres. Other agents considered that their role was more to provide a training needs and consultancy service; they sought to derive income from their activities by negotiating placement fees with training course providers. These disparate goals suited the MSC, which, after all had to prepare a case for the Treasury and needed to know to what extent the service could be self-funding.

Conscious of the scope for improving the TAP system's user interface, the MSC decided to commission a number of 'demonstrators' from small design groups. These demonstrators were to be simulations of what an interface of the near future might look like and how it would operate. As such it did not have to operate using real data – instead it could use dummy data that would simply help to provide the 'look' and 'feel' of a working system.

Four groups – three software houses and a university research group – were given contracts to build demonstrators. The idea behind this parallel funding was that different groups might choose different input media (eg mice, custom keyboards, touch screens, etc) and presentation styles (eg voice output, colour graphics, etc). All four design groups reported to members of the TAP development unit of the MSC.

THE DESIGN PROBLEM

All groups recognised the problem that would confront users with little or no computer experience when faced with a standard computer keyboard – and over a hundred individual keys. In fact the problem could easily be avoided. Much of the users' interaction with the computer could be accomplished by presenting them with 'menus' – lists of options where the user could simply select a number, just like choosing a bottle of wine in a restaurant.

Three groups chose to use a 'touch screen'. With these, users make choices and browse through information by touching predefined areas of the screen, and the keyboard is dispensed with altogether. The university research group originally favoured this idea, but became convinced that an equally good alternative would be to design a special 'custom' keyboard. This would be specifically designed for the TAP application, and comprise only those keys that were required for its use. This appealed to the MSC because it introduced more variety into the interfaces – all the other groups had opted for using touch screens. One of the prototype versions is shown in Figure 24.3.

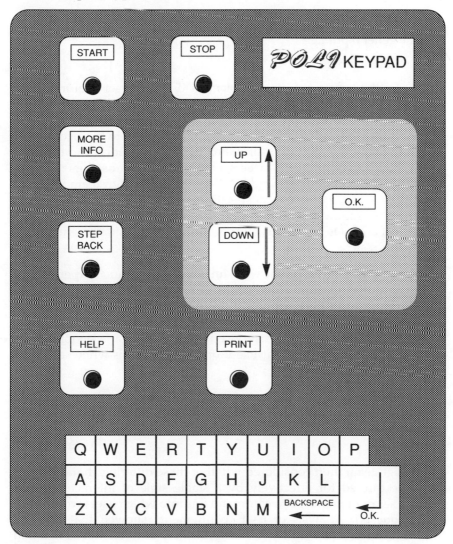

Figure 24.3   A Prototype Key Layout for the A4 Size Custom Keyboard

The remainder of this case study focuses on the university research group's design strategy. Its design team comprised a programmer, and two HCI researchers specialising in the design of computer dialogues; the team had been brought together specifically for this project. They suggested the design should be user-driven rather than technology- or data-driven. In other words, the users of the system themselves should determine and define what it should do, rather than the designers or the client. To achieve this, the designers had to carry out a task and user analysis to identify the key users of the system, what their needs were, and how these differed.

Two key groups of users were identified:

– the general public;

– the TAP agents.

However, there was a major problem in defining user requirements. Members of the public could not easily explain how they wanted the interface to function: they did not have enough experience of using similar computer systems. So the design team looked to the people best placed to know the sorts of information the public needed and the sorts of questions they asked – careers advisers and counsellors. Having interviewed careers officers and TAP agents, the design team was able to prepare a user requirements specification. This contained an explicit statement of assumptions about what different types of user would need in terms of access to functions, support from the system, presentation of information, etc.

Members of the general public were unlikely to have much experience of using computer systems. The knowledge of IT systems they did possess was likely to have been gained by using such services as bank cash dispensers, programmable video recorders, videotext and the like. They would probably use the TAP service infrequently: some people might use it only once, others might use it on a weekly basis while searching for a particular course.

TAP agents, on the other hand, would use the system day in and day out, becoming expert in its use. Some would undoubtedly be facilitators or intermediaries, acting as an interface between the client and the computer.

The design team then considered whether these differing characteristics could be catered for effectively by a single style of interaction (eg a lengthy series of menus, or a command line into which users would type their requests). Analysis of user requirements showed that a single interaction style was unlikely to satisfy the very different needs that had been identified. A person with little or no computer experience would need to be guided through the interaction; however, this same guidance might interfere with an experienced user's interaction, or become annoying.

The expert user, constantly using the system, would be able to remember commands and procedures, and would find shortcuts useful; the computer-naive person needed to have all legitimate actions available to him or her displayed at all times, thus lessening short term memory load. Furthermore, discussions with careers advisers high-lighted two different types of search strategy: one which could be described as a 'directed search', and another best described as 'browsing' for information. Some users would know exactly what information they were seeking (eg a course on central heating systems at a local technical college). Others might simply have time on their hands, and want to find out the topics available for them to study. In the latter example the key search criteria might be the town centre, on a Wednesday: the course topic might be of secondary importance. Interestingly, the existing TAP system was not flexible enough to answer this query, as the user always had to select a topic for study before being allowed to specify other search parameters.

The design of the interface demonstrator progressed by a series of iterations. Prototype versions of the system were created and shown to users for their comments, which were then analysed and used to generate a series of modifications. This approach offered considerable flexibility, and because the prototypes were quick to build, more than one style of interface was designed and tested.

The design team found it extremely difficult to judge the effectiveness of intermediate designs, and even that of the finished product. It would have been possible to develop the interface in stages (following cycles of design and build, show for comment, modify) until the project endpoint was reached, but the team felt that the effectiveness of the demonstrator should be measured more formally, using representative system users.

This committed the design team to testing the system in the field, under realistic conditions. This posed a major problem. For useful data to be collected from the trials, the system had to have some inherent usefulness; people had to be able to get useful information from it. This involved the team in creating their own, small database of local opportunities. Approximately 250 leisure courses running at local colleges and other institutions were entered on the system, which was then named POLI (Public Opportunities for Learning and Instruction) for the purposes of the field trial.

Tests of the interface were carried out in three stages. Initial designs were assessed in-house by the design team's colleagues – a process often termed expert evaluation.

Next, a fully functional (working) prototype was deposited in a public library for three weeks. A poster nearby invited passers-by to use the system and explained its facilities. Users were asked to complete a questionnaire about the facilities and the interface. As the system was unmanned, the designers wrote a computer program that recorded all the interactions with the computer, allowing them to replay user sessions and find out how many times the system had been used, what information the user had requested, and what difficulties had been encountered (inferred from the session transcripts). From the keystroke file it was evident that not all users completed a questionnaire. However, from the 50 that were returned the designers were able to build a profile of the typical user: male, under 25 years old, and possessing some experience of computers. They also gathered useful subjective data about people's reactions both to the service and to its interface.

The third and final stage of user testing was carried out in a more controlled environment. The system was set up at four sites:

- a community training and education agency for ethnic minorities;

- a TAP agency;

- a community centre used by the elderly;

- the research centre itself.

The field trials took place over a ten-day period, and members of the public were paid to participate. The exercise required them to work through a series of standard tasks, ranging from the simple (eg finding the number of courses on a particular topic) to the difficult (eg naming the tutor on a certain course at a certain location). As they worked through the tasks, they were observed by one of the design team. On completion of all the tasks, users were asked about their use of the system. In particular, they were prompted to identify any difficulties they had encountered. This discussion was assisted by replaying one of the tasks, using the replay software. Of the 31 volunteers, 27 completed the set tasks; the other four used the system and offered comments, but did not wish to work through the exercise, even through the experimenters stressed that it was the system, not the user, that was being tested.

One of the most interesting aspects of this phase was the visit to the community centre used by the elderly. No one was willing to try the system, even with the system's designers on hand to offer advice and assistance. Many people spent considerable time watching a demonstration of the system's facilities, but if they were invited to try it themselves a typical response was "Very interesting, but it's not for me."

This aside, this third phase of user testing yielded the most useful data for improving the user interface. It led to another round of modifications to the demonstrator before delivery to the client, the MSC, at the end of the six-month project.

CASE STUDY QUESTIONS AND TASKS

Some of the major issues considered by the design team are presented below. As design of computer systems is generally carried out by teams, we recommend that you work on the tasks in small groups. Prior reading of the key references will help you answer questions 4, 5, 6, and 7.

1 Different types of users have different requirements. Identify the key user groups with an interest in the TAP system, and describe how their requirements might differ.

2 The environment in which the TAP system was used made considerable demands on the way in which it was packaged, and on the hardware that was chosen. List these demands.

3 What factors govern the acceptability of a system to its intended users? Can you give examples of systems that are technically effective but unacceptable to some users?

4 The design team chose an iterative design cycle that depended on producing realistic simulations or prototypes of the eventual system. What are the advantages of using prototypes? What are the disadvantages, and how might these be lessened?

5 The design team evaluated its system with a range of techniques including interviews, questionnaires, appraisal by experts, and system logging software. Discuss the relative strengths and weaknesses of these approaches, and list any other evaluation techniques with which you are familiar.

6 Some designers argue that they are familiar with the needs of their systems' users, and that if they assume the persona of a typical user (a process often referred to as putting oneself in the user's shoes) they will produce systems acceptable to other users. What are the inherent dangers in using this approach?

7 Can IT products for casual use by the general public ever be satisfactorily designed to be capable of being used by everyone?

ESSENTIAL READING

Clegg C et al, *People and Computers: How to Evaluate your Company's New Technology*, Ellis Horwood, 1988

Rubinstein R, Hersh H, *The Human Factor*, Digital Press, 1984

Shneiderman S, *Designing the User Interface: Strategies for Effective*

Human–Computer Interaction, Addison Wesley, 1987, chapters 1, 2, 10 and 11

ADDITIONAL READING

Norman D A, Draper S W, eds, *User-centred System Design*, Lawrence Erlbaum, 1986

25 Information technology and organisational structure: Canadian Department of Informatics

Wally Mueller

BACKGROUND

The Canadian Department of Informatics (CDI) collects, analyses and reports on data about the demographic characteristics of the entire population of Canada through nationwide census surveys every five years. It also conducts a variety of surveys on random samples of the population, and gathers data from several industry and government sources to generate key economic and social indicators. Separate surveys cover such areas as mining and manufacturing, trade and shipping, agriculture, housing and construction, prices, labour markets, income and expenditure and health and lifestyle.

CDI has an excellent reputation for its statistical services among peak employer bodies in industry, federal and provincial governments, and academics. Its reputation in the community is somewhat mixed, however. Participation in the surveys is compulsory. Some surveys require citizens to produce extensive records; others have raised questions about invasion of privacy.

CDI's head office is in Ottawa, with regional offices in each provincial capital. The department employs almost 4000 staff spread over nine formal levels (see Figure 25.1). Most are males (58%), but the gender ratio changes markedly across levels. At the top three levels (7–9), over 80% of the managers are males. At Level 1, males are in the minority (37%).

The vast majority of staff have formal professional qualifications. They make up the bulk of numbers at Levels 3–5. However, the department operates not as a professional bureaucracy, but as a fairly rigid divisionalised hierarchical structure. By definition, the work of employees in a professional bureaucracy is regulated by self-imposed standards. These standards reflect extensive tertiary training in disciplines such as computer science, information systems, finance, economics, accounting, mathematics and statistics. However, in CDI much of the coordination and control of work is achieved by adherence to rigid sets of procedures, and this reinforces strong vertical lines of authority.

311

Close supervision of work at lower levels maintains data quality, while at middle and upper levels staff are monitored to ensure that procedures are being followed and data security maintained.

Turnover is relatively low. Most of the middle and top managers have been with the department for over 20 years, although not necessarily in the same office. Transfer across regional offices is a common way to gain accelerated promotion.

The professional staff are highly task-oriented, and pride themselves in keeping pace with the latest technological developments. These have led to more timely and accurate production of statistical reports in a variety of forms, including compact disc technology. Some of these changes, however, are affecting not only the way in which staff perform their individual tasks, but also interrelated patterns of work. The changes have so far been confined to the analysis of data, over which professional staff exercise a good deal of control by virtue of internalised standards. However, the most recent changes are occurring or expected to occur in the other two aspects of the department's work: data collection and reports.

IMPACT OF NEW TECHNOLOGY

At lower levels of the organisation, new technology will have a major impact on data gathering. Plans are well advanced to replace manual gathering of survey information by remote computer-assisted interviewing. As interviewees are questioned over the phone, their responses are typed directly into the computer. Front-end expert systems allow fewer questions to be asked when respondents meet certain criteria. Since some manual gathering will still be necessary for certain types of surveys and respondents, the necessary keyboard skills will enlarge the jobs horizontally. The software also enables data gatherers to control the quality of input more closely; this enlarges the jobs vertically.

The transfer from manual to computer-assisted data gathering means there will be much less need for tight operational control over interviewers. The role of the first-line supervisors will also change. Field interviews will no longer need to be planned, while supervision of data gathering and computer data entry will be unnecessary. The interviewers' work will now include planning samples, phone interviewing, data entry and verification and even low level data analysis if necessary.

Finally computer-assisted data gathering alters the traditional relationship between data providers, interviewers and first-line supervisors in a highly visible, concrete way. The manual data-gathering system included the following elements:

- face-to-face contacts during the preparation of survey samples;

- training interviewers;

- arranging transport;

- coordinating computer data entry with keyboard supervisors.

The end result, however, is the same as far as professional data analysts are concerned: the information is stored electronically on both the regional and centralised mainframe computers, and accessed in the same way, regardless of input.

A second example of the impact of new technology is the focal point of this case study. Unlike the first example, the new technology in this case is 'invisible', and (in a technical sense) appears innocuous. It affects the role of middle managers, and the relationship between head and regional offices. Previously, everyone knew their place in the centralised structure. The support systems (eg the centralised computer system) reinforced this structure. Information passed up and down the hierarchy in an orderly fashion, and under the supervisory control of the middle managers at every step of the way. The new technology now makes it possible to bypass the system.

ELECTRONIC MAIL SYSTEM

The new technology in this case study is nothing more than the humble electronic mail system (E mail). There are five main characters in the case and the action takes place in Vancouver (British Columbia) and Ottawa. The organisational chart in Figure 25.1 shows where the five individuals are located physically and organisationally. Government white collar employees refer to each other according to their formal organisational level; the same practice is adopted here.

WORK FLOW PRIOR TO E-MAIL

Ray Barrett (Level 8) is deputy director of special surveys. He receives a call early in the morning from his director, Mike Mackintosh (Level 9), advising that the federal (ie national) minister for housing, Senator Frank Rattigan, has requested the latest planning approval figures for new dwellings in British Columbia. The local member for Vancouver North has been petitioned by her constituency to investigate why the government targets for public housing are not being met. Hundreds of families are disadvantaged because of the housing shortage. Senator Rattigan wants to know how the trends for British Columbia compare with the rest of Canada.

Requests for reports from ministers of parliament are always given top priority in the department's workload. They are treated as special projects, and assigned ultimately to an officer with the appropriate authority and competence to prepare a comprehensive report in as short

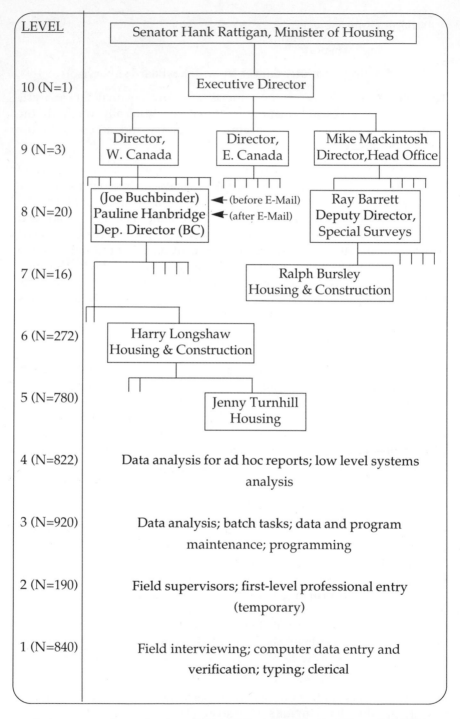

**Figure 25.1   Organisational Chart Showing the Staff Levels for the
Canadian Department of Informatics**

a time as possible. Penalties for inaccuracy are severe; the report is published in the parliamentary proceedings and often attracts press coverage if there is any 'newsworthy' material. Senior managers always countersign reports prepared by their staff, because they are directly in the minister's firing line and are held accountable for the work of their staff.

Ray receives Mike's memo in the afternoon mail; it contains the exact wording of Senator Rattigan's request. He sends a copy of the memo to Ralph Bursley (Level 7), who specialises in housing and construction statistics. Ralph is authorised to report back as soon as possible.

With the help of two Level 5 computer programmers, Ralph has little difficulty tracking down the relevant material from three separate databases and integrating them into a preliminary report.

On receipt of the report, three days after authorisation, Ray is disappointed to find the figures are at least six months out of date. He asks Ralph to obtain the latest data for the British Columbia area at least. Ralph prepares a detailed outline of the information required. This is forwarded by Ray to the West Canada director (Level 9), then on to Joe Buchbinder, British Columbia deputy director (Level 8). Joe directs the enquiry to Harry Longshaw (Level 6), who is in charge of managing the compilation of data about housing and construction. Harry takes the project to Jenny Turnhill (Level 5), who is responsible for ensuring that the data from the housing and construction industry is carefully monitored. She double-checks doubtful patterns in the data by contacting the original sources. Her data is always more current than the centralised database in Ottawa, because it is forwarded only every three months after verification processes have been completed.

Jenny has been in the job for four years, is in her late twenties and loves her work. She has an excellent degree in statistics, and a thorough working knowledge of the mainframe software systems operating at CDI. Jenny realises that presentation of statistical data is half the battle in communicating this material to non-statisticians; so she has developed desk top publishing skills on her PC as a way of keeping abreast of the latest developments. As yet she has little opportunity to use these skills, because Harry writes the reports after receiving the data requested. Harry also checks the data very closely.

Harry does not, as a matter of routine, provide Jenny with a copy of the reports that he writes. However, when the patterns in the data are not easy to interpret, he asks her to double-check the sources of data quoted in his report for Ralph:

> Jenny, there's something about this data that doesn't quite make enough sense. Are you sure you've double-checked your sources?

Since Jenny has already checked the sources thoroughly, she tries to help in another way:

> Harry, I know this data like the back of my hand. Why not let me have a look at your draft write-up? Maybe I'll be able to put my finger on something that could help.

Harry goes along with this:

> OK. I'm having trouble making sense of this data. See if you can pick up something. Here, have a crack at it.

Jenny has noticed that sometimes Harry's conclusions are a little different from her own. She puts this down to:

- her greater familiarity with the data sources;

- her greater awareness of factors affecting data reliability;

- her better understanding of the assumptions built into the raw data;

- her greater appreciation of the wider context within which the data is collected.

This last issue becomes more apparent when the report finally reaches Ralph.

His task is to integrate Harry's report with any additional material from other regions when necessary, and forward the final report for endorsement by Ray Barrett and Mike Mackintosh and the minister, Hank Rattigan. Like Jenny, Ralph sometimes draws different conclusions from Harry because the regional data has to be interpreted in the context of national patterns. The fact that interpretations are slightly different makes Ralph's work more difficult. He consumes time trying to cope with the uncertainty, knowing that the issue is sensitive and that the data finally reported in parliament has to be credible.

When he is in this state of uncertainty, Ralph phones Jenny (or others in equivalent positions in other provinces) to verify certain aspects of the data:

"Hi Jenny, Ralph here. How are things in the West?"

"Fine, how are you? What can I do for you? I suppose you've got Harry's draft for Rattigan by now."

"That's right. It's just landed on my desk. I don't know if you've seen it, but it doesn't quite add up to me. How do you read the data?"

Jenny explains the situation:

> Well, Harry did let me have a look at this one, and I pointed out that the real problem is that we're too early into the new financial year to pick firm trends. I suggested that he frame a report that

argued for a delay in judgement for two months, when the next set of data will be in.

But Ralph doesn't think this will help:

> No can do, Jenny. Rattigan will turn the heat on us, so we have to come up with an educated guess as to whether the BC data reflects a temporary hiccup or a longer-term problem. That's why Harry still had a go at it, but it seems to me in the wrong direction.

They discuss an appropriate choice of words that keeps faith with the data, and agree on a final interpretation. Ralph has complete confidence in Jenny's competence, and they often exchange ideas about alternative methods of analysis to detect more subtle patterns in the data.

By the time Ralph finalises his report and it has been countersigned by Mike Mackintosh, twelve days have passed. Senator Rattigan provides parliament with an answer to a question raised over two weeks earlier. While it is accurate and credible, the delay is a cause for much dissatisfaction.

The reasons for the delay can be summarised as:

- uncertainty about data fidelity on the part of the manager responsible for the final report;

- the need for the report to pass through several nodes of authority;

- the location of relevant competencies low down in the organisa-tional structure (ie those in positions of authority do more administration, and lag behind in working knowledge of technolo-gical developments);

- postal delays;

- misunderstanding about the intent of the original request;

- multiple processing of the data before its appearance in a report (eg inappropriate editing, selective deletions, conclusions based on the assumption that the data is context-free);

- concern about the reactions of superiors if attempts are made to bypass them when checking data quality and interpretation.

AFTER E-MAIL

Electronic mail allows staff who use personal computers on the same network to send and receive messages. The professional staff at CDI quickly discover that E-mail is more than a replacement or alternative to hard copy memo or the phone. Documents can be transferred electronically without the formalities of supervisory checks on each step of the report process.

When Senator Rattigan wants an answer to a question similar to the one above, the work flow is now quite different. Ray still sends a memo to Ralph via Mike Mackintosh, but the report now takes only three days instead of a fortnight. How did this happen?

When E-mail was first introduced, Ralph found it convenient to consult Jenny by sending data for verification. Neither of their respective superiors were aware of this communication link, nor of the increasing use of E-mail for more extensive consultation. The directors and managers on levels 8–10 made little use of the service themselves, preferring the phone for personal contacts and hard copy for memos.

Instead of forwarding a memo to Jenny via both their superiors in the organisational hierarchy, Ralph sends an E-mail message detailing his request for the latest data on housing approvals in British Columbia. Jenny is delighted at being involved in a fast-track approach to a parliamentary enquiry requiring a rapid response. It has also given her the opportunity to present the material in a suitable desktop publishing form that Ralph can reproduce for presentation to Senator Rattigan. She does not even think about clearing the procedure with Harry because:

– no set rules have been devised for such a situation;

– the time taken to explain the request and check the data would be unnecessarily long;

– duplication of effort seems wasteful.

Maintaining a simple direct electronic link between Ralph and Jenny makes good sense to both of them. The process is vastly more efficient, and in their view it is also more accurate and less uncertain. They are both close to the data, and in command of the range of statistical methods that can be brought to bear on the data.

Within a short period of time, Mike Mackintosh and Ray Barrett begin to notice that Ralph is preparing seemingly complete, up-to-date reports without receiving authorisation to obtain the latest regionally based data. They compliment both him and the deputy director (BC), who is now Pauline Hanbridge; she has replaced Joe Buchbinder, who retired shortly after the E-mail system was implemented.

Over in Vancouver, Harry is aware that his in-tray is lighter, with fewer requests from head office for reports. He is infuriated when he finds out that one of the published accounts of parliamentary proceedings makes reference to housing data that could only have been obtained through his branch of the British Columbia regional office.

Harry reprimands Jenny for bypassing his authority:

Have you seen this? There's no way anyone else but you could have got their hands on this data. What sort of game do you think you're playing? Don't you know that this is a security breach? You need authorisation from me before letting anyone else outside this office work on this data.

But Jenny stands her ground:

I can't help it if someone asks me on E-mail to help with a straightforward request for access to up-to-date figures. What harm is there in helping them? Ralph knows what he's doing. He writes reports for the minister all the time, and he seems to think we never let him down. I know you have to authorise the release of data for reports you write, but this report was written by Ralph, and he's taken responsibility for the data quality. As I see it, I haven't broken procedure. Anyway, if head office is more than happy, as they seem to be now, I can't see what the problem is.

Harry rushes off fuming to Pauline. He requests that she develop procedures for electronic mail enquiries that parallel the paper system:

This E-mail business has opened up a can of worms. If we don't come up with new procedures, security's going to go down the drain. One of my staff, Jenny Turnhill, has been dumping data directly down the line into reports being written by people in head office. I don't get to see what happens; neither do you. And I'll bet the directors in head office don't know too much about how the reports are being produced.

To Harry's horror, Pauline informs him that his colleagues at the same level of the organisation have recently reported similar problems within their functions:

Calm down, calm down. You're not the only one in this sort of predicament. It looks like staff everywhere have discovered what you can do with E-mail. Nigel, Chris and Karen [level 6 colleagues of Harry's] are also worried about the same thing.

Pauline has not yet taken action because head office has noticed the increased efficiency in report generation since the introduction of E-mail (with no increase in the leaks of confidential economic indicator data):

We can't just clamp on a squeeze, though. Head office has already given us kudos for the big time savings in responding to enquiries. And they even think the reports are a bit more accurate, for some reason. To some extent, I think we may have missed the boat. We can't introduce measures that drag out response time again. That would make me look very silly. No, we have to sit down and find a way of capitalising on what's happening.

MANAGEMENT DEVELOPMENT WORKSHOP

Being relatively new to the position of deputy director, Pauline uses the role confusion of the managers on levels 6–7 as an opportunity to organise a management development program. She asks the human resource manager to design a five-day workshop for Level 6 and Level 7 managers on the theme *Taking advantage of change*. Several outside consultants are commissioned to cover a variety of topics including:

- recognising pressures for change;

- how organisations have coped with externally imposed change (particularly government policy and new technology);

- the skills which managers need to cope with change.

Being a highly task-oriented group of managers (and missing their computers during the five days away from Vancouver!) they have found the workshop to be hard going. It does, however, serve a very useful purpose in warning managers that their roles have to change. Technology has given their subordinates the freedom and flexibility to deal with the statistical problems presented to them. By the end of the workshop, however, few have admitted that the old control procedures inhibited the more efficient methods made possible by new technology.

Pauline herself believes that authority has to be competency-based. This poses a threat to the managers reporting to her. Her predecessor, Joe Buchbinder, reinforced the administrative, procedural function of their role, whereas Pauline has left the issue open to debate and negotiation. As the managers had gradually lost touch with developments in statistics methodologies, hardware and software, and presentation techniques, and since their managerial style emphasised procedural control rather than personalised support, the concept of competency-based management raised by some in the workshop was met with decided reluctance to discuss the issues.

At the conclusion of the workshop, Pauline supports attempts by the group to form a number of small task forces. These will examine all aspects of the change process under way. This includes consideration of the new corporate plan being prepared by head office – a move to a 'fee for service' regime, attracting bright people to challenging jobs, increasing productivity and job satisfaction, and developing new rules for the processing of confidential economic indicator data in a more decentralised structure.

CASE STUDY TASKS

The following activities largely involve task-oriented small group roleplay. Minimum group size should be two, maximum six. For Activity 1, three separate groups are required. If class size is greater than 18, replicate groups can be formed. Each group should elect a 'scribe' to write down a summary of the outcomes on supplied overhead transparencies (preferably) or on flip charts. At the completion of the group activity, the class reconvenes as a plenary session. Each scribe then offers a brief presentation of his/her group's main points, with the rest of the class seeking clarification of issues. Group summaries can be discussed by the class and instructor immediately after each presentation, or delayed until all presentations have been made. Scribes should be assisted by their group members during discussions of their task outcomes.

Activity 1

Assume you are mid-way through the management development workshop arranged by Pauline Hanbridge, deputy director (BC). The facilitator of the workshop has divided the managers into three groups:

Group C

Imagine you are a group of Level 6 managers, with views similar to those of Harry Longshaw as portrayed in the case:

1 List the key features of your role at CDI before and after the introduction of E-mail.

2 Since E-mail is here to stay, what strategies do you suggest should be employed to maintain the clear lines of authority that existed before its introduction? In other words, how do you retain the control you had under the old system?

3 What new skills would you need to exercise such control?

4 How would you acquire these skills?

Group O

Imagine you are a group of Level 6 managers, similar to Harry Longshaw. You have seen the writing on the wall, and want to adjust to life after E-mail:

1 List the key features of your role at CDI before and after the introduction of E-mail.

2 What strategies would you employ to develop a new role for Level 6 and Level 7 managers in a productivity-conscious, entrepreneurial organisation that has more open communication systems, but where security of data is still a prime consideration in the organisation's charter?

3 What skills would you need in your new role?

4 How would you acquire these skills, bearing in mind that you have been in a stable organisation for 20 years?

Group P

Assume the role of Pauline. As a new appointee to the position of deputy director in charge of a regional office, you have arrived at a time of sudden technological change which has caught your managers off guard. They enjoyed excellent relationships with the previous head, Joe Buchbinder, who generally adopted an easy-going, paternalistic style of leadership during his 12 years at the helm. Joe's retirement was a sad occasion for the managers.

Head office specifically chose you for the task of modernising the professional and managerial practices of your regional office. They have promised to supply you with the necessary resources to effect the changes: you are among the first of a new breed of deputy directors, so they want you to succeed. You have excellent credentials in a technical/professional sense and have a reputation for being fairly direct (rather than directive) and forthright. You have also been chosen as the person most likely to foster an entrepreneurial climate in your department.

1 How would you like to see your department restructured, given that managers do not yet feel comfortable about your style of management, or your agendas?

2 How would operations in the restructured department differ from current practice?

3 What would the implications be for managers at Harry Longshaw's level in the department? How do you see their role changing?

Activity 2

After Groups C, O and P have completed their tasks, an alternative to the plenary session in Activity 1 is to form new groups. These groups perform new and identical tasks. Each should comprise at least one member from the original Groups C, O and P.

The task now is to negotiate new roles for Level 6 and Level 7 managers. The scribe should be a representative from the original Group O. The objective of this exercise is to see how role negotiation reflects the differing agendas of the major stakeholders.

As with Activity 1, each group presents the outcomes of the negotiations, including an account of some of the dominant process issues involved. In the discussion, it would be useful to compare the original group summaries of desired roles with the newly negotiated roles.

Activity 3

Break into new groups of around 3–5 people. Attempt the following task:

The Canadian government has recently agreed to a 6% national pay increase for all employees – but there is a proviso. At the end of 12 months, the organisations or industries must demonstrate to the federal industrial tribunal that they have carried out enough work or organisational restructuring to yield a 6% increase in efficiency or productivity. Furthermore, the Government requires evidence that any work redesign involved in restructuring has been participative:

1 In your role as Pauline, how would you manage this process?

2 Who should the stakeholders be?

3 What would you reasonably expect the outcomes to be?

Activity 4

This takes the form of class discussion. To what extent are the outcomes anticipated in Activity 3 likely to be due to the following changes?

– E-mail;

– the new deputy director, Pauline;

– federal government pressures to restructure;

– other changes.

ESSENTIAL READING

Child J, New technology and developments in management organisation, *Omega*, 1984, vol 12, no 3, pp211–224

Mintzberg H, *The Structuring of Organisations*, Prentice-Hall, 1979

ADDITIONAL READING

Bjørn-Andersen N, Management use of new office technology, Otway H, Peltu M, eds, *The Managerial Challenge of New Office Technology*, Butterworths, 1984, pp99–124

Child J, *Organisation*, Harper and Row, 1984

Danziger J N, Dutton W H, Kling R, Kraemer K L, *Computers and Politics: High Technology in American Local Governments*, Columbia University Press, 1982

Mueller W S, Computerised office systems: To centralise or decentralise?, *Human Resource Management Australia*, 1985, vol 23, no 3, pp45–51

Wainwright J, Francis A, *Office Automation, Organisation and the Nature of Work*, Gower, 1984

Index

DATE DUE

GAYLORD			PRINTED IN U.S.A.